William Faulkner

A CRITICAL STUDY

William Faulkner

A Critical Study

THIRD EDITION, REVISED AND EXPANDED

IRVING HOWE

The University of Chicago Press
Chicago and London

IRVING HOWE is Distinguished Professor of English at the City University of New York. His books include *Sherwood Anderson: A Critical Biography*; *Politics and the Novel*; *Thomas Hardy: A Critical Study*; *Steady Work: Essays in Democratic Radicalism*; *Decline of the New: Cultural and Literary Essays*; *The Critical Point: Literary Essays*, as well as several anthologies of Yiddish literature translated into English, which he has edited with Eliezer Greenberg.

The University of Chicago Press, Chicago 60637
The University of Chicago Press, Ltd., London

Published 1952. Third edition 1975
80 79 78 77 76   98765432

Printed in the United States of America
ISBN: 0-226-35483-0 (clothbound), 0-226-35484-9 (paperback)

T O

Thalia

A LIST OF

Faulkner's works

DISCUSSED IN THIS BOOK

❁

PREFACE

TO THE THIRD EDITION

THIS SMALL BOOK has a small history. First published in 1952, it was one of the earliest book-length studies of William Faulkner's fiction, and thereby necessarily tentative and incomplete. A decade later there appeared, in paperback, a second edition considerably revised and substantially enlarged. The novels that Faulkner had issued during the intervening years were discussed in the second edition, and some estimates of individual works were modified.

Now, in this third edition, I have added a section on Faulkner's last book, *The Reivers*, and have corrected some factual errors. Otherwise, this edition remains substantially the same as that published in 1962.

I have resisted the temptation to rewrite the book in light of the vast body of Faulkner criticism which has accumulated in recent years. To have done that would have meant to profit, no doubt, from the analyses, insights, and corrections of other critics; but it might also have meant to produce a composite of opinions, a book not quite anyone's. Literary criticism, I think, must rest finally on personal statement and judgment; whatever value this book has, depends largely on its being a coherent presentation of one reader's vision. So I have decided to remain with my own understanding of Faulkner's work, fully aware that this necessarily entails limits and flaws. Interested readers will find no lack of other critical works providing contrasts of understanding and opinion.

Among later Faulkner critics it has become customary to describe this book as an example of the "social" approach to literature. Perhaps so; it is not for me to say. But I do want to say that in writing the book I had no programmatic intent, no deliberate goal of exemplifying the "social" or any other approach to literature. I wrote about Faulkner's books as I saw them, through the lens of my own sensibility and experience, and in the second half of the book, wrote with what strikes me as a decided emphasis on distinctly literary issues.

It remains only to quote a few sentences from the preface to the original edition:

"The scheme of my book is simple. First, I have tried to say what Faulkner's work is 'about,' to report on the social and moral themes in his books; and then I have tried to analyze and evaluate the more important novels. ... Faulkner being a writer who particularly requires and tempts thematic analysis, it would have been cumbersome to proceed in the usual fashion from a full-scale discussion of one book to the next; I felt the need to survey such thematic materials as his attitudes toward the Negroes or his feelings about nature in compact sections. The disadvantage of this scheme, I suppose, is that the discussions of the individual books are split up into two and occasionally three separate parts. In practice, however, the separation between exegesis and evaluation cannot and should not be made very precisely. The two overlap; at least I hope so. ...

"In quoting from Faulkner's books I have left intact idiosyncracies of punctuation or emphasis, even when the reason for them is not clear out of context."

CONTENTS

(PART 1)

William Faulkner: His World and His Work

Classes and Clans

AMONG AMERICAN NOVELISTS OF THE PRESENT CENTURY only William Faulkner has created an imaginary world that is complete in itself, or perhaps one should say almost complete in itself. For while Faulkner commands the past of his Yoknapatawpha County as a fund of legend, memory, and pain, what he can summon of it in a given book tends to be partial and fragmented. As a rule, his view of the past comes to him in brilliant gasps and flashes. His central subject has remained constant, but each return to it has an air of improvisation, as if he were forever seeing his world in a new way.

The world of Yoknapatawpha, though of great fascination simply as a spectacle of drama and event, is also the setting for a complex moral chronicle in which a popular myth and an almost legendary past yield something quite rare in American literature: a deep sense of the burdens and grandeur of history. In America this kind of literary enterprise is seldom undertaken and still less frequently completed. Faulkner alone among our significant twentieth-century novelists keeps returning to the same imaginary locale: his Yoknapatawpha County, 2,400 square miles in area, bounded by the

Talahatchie and Yoknapatawpha rivers, and comprising mainly farm lands and pine hills. Faulkner's intense preoccupation with this mythical county indicates that it serves him as more than a literary convenience, a place known and used; it is related to those moral and social problems that most urgently beset him, and in his better novels locale and theme have a way of seeming almost inseparable. Therefore, merely to describe his world with some fullness and accuracy is to approach the central motives of his work.

Not since Henry James has any American novelist provided so many "living" characterizations. This fact tends to be slighted in the critical study of Faulkner's work, perhaps because it lends itself more easily to notice than to analysis. Yet the first and most fundamental test of fiction is that it yield impressions of character we can credit and retain. Even those readers distrustful of Faulkner's style or repelled by his violence must be struck by the amplitude, vitality, and high coloring of the figures that move across the Yoknapatawpha landscape. Although Faulkner's plots are sometimes too cumbersome and tricky for the matter they convey, and his reflections can become turgid and pretentious, his characters seldom fail us. They have a marvelous way of seeming to break out of their fictional bounds and of achieving the illusion of independent existence, so that in reading Faulkner's books one does not accept very easily the doctrine of modern criticism that characters "live" only between the first and last page. We know, on the contrary, that they live in memory and change in memory. One retains not only the impression of their distinctive moral traits, but one also remembers their inflections of speech, their mannerisms, their idiosyncracies of dress, the way they walk and stoop and crouch— all those synoptic gestures of body and voice by which a novelist lures us toward inner life.

The aging Negro servant, Dilsey, as she climbs the

Compson stairs, her every step an accusation; Popeye, that specter of foulness, neighing over his sexual deputy; Lena Grove, as she blandly wanders through the countryside looking for the man who has seduced her; Lucas Beauchamp, the Negro who is too proud to either accept or defy white society; Mink Snopes, the puny murderer, stumbling toward Memphis after 38 years in prison; Isaac McCaslin, the moral hero of Yoknapatawpha, as he returns for the last time to the hunting camp that has become a symbol of lost virtues—these figures stay in the mind, and their vitality does not wholly depend on the structural uses to which they are put in a particular Faulkner novel.

Impressions such as these form the true stuff of fiction: impressions of the rare moments when through motion or speech a character comes to full being. And the vividness of Faulkner's characters is magnified, as their meaning is complicated, by the variety of tones through which he approaches his world: despair in *The Sound and the Fury*, frenzy in *Absalom, Absalom!*, wry but also wild humor in *The Hamlet*, controlled wistfulness in "The Bear." The traditional resources of fiction —dramatic conflict, persuasive characterization, fluidity of narrative—are here in abundance and sometimes in excess; but even as these hold and entice us, we cannot help being aware that through them winds a pattern, partly designed and partly arising from the inner logic of the work itself.

After a private census which by now may be somewhat dated, Faulkner announced that of the 15,611 people living in Yoknapatawpha County 6,298 are white and 9,313 Negro. If the preciseness of these figures is whimsy, the proportion is not. For even without other evidence from his books, this breakdown of population would be enough to suggest how closely his imaginary world was related, at least in the past, to the South in which he spent most of his life. The shape and color of places, the changes of weather, the close knowledge of a particular range of human types—all rise from a life-long immersion in a native scene.

One of Faulkner's great subjects, human rootlessness in the modern world, is a subject made possible by the rootedness of his own life in the one part of the country which, at least until recently, could still be called a region. We see evidence of the author's intimacy with and knowledge of this subject in both his most ambitious and most casual work: in the superbly recorded Negro dialogue after the opening of *The Sound and the Fury*, as well as in the nuanced banter among the farmers in "Shingles for the Lord." Even when Faulkner twists his language into knots or drives his action into a violent confusion, the sense of place remains true. We feel dubious about some of his writing not because he has failed to establish the reality of his world but because he is manipulating style or plot in behalf of some ideological or private end so as to violate the reality of his world.

It is quite clear, however, that Faulkner is not primarily an observer of Mississippi folkways. Though his fiction rests on an assured knowledge of local feelings and objects, it engages us for reasons that have little to do with either. Most of Faulkner's critics have taken the Yoknapatawpha story as a parable of the entire South and they have been right to do so, but there must be readers of his work who have only a faint interest in the South as a problem or place and who find themselves annoyed when Faulkner slows the flood of his narrative to step forth as a Southern orator. No feeling about the South, be it friendly or hostile, traditionalist or modern, is sufficient to explain the emotion aroused by a story like "The Bear" or the richness of moral implication suggested by a novel like *The Sound and the Fury*.

If, indeed, Faulkner is as important a writer as we now suppose, his work must concern us for reasons ultimately distant from the setting he has chosen or the special problems confronting man in this setting during the past century. The more severe Faulkner's treatment of the South, the more readily does one forget he is writing about the South. *The Unvanquished* and *Sartoris*, the least impressive of the Yoknapatawpha books, are most conventionally "Southern" in sentiment while *The Sound and the Fury* seems a terrible criticism not of the recent South alone, but of the entire life of our era. To the extent that *The Sound and the Fury* is about modern humanity in Mississippi, to the same extent is it about modern humanity in New York and in Paris.

To penetrate Faulkner's work it is necessary first to look at the self-contained world of Yoknapatawpha, a world with its own social relations and moral qualities. To see this world is to come upon an important difference between Faulkner's books and the traditional social novel. From its inception in the eighteenth century, the novel has had as one of its major concerns the contrast in manners between contending classes that meet and sometimes fuse in a highly organized society. But the tensions in Yoknapatawpha, while certainly numerous and often extreme, are not primarily caused by this conflict between classes aware of their historical roles and mutual antagonisms. Faulkner is gifted at noting a play of manners which usually reflects nuances of individual character rather than the condition of social classes: most happily represented in such a figure as the sewing-machine agent, V. K. Ratliff. None of the conspicuous actors in Faulkner's world comes from the major social groups we are accustomed to meeting in life or literature. There is no genuinely wealthy class, only a remnant of an old aristocracy; no industrial proletariat; no coherent intelligentsia, only one or two provincial intellectuals; and the merest strand of a middle class, visible mostly in the later and weaker novels. Nor can one find in Faulkner's work anything of the cultural duel between European tradition and Ameri-

can novelty which forms so persistent a theme in our
literature.

Like Mississippi itself, Yoknapatawpha is a land
clawed by poverty, and while it does have social classes,
they are either vestigial or embryonic remnants of the
old aristocracy or forerunners of a new commercial
ruling class. Most of Yoknapatawpha is kept from split-
ting into distinct classes by the flattening pressures of
poverty and the absence of industrialization, but if
Faulkner continues to explore its mid-twentieth-cen-
tury life, this statement will have to be amended. A
few wealthy men do appear: Will Varner in *The Hamlet* is something of a back-country magnate, though his
wealth is impressive mainly by contrast with the poverty
of the neighboring farmers. The most recent generation
of Sartorises lives in reasonable comfort and the Mallison family of *Intruder in the Dust* enjoys ordinary
middle-class ease, but the bulk of Yoknapatawpha is
made up of hard-working farmers beneath whom hangs
a fringe of "poor whites." As for the Negroes, they are
seldom distinguished in economic terms at all, and
rightly so, since the differences among themselves are
as nothing when compared to the differences between
them and the whites.

Clan rather than class forms the basic social unit in
Faulkner's world. Pride in family and reverence for
ancestors are far more powerful motives in behavior
than any involvement with class. Such motives are, of
course, to be expected in a society where the past clings
to the present like a habitual lover, neither relinquished
nor enjoyed. Each of the major families in Faulkner's
world comes to signify a distinct kind of conduct that is
premised on a moral code. When a character like Jason
Compson, for example, turns from clan loyalty to class
aggrandizement, he is repudiating, Faulkner implies,
not only his immediate inheritance but an entire mode
of life. It is through this breakup of the clans that
Faulkner charts the decay of the traditional South.

Though the Compsons, Sartorises, and McCaslins, all landowners of prominence, begin roughly on the same social level, their histories from the Civil War serve radically different purposes. Their responses to modern life seem to illustrate the various moral courses that are, or were, open to the South: the chivalric recklessness and self-destruction of the Sartorises, the more extreme and tragic disintegration of the Compsons and, by way of resolution, the heroic expiation for the evil of the past upon which Isaac McCaslin decides. Similarly, the families on a lower economic plane—the Bundrens, Tulls, MacCallums, Snopeses—are related not so much to a range of social conditions existent among the Southern farmers and "poor whites" as they are to a series of moral contrasts worked out within the limits of those conditions.

The Yoknapatawpha story is to be read more as a chronicle than as a group of novels. It is concerned less with the struggle of the classes than with the rise and fall of the clans, and through its history of the clans it elaborates a moral fable whose source is Southern life. The meaning of the fable is, at Faulkner's best, without geographical limit. To understand this fable we must momentarily put aside our description of the Yoknapatawpha world and turn to Faulkner's personal experience and his feeling toward his native region.

II

Background of a Writer

THE ATMOSPHERE IN WHICH WILLIAM FAULKNER SPENT his boyhood was heavily laden with memories of the Southern past, and at the center of these memories stood a figure of almost legendary stature.

In 1839 William C. Falkner,[1] the novelist's great-grandfather, arrived in Ripley, Mississippi, a poor four-teen-year-old boy from Tennessee looking for work to help his widowed mother. He became a clerk and then was put to "reading law" in a lawyer's office. Later, as a young man, he rose to political and economic prominence in Lafayette County (the model for Yoknapatawpha). A man of fiery and imperious character, Falkner became involved in gunfights. He killed two men, but he was acquitted both times by local juries on a plea of self-defense. Yet he was not quite a conventional Southerner. He grew impatient with the chivalric code and in his own way tried to break out of it. Nor was Falkner really part of the plantation aristocracy. By the

[1] The novelist added the "u" to the family name.

1840's large plantations had been carved out in Mississippi—Falkner would own one himself—but there was not yet an aristocracy comparable in power, wealth, and size to that of the Southern seaboard states. Life was much rougher in Mississippi than in Virginia and South Carolina. The wilderness still lay within reach and the air of the frontier had not yet disappeared from the towns. In this atmosphere Falkner was one of the rising "new men," energetic figures who by force of circumstance would become defenders of a society they might not entirely accept.

At the outbreak of the Civil War, Falkner became Colonel of the Second Mississippi Regiment, and under his leadership it saw a good deal of action, especially in the first battle of Manassas. But when the regiment, apparently chafed by his strict discipline, replaced Falkner as Colonel at its annual election of officers, he simply packed up and went home. Back in Mississippi, he formed a guerrilla band to harass the Northern armies that were cutting deep into the rear of the South.

At the end of the war, instead of succumbing to the lethargy of defeat, the Colonel turned to new occupations: money-making and literature. With enough rolling stock for two trains, he built a sixty-mile narrow-gauge railroad which went from Oxford to a point within the Tennessee border, where it met the Memphis and Charleston line. He became active in politics, helping to organize the American Party or "Know Nothings" in Mississippi and being elected to the state legislature toward the end of his career. He wrote several books, the most notable of which is *The White Rose of Memphis*, a novel brimming with high sentiments, brave gentlemen and pure ladies; it sold 150,000 copies within thirty years.

The Colonel died in 1889, having been shot by a business associate in the public square of Ripley—much as Colonel Sartoris, a character in *The Unvanquished*, who is modeled partly upon the Colonel, is also killed.

The Unvanquished is an imaginary but in some ways faithful reconstruction of the family history, with the willful Colonel Sartoris representing the archetypal ancestor and, thereby, both the power and blindness of the remembered South. Bayard Sartoris, the boy through whose eyes the action of *The Unvanquished* is seen and who appears as a deaf and crusty old man in *Sartoris*, is also based on an actual person: Colonel Falkner's son, John, an irascible man who became Assistant United States Attorney and bank president in Oxford. John Falkner was active in the political rise of the Mississippi rednecks, the group led by Senator James Vardaman, which expressed and exploited the grievances of the tenant farmers in the late years of the nineteenth and the early years of the twentieth century. The time when his grandfather and uncle were Vardaman's spokesmen in Lafayette County coincided with William Faulkner's boyhood, and his novels show some traces of the pathos and humor of the redneck upsurge.

Murry Falkner, grandson of William C. and father of William, was a decent man, but clearly less vital than the Falkners before him. For some years he ran a livery stable and a hardware store; then he became assistant secretary for the University of Mississippi, which is located in Oxford. Apparently, he has not appeared as a model for any of the Yoknapatawpha characters, perhaps because his life was not very rich in drama. In any case, this completes the line of family descent, and at least by the standards which in his early work Faulkner associates with the old South—standards of recklessness and daring—it clearly *is* a descent.

Born in 1897, William Faulkner heard an endless number of stories during his childhood about his great-grandfather and other heroes of the South—stories about gallantry, courage, and honor, told with all the greater emphasis as the past seemed less and less retrievable. In *Sartoris*, Faulkner describes with gentle sar-

casm the gradual inflation of a family memory into a
knightly legend:

> . . . as [Aunt Jenny] grew older the tale itself
> grew richer and richer, taking on a mellow splendor
> like wine; until what had been a hare-brained prank
> of two heedless and reckless boys wild with their
> own youth had become a gallant and finely tragical
> focal point to which the history of the race had
> been raised from out the old miasmic swamps of
> spiritual sloth by two angels valiantly fallen and
> strayed, altering the course of human events and
> purging the souls of men.

As a boy Faulkner did not need to study the history
of the South; he lived in its shadow and experienced its
decline. There were still many survivors of the war for
whom it formed the dominant point of memory: aging
veterans whose years after the surrender seemed drab
and diminished. Faulkner would later recall that during
his childhood he and his friends had played Civil War
games under the guidance of old men who set out "the
rules" by telling them exactly how the famous battles
had been fought. It was inevitable that the figure of
his great-grandfather should come to loom splendid in
his boyhood mind and that he should saturate himself
in legends of the past: a past that may or may not have
been more virtuous but certainly seemed more spacious
and vigorous than the present.

Faulkner's education was erratic. He left high school,
without being graduated, to work in his grandfather's
bank. He read widely if narrowly, and dabbled in poetry
and painting. He was enraptured by romantic verse,
which "completely satisfied me and filled my inner
life." Equally nourishing for his inner life was a friendship he began in 1914 with Phil Stone, a young Missis-
sippian studying to be a lawyer but already lost to a life-
long passion for literature. Stone, by the standards of

his time and place, was a very sophisticated young man. From Stone—later a model for Gavin Stevens in several of Faulkner's novels—the young Faulkner learned about a whole new world of modern culture. With Stone he held many long conversations about the problems of the South: conversations which blended criticism and nostalgia.

When the United States entered the First World War, Faulkner tried to enlist in the Army Air Corps but was rejected because of his size. He did manage to join the Canadian Air Force and go to Toronto for his flight training. A legend—enshrined, among other places, in the first edition of this book—has grown up that Faulkner served as a pilot in France and suffered severe wounds when his plane crashed in combat; but the truth is that the war ended while he was still in Canada and his only wound came as the result of an Armistice Day prank.

Upon his return to Mississippi, Faulkner took some courses at the state university. He did poorly in English and remained a student only for a year. Then he drifted to New York City, where he worked in Lord & Taylor's book department, and drifted back to Oxford. For a while he became a town "character," walking about barefoot, wearing, it is said, a monocle, and supporting himself by doing odd jobs as carpenter and housepainter. He then held a brief appointment as university postmaster, but a certain reluctance to distribute mail cut this career short. His letter of resignation contains a marvelous sentence, probably more revealing of his later mind than most of the juvenilia and apprentice sketches which have been assembled and studied by literary scholars: "Thank God I won't ever again have to be at the beck and call of every son of a bitch who has two cents to invest in a postage stamp."

It is now that Faulkner seems to enter upon a state of mind which, for lack of a better word, might be called a crisis. He had no training or visible prospects;

he showed little interest in hard work; he did not know what to make of himself; and he shared the vague discontent that was felt by other sensitive young men home from the war. But he could not release this feeling as the other sensitive young men did. The Left Bank, the New York literary world, political radicalism—these seldom stirred his interest and never satisfied his needs. The land to which he had returned was itself like an old battlefield striped by scars of war, and its people seemed still to be living with a flawed but cherished past. The evidence of his early novels suggests that to Faulkner the two wars, the old war of his homeland and the recent war in Europe, had a way of melting into one desolation. And perhaps most disturbing of all, the South of the twenties was changing in ways difficult to specify but immediately felt. The traditional sense of Southern homogeneity was cracking. The agrarian economy was being pierced by salients of industrialism, though not yet in Faulkner's part of the country. And while the South was more prosperous than it had been for decades, a young man of Faulkner's reflective bent might feel uneasy about the new faces that were rising to the social top, faces he would later draw with bitterness and dismay in Jason Compson and Flem Snopes.

With the help of a subsidy from Phil Stone, Faulkner published in 1924 a little book of poems called *The Marble Faun*. These Swinburnian verses are little more than exercises in provincial romanticism, and they have met with deserved neglect. Faulkner's whole career demonstrates that he commands a major gift for poetic evocation, but it is not a gift that can be contained within the limits of verse. Apparently untroubled by the failure of his book, Faulkner kept up his "undirected and uncorrelated" reading (the adjectives are his), particularly in Shakespeare, Shelley, Keats and Housman, and continued to write an occasional pale lyric.

Oxford was hardly the town to feel sympathetic toward Faulkner's literary ambitions; without too great malice but with characteristic shrewdness, it mocked him for trying to break away from the ruts of conventional life. Perhaps to find a more sympathetic environment, perhaps simply out of boredom, Faulkner left Oxford in 1924 and settled for a time in New Orleans. There he met Elizabeth Prall, who had been his superior at Lord & Taylor's and who was now the wife of Sherwood Anderson. The two men became friends, meeting in the afternoons to talk, quarrel, drink, drift through the hot streets, and exchange the tall tales they both loved to tell. Anderson later published his poignant but inaccurate sketch, A *Meeting South*, which concerned "a little Southern man [who] lived always in the black house of pain" because of injuries suffered in the war and who now hoped to write poetry: " 'If I could write like Shelley I would be happy. I wouldn't care what happened to me.' "

Anderson, who had a genuine gift for divining talent, suggested to Faulkner that he try his hand at a novel. Years later Faulkner would recall that when he saw how comfortable life was for Anderson (which suggests he was not yet in the habit of seeing very deeply) he decided that writing would be a pleasant way to earn his living. Six weeks later he came to Mrs. Anderson with the manuscript of a novel which Anderson agreed to recommend to his publisher provided he would not have to read it first.

Or so the story goes. It is a pretty story and may be true, but one must remember that Faulkner and Anderson shared a bland indifference to routine fact—especially when it concerned their own past—and a great fondness for fabricating tall tales. The story may just possibly be the result of an unplanned collaboration in pulling the public leg, much as their correspondence about Al Jackson, that fine old river-man whose sheep kept turning into fish, was a wild private joke. That Anderson did not look into Faulkner's manuscript seems

most unlikely, particularly in view of his native courtesy
and curiosity; but it may have struck him as a marvelously funny touch, a way of confounding the highbrow
critics, to say he had sponsored Faulkner simply because
of his "sense" of the man. And to Faulkner the story
would also have had an attractive savor, suggesting as it
does that the very act of becoming a writer, so often regarded as a solemn dedication, can be casual and for-
tuitous.

I offer this surmise for one reason: to cast some doubt
upon Faulkner's claim that he began writing his novels
as a pleasant maneuver, a casual mimicry in behalf of
comfort. (The issue is a recurrent one in Faulkner's
career, right up to his fabulous remark, at the time he
won the Nobel Prize, that he was merely "a farmer"; it
has to do with the fear of a certain kind of self-educated
American writer that casting himself as an intellectual
or man of letters will somehow dry up the sources of
his creativity.) Yet, even if Faulkner did "dash off"
Soldiers' Pay, even if he had not yet learned to give
full credence to his gifts and ambition, the book clearly
rises from his deepest feelings, the feelings which had
been with him since at least the time of the war and
which had received only tepid expression in his poems.

Both of Faulkner's early novels, *Soldiers' Pay* and
Mosquitoes, are much more interesting as biographical
and literary evidence than as works of art. Like Hemingway's early novels, but with hardly a grain of their fierce
authority, *Soldiers' Pay* announced the discovery of a
generation that has been sold and is "lost." No longer
very striking or fresh by the time Faulkner came to it,
this theme is embodied in a story about a war veteran,
Donald Mahon, on his way to Georgia. Mahon is so
badly wounded, so little able to respond either to his
own condition or the people clustered about him, that
he cannot possibly sustain the significant burdens the
story thrusts upon him. Strong emotions, uncontained
and without attachment, swirl through the book, while

at the center lies an inert victim—suggesting a pathos
so extreme that the writer cannot direct it toward any
end but itself. After the opening pages, all that can
happen is a footnoting of Mahon's known and irrevocable plight. The circle of characters surrounding him,
despite Faulkner's efforts to set up some ironic by-play,
really cannot do much but wait until he dies. So pitiful
a figure offers small incentive to dramatic or moral development, and one comes to suspect that for Faulkner
the true value of the book lies not in anything he can
make of the returned veteran, but in some anterior
image of him as victim.

The writing consists of a bright rhetorical impasto,
the style of a young man who adores style. There are
many pasteboard gems: "a pure quivering chord of music wordlessly and far away," "moon-silvered ridges
above the valleys where mist hung slumbrous," and
more. When set against the subject matter, it seems a
style strangely, even flauntingly, incongruous. Perhaps
the explanation is that the style comes from Faulkner's
reading of Swinburne, Housman, and *The Rubaiyat,*
while the subject reflects his own unsettled feelings.

Yet the book has a certain interest, not so much in its
own right as for signs and anticipations of the writer
to come. There are passages, bits of description and
miniature set-pieces, that show a decided verbal talent.
There are other passages that display Faulkner's gift for
precise evocation of place and moment. In the opening
scene, in which Mahon is being taken home on a train,
Faulkner records some fine talk among the soldiers and
other passengers, neatly capturing the post-war atmosphere, if not as it really was in American life, then as it
was being stylized in American literature. And in the
final scene two of the more sympathetic characters, saddened by the consequences of Mahon's death and the
general air of desolation which surrounds them, wander
toward a Negro church—the first of several episodes in

Faulkner's novels where white people, sick with self
awareness, turn for cleansing to the Negroes:

> listening, seeing the shabby church become beauti-
> ful with mellow longing, passionate and sad. Then
> the singing died, fading away along the mooned
> land inevitable with tomorrow and sweat, with sex
> and death and damnation; and they turned town-
> ward under the moon, feeling the dust in their
> shoes.

This is hardly distinguished writing, if only because of
an excessive reliance on the moon; but even in these
self-conscious periods there is a faint anticipation of the
later Faulkner.

Not as much can be said for Faulkner's second novel,
Mosquitoes, an attempt to satirize the literary intelligentsia of New Orleans, particularly the group that
published the little magazine, *The Double Dealer*, in
the early twenties. The spirit of Aldous Huxley hovers
over the novel, and Faulkner knows no way of making
peace with it. He lacks Huxley's gift for letting ideas
spin and speed off on their own, flares of the mind that
for a moment seem to acquire an autonomous being
and, thereby, a kind of concreteness. Nor does he command Huxley's gift for marshalling ideas for conflict.
Ideas are surely important to Faulkner's work, both as
they inspire his own enterprise at some very deep level
and as they spark the obsessions of his characters. But
when he comes to a direct expression of ideas Faulkner
turns sluggish and solemn, and when he tries his hand
at satire, the trouble is simply compounded. Some of
Faulkner's more worshipful critics, intent on beating
blood out of stones, have found things to praise in
Mosquitoes; namely, the theme they extract from it:
that there is a radical disparity between words and action and that the former become empty, vain, and
trivial when split away from the latter. No doubt this is

the case, and if *Mosquitoes* hardly embodies this idea, it surely exemplifies it.

This novel, the weakest Faulkner has written, is essentially a symptom of the unacknowledged envy felt by a provincial young man as he measures himself against those he takes to be cosmopolitan intellectuals. I use the term "provincial" merely to indicate that, by reason of social and geographical limitations, Faulkner at the age of 27 lacked the cultural resources that would be at the disposal of many European (I leave aside Northern) writers of a similar age. This provincialism is simply a fact to be recorded and assessed, the source not only of Faulkner's weaknesses but also of much of his strength.

Since neither *Soldiers' Pay* nor *Mosquitoes* sold very well, Faulkner found himself in the position, familiar enough to writers, of being unable to live by his writing. Disillusioned by his glimpse of the New Orleans Bohemia, he returned to Oxford, where for a while he took a job as a night superintendent of a power plant. There, in the town soon to figure in his novels as Jefferson, he wrote the books that would bring him a world-wide reputation.

The situation is noteworthy. A young writer whose distaste for the life of his moment is beyond direct expression; a writer who can find release in his first novel only as a fantasy of persecution; a satirist who in his second novel stumbles into dull malice; a romantic provincial who approaches the literature of the past somewhat like those chivalrous Confederate officers he would later depict in a raid on Northern stores; a man of large undisciplined gifts, able to spur a narrative and blessed with a flow of language—all this is impressive, but hardly enough to prepare the reader for the flood of first-rate writing that is soon to come.

What happened to Faulkner between *Mosquitoes* and the novel that came a few years later, *The Sound and the Fury?* What element of personal or literary experience can account for such a leap? At the door of this mystery there is no use pretending entry. But one thing may be said: the early Faulkner is a man in quest, both of some organizing principle in experience and of a subject by which to test this principle in his writing. There is no lack of talent in his early work, only the lack of an occasion to employ it fruitfully. And the extraordinary growth in the books to come will arise from his discovery of his native subject: the Southern memory, the Southern myth, the Southern reality. From this subject he will not stray for long, and in his loyalty to it he will show the true artist's tact—the Greeks might have said virtue—for using to the full those resources uniquely his own.

III

The Southern Tradition

UNTIL VERY RECENTLY, REGIONAL CONSCIOUSNESS HAS RE mained stronger in the South than in any other part of the United States. This "historical lag" is the source of whatever is most distinctive in Southern thought and feeling. After its defeat in the Civil War, the South could not participate fully and freely in the normal development of American society—that is, industrialism—and large-scale capitalism arrived there later and with far less force than in the North or West. By the Reconstruction period New England regional consciousness was in decline and by the turn of the century the same was probably true for the Midwest; but the South, because it was a pariah region or because its recalcitrance in defeat forced the rest of the nation to treat it as such, felt its sectional identity most acutely during the very decades when the United States was becoming a self-conscious nation. While the other regions submitted to dissolution, the South struggled desperately to keep itself intact. Through an exercise of the will, it insisted that the regional memory be the main shaper of its life.

Perhaps because it had so little else to give its people, the South nurtured in them a generous and often obsessive sense of the past. The rest of the country might be committed to commercial expansion or addicted to the notion of progressive optimism, but the South, even if it cared to, was unable to accept these dominant American values. It had been left behind. It was living on the margin of history—a position that often provides the sharpest perspective on history. Some decades after the defeat of the South, its writers could maintain a relation to American life comparable, in miniature, to the relation in the nineteenth century between Russian writers and European life. For while nineteenth-century Russia was the most backward country on the continent, its writers managed to use that backwardness as a vantage-point from which to observe West-European life and, thereby, to arrive at a profound criticism of bourgeois morality. Precisely because Russia was so far behind the West, the Russian writers could examine the bourgeois code without hesitation or illusion. It was this crucial advantage of distance, this perspective from the social rear, that was the major dispensation the South could offer its writers. And it gave them something else: a compact and inescapable subject. The Southern writer did not have to cast about for his materials; he hardly enjoyed a spontaneous choice in his use of them, for they welled within him like a dream recurrent since childhood. Faulkner has given a vivid if somewhat romantic description of this subject in *Intruder in the Dust*:

For every Southern boy fourteen years old, not once but whenever he wants it, there is the instance when it's still not two o'clock on that July afternoon in 1863, the brigades are in position behind the rail fence, the guns are laid and ready in

the woods and the furled flags are already loosened
to break out and Pickett himself with his long oiled
ringlets and his hat in one hand probably and his
sword in the other looking up the hill waiting for
Longstreet to give the word and it's all in the balance, it hasn't happened yet, it hasn't even begun. . . .

But of course it has happened; it must begin. The
basic Southern subject is the defeat of the homeland,
though its presentation can vary from the romancing of
parts of *Sartoris* to the despairing estimate of social loss
in *The Sound and the Fury*. Nor does it matter, for the
moment, whether one defines the Southern subject as,
in Allen Tate's words, "the destruction by war and the
later degradation by carpetbaggers and scalawags, and a
consequent lack of moral force and imagination in the
cynical materialism of the New South," or as the defeat
of a reactionary slave-owning class followed by its partial recapture of power through humiliating alliances
with Northern capital and a scrofulous commercial class
of local origin. Regardless of which interpretation one
accepts, the important point is that this subject, like a
thick cloud of memory, has been insistently and im-
placably there. The Southern writer could romanticize
it, reject it, enlarge it into an image of the general
human situation; he could not escape it. And precisely
this ubiquity of subject matter provided him with some
very considerable advantages. Not so long before the
Civil War Hawthorne had remarked on "the difficulty
of writing a romance about a country where there is
no shadow, no antiquity, no picturesque and gloomy
wrong, nor anything but a commonplace prosperity."
But now the War and Reconstruction gave the Southern writers all that Hawthorne had found lacking—all
but antiquity. And there were ruins to take its place.

It was not until the First World War that serious
Southern writing began to appear—that is, not until

Southern regional consciousness had begun to decay. A
land bent by defeat was unlikely to turn to letters with
an urgent passion or enthusiasm. Nor could the South
look back upon a serious literary tradition of its own,
certainly none comparable to that of New England;
ante-bellum Southern writing had for the most part
been sentimental, genteel and insipid. Talented men in
the pre-Civil War South had given themselves to politics and oratory and had looked upon literature as a
minor pastime hardly sufficient to engage their intellectual capacities. Only some decades later, when the most
sensitive minds of the South would be appalled by the
Snopesian vulgarity of its commerce and its politics,
would they turn to the arts—half in hope, half in
desperation.

For it was the reality of twentieth-century life, in all
its coarse provocation, which drove so many Southern
writers to a regional past that in happier circumstances
they might have learned peaceably to forget. The mottoes of Southern agrarianism which became popular
some decades ago were hardly to be taken seriously as
social proposals for the most industrialized country in
the world; but as signs of a fundamental quarrel with
modern life, an often brilliant criticism of urban anonymity, they very much deserved to be taken seriously.

Before the Southern writers could make imaginative
statements about their own past, they had to be exposed to intellectual drafts from beyond their regional
horizon. Southern literature at its best—the work of
Faulkner, Caldwell, Ransom, Tate—was conceived in
an explosive mixture of provincialism and cosmopol-
itanism, tradition and modernity. To measure the stature and local value of their ancestor, Poe, the Southern writers had first to understand what he had meant
to Baudelaire, and for that they had to possess a sophisticated awareness of the European literary past.
For the Southern imagination to burst into high flame
it had to be stimulated, or irritated, by the pressures of

European and Northern ideas and literary modes. Left to itself, a regional consciousness is not likely to result in anything but a tiresome romanticizing of the past and, thereby, a failure to understand the present. Once, however, the South reached the point at which it still remained a distinct region—though already cracking under alien influences—it could begin to produce serious works of art. As Allen Tate has shrewdly remarked, "the distinctive Southern consciousness is quite temporary. It has made possible the curious burst of intelligence that we get at the crossing of the ways, not unlike, on an infinitesimal scale, the outburst of poetic genius at the end of the sixteenth century when commercial England had already begun to crush feudal England." What Tate seems to be saying here is that Southern literature took on seriousness and grandeur only when the South as a region began to die, when its writers were forced to look back upon a past that was irretrievable and forward to a future that seemed intolerable.

It is, therefore, insufficient to say, as some critics do, that Faulkner is a traditional moralist drawing his creative strength from the Southern myth. The truth is that he writes in opposition to this myth as well as in acceptance of it, that he struggles with it even as he continues to acknowledge its power and charm. As he moves from book to book, turning a more critical and mature eye upon his material, the rejection of an inherited tradition acquires a much greater intellectual and emotional stress than its defense. At no point, neither in his early romanticizing nor his later moral realism, is Faulkner's attitude toward the past of the South a simple or fixed one. The direction or drift is certainly away from romanticizing and toward realism. His relation to his own beliefs, characteristically "modern" in its ambivalence and instability, is far more difficult than was the case with most nineteenth-century American writers. We may safely assume that in their major work Melville and Whitman were moved by the democratic yearnings of nineteenth-century America; one feels of *Moby Dick* and *Leaves of Grass* that they are books written with the resources of an entire age behind them. Melville's epic conceptions and Whitman's rolling declamations follow, in part, from their adherence to a myth that is still viable and, therefore, likely to stir men to dedicated action. Faulkner, however, is working with the decayed fragments of a myth—the somewhat soured pieties of regional memory—and that is one reason his language is so often tortured, forced, and even incoherent. Unquestionably Faulkner has been influenced by Melville, but in their uses of language one can see reflected the difference between a belief still vigorous and a belief picking at its own bones. Yeats's definition of rhetoric as the will doing the work of the imagination is pertinent to both Melville and Faulkner, but particularly to Faulkner. For what is the soft shapeless rhetoric of *Sartoris* but the sign of a strained will floundering in sentimentality, and what is the agonized rhetoric of *Absalom, Absalom!* but the sign of a strained will confronted with its own intolerably acute awareness?

The Southern myth is a story or cluster of stories that expresses the deepest attitudes and reflects the most fundamental experiences of a people. Its subject is the fate of a ruined homeland. The homeland—so the story goes—had proudly insisted that it alone should determine its destiny. Provoked into a war impossible to win, it had nevertheless fought to its last strength, and it had fought this war with a reckless gallantry and a superb heroism that, as Faulkner might say, made of its defeat not a shame but almost a vindication. Yet the homeland fell, and from this fall came misery and squalor: ravaging by the conquerors, loss of faith among the descendants of the defeated, and the rise of a new breed of faceless men who would batten on their neighbors' humiliation.

From these stories there follows that pride in ancestral glory and that mourning over the decline of the homeland which constitute the psychology of the "lost cause." Thus, for one intermittently Southern writer, John Peale Bishop, the South found its highest distinction in "a manner of living somewhat more amiable than any other that has ever been known on the continent." And for another Southern writer, Allen Tate, the South is the one place that "clings blindly to forms of European feeling and conduct that were crushed by the French Revolution." Where else, he asks, "outside of the South, is there a society that believes even covertly in the Code of Honor?"

A myth which pervades a people's imagination is hardly open to rational attack or defense, particularly when it is considered as a part of a work of literature. The historian, no doubt, would have to compare the claims of the Southern myth with the actual course of Southern history. He would evaluate the tradition and order so often ascribed to the old South; inquire exactly for whom its way of living could be somewhat more amiable; speculate on the extent to which the Southern emphasis on honor may have been a means of salvaging pride from defeat or a token of uncertainty about the moral value of its cause. And if our historian were inclined to moral reflection he might ask the one question that, by its very nature, the myth cannot tolerate: Granted heroism, granted honor, was the homeland defending a just cause? For the literary critic these questions, while important, are not the crux of the matter, since it is hardly necessary to take at face value the claims of the Southern myth. I certainly do not accept these claims in order to acknowledge the creative uses to which this myth can be put by a sympathetic imagination. The Southern myth, like any other, is less an attempt at historical description than a voicing of the collective imagination—perhaps of the collective will. The old South over which it chants in threnody is an ideal image—a buried city, as Allen Tate has called it. Both the violence and the poignancy with which this ideal image has been employed suggest an awareness that the buried city can never be found.

The writer often comes to a myth eager for acquiescence, but after articulating its assumptions he may begin to wonder about its meaning and its value. During recent decades Northern writers have been engaged in a large-scale examination of myths of industrial capitalism such as enterprise, accumulation and success; the rejection of these myths has motivated a great many of the older contemporary writers. Somewhat similarly, Faulkner in his stories and novels has been conducting a long, sometimes painful and at other times heroic examination of the Southern myth. He has set his pride in the past against his despair over the present, and from this counterpoint has come much of the tension in his work. He has investigated the myth itself; wondered about the relation between the Southern tradition he admires and that memory of Southern slavery to which he is compelled to return; tested not only the present by the past, but also the past by the myth, and finally the myth by that morality which has slowly emerged from this entire process of exploration. This testing of the myth, though by no means the only important activity in Faulkner's work, is basic to the Yoknapatawpha novels and stories, and from it comes his growing vision as an artist.

IV

Outline of a World

THE EVENTS OF THE YOKNAPATAWPHA WORLD ARE hardly meant to illustrate social relations or tendencies, nor do they stem from a methodical scheme for the representation of Southern history. They may be reduced to such a scheme by the critic and perhaps they have to be, but in doing this, one runs the danger of exaggerating the extent to which they have been designed and risks underestimating the extent to which they have been summoned. For we are not in the presence of those strategies which make possible the fine coherence of a Henry James novel or, on a large and somewhat looser scale, of the *Comédie Humaine*. Despite the virtuosity that goes into most of Faulkner's books, their fundamental source is less the artificer's plan than the chronicler's vision.

The comparison frequently made between the Yoknapatawpha novels and the *Comédie Humaine* is therefore of limited value. In energy of presentation and inclusiveness of material Balzac and Faulkner do have much in common, but the genesis, and intent of their work are quite different. In the *Comédie Humaine* a powerful directing mind molds the individual novels

into a comprehensive portrait of nineteenth-century
French society, and brings to bear upon that portrait a
precise social point of view. Almost always in control of
his materials, Balzac isolates those elements of conduct
which reveal the status of a social class at a given moment in history. Faulkner is not nearly so often the
executive artist; some of his best work results from submission to rather than control of his materials. The
"idea" of society does not entice him as it does Balzac,
and he approaches it only when it thrusts itself upon
his line of sight. No consistent or precise social point of
view runs through his work. From book to book his attitude toward the South undergoes change and modulation, often without acknowledgment and sometimes
against the resistance of his will. In the end he offers
less an opinion about society than a view of man.

Though neither social photography nor historical record, the Yoknapatawpha chronicle is intimately related
to the milieu from which it is derived; it is an appropria-
tion from a communal memory, some great store of
half-forgotten legends, of which Faulkner is the last,
grieving recorder. It is as if the whole thing, no longer
available to public experience, lived fresh and imperious
in his mind, as the memory of the Civil War lives in the
mind of the Reverend Hightower in *Light in August*—a
tragic charade of the past. Thus the difficulty and ultimately the unimportance of dating events or of recon-
ciling the many contradictory datings in the Faulkner
world—in a vision sequence melts into simultaneity. So
too with Faulkner's productivity; he has little need to
construct, he needs only to call upon what is already
waiting for him. But even while it serves him as a private and luminous reserve, this vision impinges at every
point on the world in which he lives.

We are confronted, then, not with an imaginary
world of which every aspect is carefully designed, but
with a complicated story known in its essentials to
the narrator but still unordered in his mind—a story of

confused family records that can be unraveled only with difficulty. Behind the telling of this story there is always a desperate search for order, not merely as a strategy in narrative but also as a motive for composition. Incidents reappear from one book to another, their meanings changed and their tenor modified; characters, insignificant in one book, reach major dimension in another; narrative bits left fallow for years are suddenly worked over with ferocious energy. Less happily, in the later books, episodes that have been brilliantly unfolded are summarily repeated. As the Yoknapatawpha story grows there are accretions, rejections and afterthoughts. For reasons he need not continually trouble to make explicit, Faulkner returns to neglected strands of his story, working less by intent than impulse, and his occasional slips in chronology or names are due less to carelessness than the indifference to consistency that is typical of legends.

Faulkner's vision is hardly to be formulated in simple terms, nor is it at all the same as the resolution of his attitudes toward the South. But, for the moment, let us agree to consider mainly the latter. Malcolm Cowley has described Faulkner's social view as that of an "anti-slavery Southern nationalist," while George Marion O'Donnell, a pioneer Faulkner critic, finds him a "traditional moralist" defending the "Southern socio-economic-ethical tradition." Perhaps if Faulkner's responses to the South were kneaded into a tight ideological ball it would resemble anti-slavery nationalism, but actually his work contains almost every conceivable attitude toward the South, from sentimentality to denunciation, from identification to frigid rejection. While in his earlier books Faulkner may, at the price of simplification, be designated a "traditional moralist," and in parts of *Sartoris* and *The Unvanquished* the author apparently thinks of himself as a defender of the old South, his work shows a gradual recognition that his values can now be realized only in new and untested social groups. The Yoknapatawpha novels range in attitude from the suicidal romanticism of Bayard Sartoris to the grave ethical responsibility of Isaac McCaslin, and in the contrast of these extremes, as well as in the numerous shades between them, one can see a controlling preoccupation of Faulkner's work: the relation of the sensitive Southerner to his native myth, as it comforts and corrodes, inspires and repels. The myth appears in its simplest version in *The Unvanquished,* in which a few of the stories are hardly distinguishable from the romancing of popular Southern fiction. By the time *Intruder in the Dust* was written, Faulkner has almost broken away from his lifelong struggle with the Southern myth and re-entered the province of ordinary affairs. In *Absalom, Absalom!* he is often overcome by his struggle with the myth—which is one source of the magniloquent rhetoric of that book. But in his greatest novel *The Sound and the Fury* and in his greatest story "The Bear" there is a rare balance: the tension neither excessive nor slack.

[1]

The Yoknapatawpha novels did not appear in historical sequence. Though set in the Civil War period, *The Unvanquished* was published later than several books about twentieth-century Yoknapatawpha. And since he kept modifying, revising, and at some points, radically transforming the whole Yoknapatawpha story or legend, any effort to trace a clear or unbroken line of development in Faulkner's books becomes extremely risky. They can be discussed in order of internal chronology, which yields a history of Yoknapatawpha, or in order of publication, which may provide a history of Faulkner's attitudes toward his subject matter. In practice, a blend of the two is inescapable.

Sartoris is the necessary beginning. Its action takes place directly after the first world war, when Bayard Sartoris comes home from battle, sick in mind, without hope or purpose, and haunted by the death of his twin, John, who has been shot down in aerial combat over France, while he, Bayard, watched helplessly. The morbid relation between the brothers is important for the novel, but soon it becomes clear that Faulkner means this problem to lead toward, or be symptomatic of, a still larger one. As in *Soldiers' Pay*, he struggles with the difficulty of trying to impose an enormous weight of meaning on a character who is virtually speechless and incapable of any large or transforming action. Bayard is to serve as a focus of estrangement and discontent, but whenever we are required to observe him closely, we are more likely to be struck by his private troubles than their public reverberations. And since a good many of the events in the novel are measured by their impact on Bayard, the fault proves to be a serious one.

More a cluster of set-pieces than a compact narrative, *Sartoris* reads like a notebook packed with bits and pieces of novels still to be written, as if Faulkner cared only about hurrying it all onto paper. Several of the Yoknapatawpha social groups are summarily introduced: the ebbing patriciate in the Sartorises, the independent hill farmers in the MacCallums, and, secondarily, the Snopeses and the Negroes. Though the Yoknapatawpha world is not yet seen distinctly, the feelings it will elicit from its creator lie about in profusion, often in excess of what the book itself requires. It is a book heavy with the air of sickness, but neither diagnosis nor cure is suggested; the characteristic tensions of Faulkner's world begin to emerge, but they are still incipient and undefined. Perhaps this is one reason *Sartoris* is so sluggish in pace, as if it were neurotically circling its material rather than extending it through narrative.

Bayard's inability to achieve a sustaining relationship with the tradition of his family and native region forms a central theme of the book. In Faulkner's world the Sartorises stand for the Southern patriciate, the group

in whom the values of the homeland should presumably
find a vital agent; but Bayard, a sullen and muddled
young man, does not understand what the tradition is
or is supposed to be. That it once was there, he knows;
that something should replace it, he also knows. But he
cannot move beyond his awareness of loss. In his "false
and stubborn pride" he burns with a sense of depriva-
tion. He drinks, he mopes, he mourns the death of his
twin. All of his concerns seem to be immediate ones,
brought on by his time in the European war.

Whatever artistry Faulkner commands in this novel is
largely directed toward reinforcing the suggestion that
Bayard's problems are ultimately related to those of the
family and the homeland. There are vivid scenes—vivid
because here Faulkner need not trouble himself with
Bayard as a "problem"—in which he goes off on a
drunk with town cronies and ends feeling more cha-
grined, more "cheated" than ever. With barely a sign
of emotion—for he loves only his dead brother, only the
fact of death in his dead brother, perhaps only the heritage of death which is all the family tradition yields him
—Bayard marries one of those placid females who appear regularly in Faulkner's books. This one is called,
not accidentally, Narcissa, and she makes a number of
efforts to pull Bayard into the comfort of ordinary life.
But she does not succeed, the distance between husband and wife, as between a wish for death and con-
tentment with life, being too great. Brought up in a
milieu where introspection has seldom been valued,
Bayard suddenly faces a need for a self-awareness he
cannot even define, let alone discover. His intelligence
is unequal to his despair.

Bayard's situation is clarified through several contrasts
with other Sartorises. His grandfather, also named Bayard, has lived through the Civil War and experienced
the collapse of the homeland, but is no longer morally
competent to help young Bayard. The older Bayard has
retained little of tradition except a clutter of sentimen-

tal details. Once, apparently, there was a great story, an heroic legend, but even those who lived through it can no longer remember. Indeed, one way of defining young Bayard's problem is to note that the older Bayard no longer has anything to tell or hand down to him. Through wild automobile rides, the two court death together, each releasing his own bafflement in a search for violence. Faulkner notes the parallel with some skill, and through the similarities of character implies that young Bayard's self-destructiveness has roots in the very past from which he feels cut off. His deracination comes to be an oblique criticism of the lost tradition.

A more emphatic comparison with the past is provided by another Sartoris, an ancestor who fought with Jeb Stuart in the Civil War. This is *the other Bayard*—what the living Bayard might have been in more heroic times. How the other Bayard lived and died has become a family legend, a standard of the ideal past by which to measure the smallness of the present.

During the war (the important war) the other Bayard had been witness to the capture of a Northern major and had heard General Stuart apologize for being unable to furnish him a horse. Half playfully, Stuart added that a horse might be had by another raid on Northern lines—to which the major replied that the comfort of an insignificant prisoner hardly warranted the risk of Southern soldiers. There follows a pivotal passage:

"Not for the prisoner, sir," Stuart haughtily replied, "but for the officer suffering the fortune of war. No gentleman would do less."

"No gentleman has any business in this war," the major retorted. "There is no place for him here. He is an anachronism, like anchovies. At least General Stuart did not capture our anchovies. . . . Perhaps he will send Lee for them in person."

Hearing the Northerner's ungallant rejoinder, the other
Bayard wheeled his horse, rode back to the Northern
lines in quest of the now symbolic anchovies, and was
killed.

In spiritual composition the other Bayard and the
young Bayard are much alike, but the former's death,
while an act of outrageous bravado, is also an effort to
vindicate a principle through a willed gesture. The
other Bayard can still give his death a chosen, personal
quality, while for the modern Bayard death has become
anonymous and mechanical. At the end of the book,
the modern Bayard will die without purpose or dignity, simply by arranging for his own destruction.

In this contrast between ways of dying, we see the
decline of a world and the code that once kept it vital.
Or do we? Can the meaning of the Southern tradition
be realized in what Faulkner himself calls the other
Bayard's "hare-brained prank?" Does the contrast between the two Bayards yield quite the significance it is
apparently meant to? Such questions are not easy to answer, since Faulkner's own attitude toward the world of
the Sartorises is ambiguous. But the objection to the
novel is not that Faulkner's feelings toward the homeland are either more or less ambiguous than in his
later works; it is that he fails to confront the ambiguity
with the seriousness which characterizes the best of his
later works. Seldom in *Sartoris* does Faulkner rise above
the limit of his characters' perception—and, given the
Sartorises, this is a severe limit. Seldom can Faulkner
summon, in any strong imaginative way, more of the
lost tradition than the deprived Bayard himself.

The contrast between the Bayard of anchovies and
the Bayard of airplanes becomes open to an excessive
range and number of interpretations. For surely the
other Bayard's dash toward the Northern lines, while
admirable enough within the limits of adolescent feeling, cannot be made to carry the burden of a lost tradition—to say nothing of that awareness of human issues

we identify as the moral sense. There is reason to suppose that Faulkner knows this, since none of the Bayards escapes some measure of critical irony; but he knows it only for part of the time and his irony lacks adequate force or intellectual coherence. As a symbol of the past, the other Bayard will not do—or perhaps, by destroying the notion that the past of the homeland contained a profound if now buried value, he does too well.

We face here a difficult problem in criticism. It is hard to make a clear or confident distinction between the ambiguities a writer perceives and controls and the ambiguities which, even if he perceives, he does not control. The dash and glamor of the other Bayard are treated by Faulkner with a mixture of admiration and deprecatory amusement, yet the pattern of the book and its romantic style persuade us to put at least some positive stress on that crucial dash for the anchovies. In the exchange between General Stuart and the Northern major, Faulkner's understanding is at least partly with the major, while his sympathies are largely with Stuart.

This difficulty in locating or embodying the values of the past troubles the entire novel. The South, writes Faulkner, fought "in a spirit of pure fun; neither Jeb Stuart nor Bayard Sartoris, as their actions clearly showed, had any political convictions at all." One may be allowed to doubt this, or at least to remark that between pure fun and political convictions there can be a great many other motives for fighting a war. But if Faulkner is right, then why are we to suppose that Bayard's inability to find his place in the tradition of the homeland is as great a loss as Faulkner would have us suppose? The question matters not in the abstract—we are not rehearsing old wars—but insofar as it touches upon the meaning and value of the novel.

A similar difficulty in furnishing moral substance for the tradition can be observed in another passage, an exchange between Bayard's grandfather and an old Civil War veteran:

> Old Bayard shook the ash from his cigar. "Will," he said, "What the devil were you folks fighting about, anyway?"
>
> "Bayard," old man Falls answered, "be damned ef I ever did know."

Some allowance should be made here for the playful caginess of old men sparring with one another. Perhaps, too, the failure of old man Falls to say what the great war was about, should not be taken to mean that he didn't once know or, at some deep level, still doesn't know. And it can even be argued, as Alfred Kazin has argued, that Faulkner wishes here to elegize "the heroic traits called out by war, the intimate solidarity and unconscious beauty of a common effort." My own reading of the novel is a different one. In the context of the book, where so much is made about the tacit relation between Bayard's troubles and the disintegration of the Southern or Sartoris code, it is precisely "the intimate solidarity and unconscious beauty of a common effort" that will no longer do. That kind of rhetoric seems a little wilted by the time the young Bayard comes home, and if his inarticulate rage and desperation have any meaning at all, they suggest a need to find something more substantial.

It may then be that old man Falls answers better than he knows, particularly since none of the more intelligent characters in the book can provide a more significant answer to old Bayard's question. And in the absence of such an answer, little remains but the trite sentimentalism to which Faulkner succumbs:

> The music went on in the dusk softly; the dusk was peopled with ghosts of glamorous and old disastrous things. And if they were just glamorous

enough, there was sure to be a Sartoris in them,
and then they were sure to be disastrous . . . For
there is death in the sound of [Sartoris] and a glamorous fatality, like silver pennons downrushing at
sunset, or a dying fall of horns along the road to
Roncevaux.

Such passages lead one to question the reading proposed first by George Marion O'Donnell and then accepted by many Faulkner critics. "The Sartorises," according to O'Donnell, "act traditionally; that is to say,
they act always with an ethically responsible will. They
represent vital morality, humanism." It is hard to reconcile such statements with an attentive reading of *Sartoris*, for at least one of the meanings of the novel is
that the family has always been under a compulsion to
glamorous self-destruction—which is to say that the
Southern tradition, flawed from within, drives toward
its own death. And whatever the undoubted attractions
of glamorous self-destruction, it should really be kept
distinct from "vital morality." Somewhere there may
be a tradition for Bayard Sartoris to find, but the novel
indicates, even if not wholly in the way Faulkner seems
to intend, that the chaos of the Sartoris family is hardly
the place to look for it.

Bayard must go elsewhere, to another family. (All
through the Yoknapatawpha chronicle, as a recurrent
rhythm, the search for a new morality means a turning
to another family.) In the only first-rate section of
Sartoris, Bayard turns to the MacCallums, a clan of
hillsmen and small farmers. Here Faulkner's style also
changes; it becomes firmer, harsher. Somewhat similar
in function to the hunt scene of *War and Peace*, this
section anticipates a main direction of Faulkner's work:
from the feeble aristocracy of the Sartorises to the Mac-
Callums, proud plebeian farmers.

Old Mr. MacCallum and his unmarried sons form a
family rigorous in standards of behavior yet bound in

grave affection,—their unity a powerful contrast to the crumbling of the Sartorises. Here, amidst the possum hunts and freezing breakfasts and blazing fires, Bayard finds propriety and peace; life takes on a warming equanimity, a tolerable rhythm.

And he lay, at ease at last, intending to rise and go to [the MacCallums] the next moment, putting it off a little longer while his blood beat slowly through his body and his heart was quieted. Buddy breathed steadily beside him, and his own breath was untroubled now as Buddy's while the human sounds came murmurously into the cold room with grave and homely reassurance. It comes to all, it comes to all, his tired heart comforted him, and at last he slept.

This composure lasts but a moment. Among the Mac-Callums too there are signs of decay: the sons unmarried, the youngest one envying Bayard his town privileges, the family vigor dependent mainly on the will of an aging father. On Christmas day, grateful for their steadying influence, but restless with the thought of home, Bayard leaves the MacCallums and wanders through the countryside. He takes shelter in the cabin of a Negro family with whom he shares a modest holiday meal, and here again he savors an interlude of quiet and decorum. But again, he cannot stay.

Home from the war and in search of a way to live, Bayard Sartoris finds neither guidance nor release from his need. Somewhere, something has been lost, and, as he plunges wilfully to his death, that is all he knows.

[2]

One of Faulkner's few efforts to fill in the Sartoris past and, thereby, to populate his myth, is the loose episodic novel *The Unvanquished*. Yet, even here, Faulkner does not show the Southern tradition brought to life through a normal passage of society nor, for that matter,

through the excitements of war. If, as Robert Penn Warren tells us, Faulkner places a high value on the old
order because it allowed man "to define himself by setting up codes, concepts of virtue, obligations, and by accepting the risks of his humanity," it is remarkable how
little embodiment this value finds in the novels themselves. Nowhere in Faulkner's work is there a copious
and lively image of the old South. It remains forever a
muted shadow, a point of reference rather than an object for presentation, perhaps because the effort to see it
in fullness would be too great a strain on the imagination. The founding and later fall of Yoknapatawpha
Faulkner can confront imaginatively, the first in a number of splendid stories and the second in several of the
novels, but in *The Unvanquished,* one of the few novels in which he ventures a glimpse of the old South, he
begins at the moment where its defeat is a certainty.
From another point of view, however, this absence of
the old South is no weakness at all, since it reveals a
sense of reality triumphing over a writer's preconceptions—wisdom as omission.

Often mildly entertaining, *The Unvanquished* is the
least serious of the Yoknapatawpha novels. Most of it
was written for the slick magazines, and not only does
the book show this, it also shows how economically a
gifted writer can parcel out his major themes for trivial
occasions. The craftsman's shrewdness which, upon
need, could make Faulkner into an efficient Hollywood
scriptwriter, is also visible in *The Unvanquished.*

In the book's earlier episodes the Civil War is seen
through the eyes of Bayard Sartoris (the grandfather in
Sartoris), a boy whose level of response—usually also
the book's level of response—seldom rises above that of
Tom Sawyer. This is surely no accident, since the closer
Faulkner comes to the old South as an actual society,
the more his writing runs to coyness. But where the
world of *Tom Sawyer* is essentially a boy's world, so that
there is no reason whatever to be troubled by the lim-

its of Tom's vision, the world of *The Unvanquished* is
an adult's world, so that there is frequent reason to be
troubled by the limits of Bayard's vision. It is as if *The
Unvanquished* had been composed to deal with the
matter of *Huckleberry Finn* in the terms of *Tom Sawyer.* This is not the case, however, through the whole
book. Toward the end, as the tone darkens, Faulkner
abandons the manorial adventures of Bayard's grand-
mama, Miss Rosa Millard, as well as the antics of Bayard and his Negro pal, Ringo, and writes about the troubles of the defeated South with some authenticity. In
the death of the Southern tradition he believes passionately; its life is harder to imagine.

The characters meant to embody the tradition are
credible only when seen as agents of wartime resistance,
though even here Faulkner indulges in popular trivial-
ities: Bayard and Ringo firing at Yankee troops and
then hiding beneath the capacious skirts of Miss Rosa,
while a sharp-eyed Yankee officer pretends not to see
them; Cousin Drusilla getting herself up as a man in
order to ride with Colonel Sartoris' raiders; Granny Millard badgering her slaves to bury and then dig up the
family silver to protect it from the Yankees. In her role
as Southern lady Granny Millard is a creature of popular fiction rather than adult imagination. She takes on a
measure of reality, however, when she turns to mule-
stealing as a way of feeding her neighbors and discovers
the moral complications that follow from a partnership
with a rascal like Ab Snopes. Most of the time she seems
essentially a figure of the theatre, and, as a representative of a way of life, is memorable less for the quality of
her soul than the rigor of her carriage.

Colonel John Sartoris, a character of greater substance, is seldom seen full-face, since Faulkner is curiously disinclined to confront him. At one moment the
Colonel is a Lochinvar, riding off to plague the enemy
with his bellicose sweetheart, dressed as a man, on the
saddle behind him; at another moment he is a surpris-

ingly thoughtful student of Southern economy who approves a neighbor's experiment in replacing slavery with cooperative farming. In one story he is leader of a cabal to keep Negroes from voting,[2] in another he appears as a sudden advocate of a moratorium on violence: "I am tired of killing men, no matter what the necessity nor the end."

Since Colonel Sartoris resembles Colonel William Falkner in a number of ways, it seems likely that Faulkner had a consistent portrait in mind when he sketched these various aspects of Sartoris. But the consistent portrait does not emerge in the book, for it is a limitation of the popular mode in which Faulkner is working that it discourages those broodings and worryings through which he usually enriches an incident. Still, the Colonel is the most impressive of the Sartoris clan: a figure of some intelligence, endowed with a sardonic sense of self-limitation, and capable of a sustained action. Had the general tenor of the book been somewhat more serious, Faulkner might have been able to render him as a tragic or at least imposing personification of the power and weakness of the old order, but the novel is so organized as to evade that possibility. When so much of the action is presented in a slick and jolly manner, no adequate treatment is possible of such themes as civil war, the disruption of a society, and the cost of immoral behavior in behalf of urgent human needs.

In the unfolding of the Yoknapatawpha chronicle

[2] Though obviously needing an evaluative context, this incident is presented as a neutral anecdote: charm replaces moral responsibility. By the time he came to write *Light in August*, where the incident is briefly recalled, Faulkner had grown into a more mature writer, so that Colonel Sartoris's killing of two "carpetbaggers" and his intimidation of the Negroes is seen in quite another way. Joanna Burden, a descendent of one of the "carpetbaggers," remarks: "I suppose that Colonel Sartoris was a town hero because he killed with two shots from the same pistol an old one-armed man and a boy who had never even cast his first vote."

The Unvanquished would seem to occupy a strategic
introductory position, but the work itself is too feeble
for that role. One must remind oneself that this is
Faulkner's book about the Civil War. These coltish
anecdotes form a narrative presumably reflecting the
homeland's catastrophe. As Bayard and Ringo nestle
beneath Granny's skirts and trick the whole damned-
yankee army into supplying them with mules, one is
tempted to ask: was this the war that roused William
Tecumseh Sherman to his burst of eloquence?

There are, to be sure, effective bits throughout the
book: Negro slaves in flight after the collapse of the
Confederate Army, the rise of Grumby's bushwhackers
from the social flotsam of the South, Bayard's rejection
of the violence which is the heritage of his family. Most
of the incidents, however, remain inadequate for Faulkner's occasional perceptions, and the perceptions themselves inadequate for the heroic potential of the subject.

Why then is the portrait of the homeland's agony
little more than a trivial sketch of adolescent adventure?
The Sartorises can engage Faulkner's serious attention
when they are heroically and stubbornly embattled in
behalf of a lost cause, but as representatives of a social
order, they elicit from him a mixture of amused fondness, family pride, a somewhat quizzical effort at belief,
and what Allen Tate has caustically described as "Confederate rhetoric." Faulkner's failure in *The Unvanquished* to write about the South and the Civil War in
accents of tragedy or sustained seriousness must call to
question the view that he values the Sartoris world as
one that allows man to define himself as truly "human."
Perhaps Faulkner once believed this, surely he once
wanted to, but he has been singularly unable to project
it in a work of art. At times the traditional order wins
his formal acquiescence, but it cannot arouse his most
serious feelings, and the Sartoris clan, like the world for
which it stands, fails to release his most deeply felt and
radical images of life.

[3]

We are now close to an initial statement of the Yoknapatawpha theme, at least insofar as it is social in nature.
Sartoris reveals a need to search for moral guidance in
the past, but does not adequately locate the source of
that need in the present. *The Unvanquished* suggests
that the conventional Southern past, while still an object of some affection, cannot furnish Faulkner with
what he seeks. Later he will turn more deeply, beyond
the Sartorises, to that past again, in *Absalom, Absalom!*
In *The Sound and the Fury* discontent with the present
and a search for the past are presented by a writer in full
control of his material. These three books form the ma-
trix of the social theme in the Yoknapatawpha chronicle.
Three others—*As I Lay Dying, Sanctuary* and *Light in
August*—are variations and elaborations, not so much
on the legend of the homeland as on the consequences
of its decay. In *Absalom, Absalom!* Faulkner returns
with an overwhelming ferocity to his central subject:
the ordeal and collapse of the homeland. In *Go Down,
Moses* the problems raised in his work approach a resolution, previously hinted at in *The Hamlet* and later to
be imperfectly echoed in his more recent novels.

The Sound and the Fury records the fall of a house
and the death of a society. Here, as nowhere else in his
work, Faulkner regards Yoknapatawpha from a historical perspective, yet there is little history either told or
shown—not nearly so much as in *Absalom, Absalom!* or
the rhapsodic interludes of *Requiem for a Nun*. Perhaps the most remarkable fact about this remarkable
novel is that its rich sense of history comes from a story
rigidly confined to a single family, a story almost claus-
trophobic in its concentration on a narrow sequence of
events. Faulkner has said that *The Sound and the Fury*
had its origins in "the impression of a little girl playing in a branch and getting her panties wet." That impression is to be central in the book, as a moment com-

pletely felt and seen, and from it will follow a series of
actions ranging in significance far beyond the little girl
with the wet panties, her family, or her homeland. In
The Sound and the Fury Faulkner persuades us, as
never before, to accept Yoknapatawpha as an emblem
of a larger world beyond, and its moral death as an act-
ing-out of the disorder of our time. But he remains in
and of this local place, his feeling toward Yoknapatawpha a fluid mixture of affection and disgust. The material is seen from a perspective which in times of social
decline is most useful to a writer: that simultaneous involvement with and estrangement from a native scene
which allows for both a tragic and an ironic response.

Each character is unique—an entity. All of them together represent the sum of the loss which Faulkner
measures in the history of Yoknapatawpha. In their
squalor and pathos, the Compsons are the Southern
patriciate *in extremis*. Stripped of whatever is contingent in their experience, they come to suggest a dominant quality of modern life. They are of the South, signifying its decay and its shame, but the decay is universal and, therefore, the shame should also be universal. To confine the meaning of their story to a seg-
ment of Southern life is sheer provincialism, as fatuous
as an attempt to isolate a plague by drawing a line on
the map. This book is a lament for the passing of a
world, not merely the world of Yoknapatawpha and not
merely the South.

The sense of diminution and loss is intensified by
Faulkner's setting the action on Good Friday, Saturday, and Easter Sunday, so that the values of the Christian order provide a muted backdrop to the conduct of
the Compsons. These Christian references are handled
with delicacy and modesty, a triumph of tact Faulkner
does not always repeat in his later work. They rarely
break past the surface of the story to call attention to
themselves and tempt us into the error of allegory; they
never deflect us from the behavior and emotions of the

represented figures at the center of the book.[3] Toward
the end there is a scene in a Negro church, in which all
that has happened is brought to a coda by the marvelous sermon of a Negro preacher—"I got de ricklickshun en 'de blood of de Lamb!' "—and the simple kindliness of some Negro figures. Here the foreground action and the Christian references seem to draw closer,
not in order to score any religious point or provide critics with occasions for piety, but to allow the language
of the Christian drama, as it has been preserved by the
Negroes, to enforce a tacit judgment on the ending of
the Compsons.

For the Compsons the family is less a tie of blood
than a chafe of guilt. Love can exist only as a memory
of childhood, and memory only as a gall. Morality becomes a conscience-spur to the wish for death. Money is
the universal solvent, replacing affection, integrity, and
every other sentiment beyond calculation. All this, of
course, is notoriously morbid and excessive, as literature
so often is; but morbidity and excess apart, the world of
the Compsons should not be too difficult for us to acknowledge.

Among the Compsons the past lives in the broken
images that crowd the mind of Benjy, the idiot son, to
whom the past is indistinguishable from the present.
The past is sensation: the excitement of the Compson
children when their "Damuddy" dies, the pleasure of
sister Caddy crawling into bed with him while Dilsey
scolds that a boy of thirteen is too big to "sleep with
folks," the exhilaration of drinking "sassparilluh" at his
sister's wedding. These are memories Benjy cannot

[3] The following exchange comes from a recorded interview
with Faulkner at the University of Virginia:

"Q. . . . . . did you make any conscious attempt in *The
Sound and the Fury* to use Christian references, as a number of
critics have suggested?"

"A. No. I was just trying to tell a story of Caddy, the little girl
who had muddied her drawers. . . ."

wholly retrieve, but the limited number that he does retrieve is pure. He is affection barely qualified, and like other great idiots of literature provides a standard by which to measure sanity. Only in an idiot can love and loyalty survive. To this traditional hyperbole Faulkner adds the bitter footnote that these virtues survive in Benjy because he lacks the capacity to reject them.

That which Benjy knows—his sister smelling like trees, the pasture near his home, the fire burning cleanly, the jimson weeds he carries as his private graveyard for the dead Compsons—he cherishes without stint or reservation. Because he loves; because the sound of Caddy's name makes him moan over her loss; because the funeral of grandmother and the wedding of sister blend in memory, with dirge and epithalamium becoming one; because even now, at thirty-three, he is again the fifteen-year-old straining at the gate and looking for Caddy after she has left with her banker-husband— "*You cant do no good holding to the gate and crying*," his Negro keeper tells him, "*She cant hear you*"—because his sense of smell is a finer instrument than the moral sense of the other Compsons; because he cannot conceive of disloyalty, let alone commit a disloyal act; since in him the passage of time neither abates affection nor assuages woe; because of all this, Benjy is clearly an idiot. He must be.

Quentin Compson is Faulkner's image of a man aware of his dispossession, but unable to endure or transcend it. Living at an extreme of exacerbated consciousness, Quentin cannot dispose of the problems thrown up by that consciousness. Without an ordering code of belief, he is left entirely to the mercy of his perceptions, and these bring him little but chaos and pain. The "fine, dead sounds" he has heard throughout his youth, the words that form his heritage, he can neither abandon nor quicken into life.

Quentin feels that a familiar sin, because it would be there, undeniable and gross, is preferable to the routine of drift. He tries to persuade himself that he has had incestuous relations with Caddy. His story of incest is fictitious, but not merely a fantasy: " 'yes," says Caddy, "I'll do anything you want me to, anything.' " When he turns to his father for help, the elder Compson can offer him only the stale ends of country-store skepticism. His father is lost in a sterile affection for the classics, his mother in absurd pretensions to gentility. What reason, she whines, did Quentin have for committing suicide? "It can't simply be to flout and hurt me. Whoever God is, He would not permit that. I'm a lady."

Beyond everything, Quentin yearns for death—the "clean flame" that will burn out consciousness and guilt —for he can exist neither in the realm of the senses, which he fears, nor in the realm of the intellect, where he stumbles. Unable to forge the conscience of his race, he ends as a wanderer in an alien city; the lost son of Jefferson, Mississippi finds death in the Charles River of Massachusetts.

One Compson survives his family: Jason, the submoral man, rid of all supererogatory virtues, stripped to economic function and a modest, controlled physical appetite. He scorns the very notion that one human being can willingly assume and discharge obligations to another. He lives rigorously, even pedantically by the letter of his bargains. It is not that he is unkind, it is simply that he has no use for and does not believe in kindness. When the Negro boy Luster cannot produce a nickel to pay for a circus ticket, Jason prefers to burn it—with the diseased sardonic pleasure of a man turned cruel from consistency.

Like those quasi-intellectuals who abandon old allegiances to become the spokesmen of a rising new class, Jason formulates the values of Snopesism with a cleverness and vengeance which no Snopes could express. His motivating principle is never to be taken in, never to be distracted by sentiment or claims to selflessness; he knows better. Benjy he calls the "great American Gelding." Caddy he characterizes, "once a bitch, always a bitch." When the Negro servants leave for church and his mother whimpers "I know you will blame me" for the dinner being cold, Jason replies with invincible logic, "For what? . . . You never resurrected Christ, did you?" He and Mrs. Compson are the only members of the family who retain some tie at the end of the novel, he cynically using her and she fatuously deceived by him. The relationship is apt, a sign of the union between the decadent old and vicious new, with the gentility of the former veiling the rapacity of the latter. In the final passage of the section devoted to Jason, Faulkner brilliantly evokes his *Weltanschauung* as a blend of frustrated greed, coarseness, and the two most important forms of American prejudice. Dreaming of a stock-market coup, Jason says: "And just let me have twenty-four hours without any damn New York Jew to advise me what it's going to do. . . . I just want an even chance to get my money back. And once I've done that they can bring all Beale Street and all bedlam in here and two of them can sleep in my bed and another one can have my place at the table too."

To these figures of disorder and corruption, the remaining Compsons are secondary: Caddy, for whom sex is a fate rather than a temptation; Mr. Compson, who knowingly retreats from responsibility; and Mrs. Compson, always a lady and never a mother. In contrast to them stands the Negro servant Dilsey, strong, whole, uncorrupted—a voice of judgment over the Compsons and their world: "I've seed de first an de last." As she brings Mrs. Compson her hot-water bottle, as she warns her grandson not to "projeck" with Benjy's graveyard, as she blocks the thrusts of Jason's spite, she towers over the puny Compsons like some immense hieratic figure of integrity. At the end, when Dilsey brings Benjy to the Negro church, they stand alone in a landscape of ruins: the meek and the oppressed, the insulted and injured.

In the midst of the voices and the hands Ben sat, rapt in his sweet blue gaze. Dilsey sat bolt upright beside, crying rigidly and quietly in the annealment and the blood of the remembered Lamb.

[4]

As I Lay Dying is the story of another family. Since it is largely devoted to the life of the Bundrens as they respond to their mother's death, the book suffers if read merely as an episode in the Yoknapatawpha story; and most of the critical observations I wish to make about it will appear in a later section. But that side of the novel which does permit placement in the historical and legendary setting of Yoknapatawpha, quickly calls for comparison with *The Sound and the Fury*. The Bundrens are wretched, sometimes to the point of absurdity, but because they retain some feeling for the land and have not yet succumbed to town manners and "culture," they can find in themselves a portion of the strength needed for survival as a family. The Compsons cannot hold together, even for the most urgent needs of self-preservation, while the slothful Bundrens, in their own pitiful way, can.

Though in some respects Faulkner's most difficult and enigmatic novel, *As I Lay Dying* has an apparently simple plot. Addie Bundren, wife of a poor farmer, has come to the end of her existence. As the family waits for her death, Anse, the husband, ruminates and whines, Cash, the eldest son, phlegmatically builds a coffin beneath the window of her room, and the other children hover about with a mixture of selfishness, fear, and distress. Dewey Dell, the daughter, is pregnant and in order to get some abortion pills cannot help wishing that the journey to bury Addie in the Jefferson cemetery may soon begin. Jewel, Addie's illegitimate son, and Darl, the son given to introspection, both feel that the death of the mother will force a crisis in their relationship to each other and to the family. Vardaman, the youngest boy, is terrified, perhaps deranged by the whole experience. When Addie finally dies, the family sets out on a nightmarish—yet outrageously comic—journey to bring the body to Jefferson. In the end Addie lies buried with her kin and each of the Bundrens moves off to his own fate.

That the Bundrens should not be idealized is essential to Faulkner's purpose: he juxtaposes them to several farm families that are socially sturdier and morally healthier. Unlike the poor farmers neighboring them, the Bundrens scrape Yoknapatawpha's social bottom and may properly be called "poor whites." They suffer a great number of the plagues that traditionally descend upon "poor whites," especially in Southern literature. Anse the father is shiftless, and among the children Jewel is obsessive, Dewey Dell placidly vegetable, and Darl finally mad. Yet they are capable of an act in common, an act of piety. Each has private motives for wishing to obey the mother's request to be buried in Jefferson, but to list these motives is not to exhaust the meaning of their journey. Anse wants his store teeth and new wife, Cash his phonograph and Dewey Dell her abortion pills, but all of them still feel an obligation to the dead woman.

The comparison with the Compsons is so striking, precisely because the Bundrens are so shabby. Had Faulkner written about one of the other farm families, its moral superiority to the Compsons would have been immediately apparent and, therefore, of small dramatic value. As it is, Faulkner seems to be saying—and with the power of shock—that even the Bundrens, looked down upon and pitied by the poorest of their neighbors, are able to come together in a brief act of humanity in a way the Compsons cannot. What is involved here, be it consciously intended by Faulkner or not, is a shift in social interest and concern, perhaps in social allegiance: a shift, I believe, that will have major consequences throughout Faulkner's later work.

Even Anse, the least worthy member of the family, is capable of saying about his dead wife: "The somebody you was young with and you growed old in her and she growed old in you, seeing the old coming on and it was the one somebody you could hear say it don't matter and know it the truth. . . ." These, to be sure, are words, and we soon learn to discount Anse and his words. We learn to discount them partly because there rings through the book the fierce outcry of Addie, heard in a flashback to an indefinite time before her death:

> "And so when Cora Tull would tell me I was not a true mother, I would think how words go straight up in a thin line, quick and harmless, and how terribly doing goes along the earth, clinging to it, so that after a while the two lines are too far apart for the same person to straddle from one to the other; and that sin and love and fear are just sounds that people who never sinned nor loved nor feared have for what they never had and cannot have until they forget the words. Like Cora, who could never even cook."

That Anse finds another wife at the end of the journey, reveals the obvious limits of his selflessness; but his tribute to the dead woman, at least for the moment it is spoken, has a speck of the genuine, it does cling a little to the earth. Anse is emotionally withered and feckless, but he is not, in any usual sense, a hypocrite.

Similar though less severe judgments can be made about the rest of the family. Whatever their inadequacies of consciousness, the Bundrens do feel a need to offer some token of responsibility to the dead and exhibit some awareness of the claims of kinship. From one point of view, the novel releases a series of wildly grotesque misadventures which test and separate the members of the family; from another point of view, all that matters is that somehow the ethical duty of the Bundrens is fulfilled—poorly, stupidly, absurdly; but fulfilled.

The Compsons command the words of the past, the memory and the rhetoric of honor, while the Bundrens are ignorant, obscure, benighted. Yet the "fine, dead sounds" raise stronger echoes among the Bundrens than the Compsons. Moral values, so desperately violated in *The Sound and the Fury*, find a precarious and quizzical embodiment in *As I Lay Dying*, if only because the Bundrens show an occasional will to struggle. Some of Faulkner's critics have quoted, in order to illuminate Quentin Compson's despair, the famous sentence of T. S. Eliot: "It is better, in a paradoxical way, to do evil than to do nothing: at least we exist." The remark is also relevant to *As I Lay Dying*, for the Bundrens: at least they exist.

That they pay so high a price for their existence, that they must do everything the painfully hard way, that they are so victimized by a maddening literalism—all this becomes a source of the novel's poignant comedy. Their failure to distinguish between formal promise and actual responsibility is a moral undercurrent of the wretched journey, complicating yet not cancelling out the significance of their collective act. Only Darl senses how preposterous the journey has become, and to end it he fires a barn in which the rotting body has been sheltered. His motives are not entirely pure, one suspects, and his feeling that he is an unwanted son surely has something to do with this act; yet it is conceived, pitifully, in terms of kinship—the kinship that binds even as it disrupts the family. Among the Bundrens it is at least possible for one member of the family to reach another, perhaps to please, more often to hurt, but still to reach.

As I Lay Dying records Faulkner's discovery of new resources, and with this comes a new closeness and even kindliness toward his characters. The boy Darl goes mad, but his straining for an ordered knowledge of the family's inner life is often on a higher moral plane than the similar efforts of Bayard Sartoris and Quentin Compson: he is more disinterested than they, purer in spirit. Critics have sometimes complained that Faulkner overwhelms his poor whites, particularly Darl, with unlikely philosophical reflections. The complaint itself I shall discuss later, but here it should be noticed that Darl's more extravagant passages are motivated by a feeling that ultimately these poor whites have their possibilities of consciousness.

Finally, *As I Lay Dying* serves another purpose in the Yoknapatawpha chronicle; it serves as an image of the basic Southern experience. The wretched Bundrens, carrying their mother's putrescent corpse through the summer sun, wandering across the torpid land, defeated by obstacles both induced and inescapable, torn by obscure inner rivalries—all this suggests the condition of the homeland itself: unable to dispose of or come to terms with the dead.

[5]

The accusation against modern life at the heart of *The Sound and the Fury*, for which *As I Lay Dying* forms both confirmation and contrast, recurs in Faulkner's next two novels. Though of unequal merit, *Sanctuary* and *Light in August* have several things in common: both examine the failure of a serious man to oppose injustice with the vigor his conscience and social place require; both can be read as fables of modern as well as Southern life in which innocent men are ground between a decadent past and an inhuman present, and in both violence of tone serves as a barometer of the moral atmosphere. But *Sanctuary*, unlike *Light in August*, is primarily a tour of society's criminal recesses, with Faulkner descending to his local inferno—the underworld of Popeye, as it forms in the backwoods of Yoknapatawpha.

Sanctuary is a book of disgorgement. It overflows with black bile, that horror before the ugliness of twentieth century life which is a dominant theme of modern literature. Reading the novel, one finds oneself searching uneasily for comparisons in the literature of disgust. Jonson, Swift, Celine, Brecht, Eliot, all come to mind but only to be dismissed, for none of these has quite the brittle despair which characterizes *Sanctuary*. Never in his career as a writer is Faulkner more estranged from, more insistently hostile to, the modern South in particular and modern life in general.

Sincere in conception though often tricky in execution, *Sanctuary* lacks the exquisite control of *The Sound and the Fury*: what is absent is the family, usually the one secure frame for Faulkner's novels and the last redoubt for his more sensitive characters. And whatever fragments of family life do remain in *Sanctuary* soon come to seem morally indistinguishable from the hypocrisy of "the free Democratico-Protestant atmosphere of Yoknapatawpha." When Ruby Goodwin, the rather likable wife of the bootlegger, is driven out of a hotel, the act is committed by a passel of Baptist ladies, respectable harpies of the church. When Narcissa Benbow urges her brother, Horace, not to defend the victimized Goodwin, she speaks with the deepest bias of the middle-class soul: "I dont care where else you go nor what you do. I dont care how many women you have nor who they are. But I cannot have my brother mixed up with a woman people are talking about."

There is an important relation in *Sanctuary* between the foulness of characters like Popeye and the rottenness of characters like Narcissa; each, so to say, nourishes the other, and the two together, the agent of the underworld and the agent of the respectable world, drive Faulkner to that sense of nausea which dominates the novel. Popeye and his world would not be nearly so threatening were it not for the presence of Narcissa and her world. There are, to be sure, other choices, a few of them even glimpsed in *Sanctuary*, but at least in this novel only these two communicate the possibility of power.

Malcolm Cowley has acutely observed that the book is "full of sexual nightmares that are in reality social symbols." In themselves, these nightmares are but of moderate interest, for Temple Drake's behavior is too special in kind, and Popeye can hardly be understood in terms of the usual variants of human character. Both of them are severely controlled figures in a social charade which, far from being an exercise in the lurid or sensational, is moralistic to a fault. Though it has often been taken as a mere thriller, *Sanctuary* can profitably be read as a Manichean morality play.

Two standards of conduct are counterposed in the novel: those of Horace Benbow, the Jefferson lawyer, and Popeye, the gangster. It is not an even contest.

Benbow, a man of cultivation who can attain moral judgment but cannot act upon it forcefully, comes from one of the old Southern families and in his enfeebled way represents traditional values in modern Yoknapatawpha. When Benbow acts in defense of Lee Goodwin, a bootlegger falsely accused of murder, and tries humanely to help Ruby, Goodwin's common-law wife, he suffers the disapproval of Jefferson, which cares more for the surface of decorum than the substance of truth. Benbow's sister, Narcissa, uses every device of feminine cunning—she is finely drawn as an American female of ruthless placidity—to persuade him to abandon the case. At one point she breaks out with the voice of middle class pharisaism: "I don't see that it makes any difference who did it [the murder.] The question is, are you going to stay mixed up with it?" Benbow does stay mixed up with it, enough to suffer but not enough to win. His inability to save Goodwin and defeat Popeye is due not only to Popeye's superior guile, but to a fundamental Benbowish failure: he cannot tear away the bonds of propriety and caution in which his women keep him.

Popeye, the dominating specter of the novel, is less a man than a visitation—though Malcolm Cowley, in his fine essay on Faulkner, is surely wide of the mark when he says that Popeye is "the compendium of all the hateful qualities that Faulkner assigns to finance capitalism." One can share the opinion Cowley assigns to Faulkner, yet find it difficult to believe that so complex and cosmopolitan a system as finance capitalism could be adequately symbolized by this inexpressive psychopath. To a very large extent, Popeye is a pure apparition of evil, not an image of a possible man but a concentrate of a quality in modern mankind. Beyond that—if he is anything beyond that—Popeye suggests the slum *lumpenproletariat*, the scum of the earth outside all classes and threatening all classes; and within this *lumpenproletariat* he falls not among the demoralized victims but among the petty criminals. Popeye is the refuse of the city pouring over the countryside; his natural habitat is not Frenchman's Bend but the red-light district of Memphis. In his description of Popeye, Faulkner is precisely evocative: "His face had a queer blood-less color, as though seen by electric light; against the sunny silence, in his slanted hat and his slightly akimbo arms, he had that vicious depthless quality of stamped tin." Without family roots or personal culture, unbound by human affections, lacking in fluency of feeling or resource of mind, Popeye resists a full explanation in terms of social antecedents or psychological categories. His power as a character in the novel depends on not forcing him into such an explanation, but allowing him to remain, ominously, what he is.

Sanctuary is the story of an invasion. Into the social space left by the collapse of the Compsons and Sartorises, the Snopes clan creeps from the backwoods and

Popeye descends from the city. Unlike Popeye, Flem Snopes will survive in his triumph, because—to anticipate Faulkner's later novels—Flem will learn to mimic the sounds of respectability, an art beyond Popeye's range or desire. *Sanctuary*, however, focuses on Popeye's brief victory in and over Yoknapatawpha, his ability to set off a sequence of catastrophe which ends in death for an innocent man and defeat for a decent one. No force in Yoknapatawpha can successfully resist Popeye, at least none shown in *Sanctuary*. Most of Jefferson is frigidly hostile to stray victims like Lee Goodwin, and those few who do react morally are crippled by their gentility and isolation.

Of all this the title is an ironic reinforcement: nowhere in Yoknapatawpha, nor elsewhere in the modern world, is there sanctuary against invasion. The bootlegger's house in Frenchman's Bend, a seat of relatively harmless and old-fashioned crime, cannot withstand the evil Popeye brings and Temple Drake ignites; Benbow's home and the skirts of his women provide no shelter from the indignities of the world or the nagging of conscience; and Temple, a sanctuary only in name, has no sense of consecration about herself or anything else. The opening scene of the novel confirms Popeye's triumph over Yoknapatawpha, the climax shows his destruction of Temple's will. In between, except for a few brilliant comic interludes which I shall discuss later, the novel steadily accumulates horror and shock, from Popeye's corncob rape of Temple to her eager acceptance of depravity when he brings her to a Memphis whorehouse, where he hovers and neighs over her lovemaking with a young tough he has provided.

It is hard to avoid the impression that in the relationship between Popeye and Temple Faulkner has come close to allegorical explicitness. In terms of personal morality, Temple's surrender carries a significance in the novel which is very much like Jason Compson's adherence to Snopesism. In the world of *Sanctuary* the depraved and evil have at least a certain power of the will, a defined purpose; and this semblance of strength attracts to them creatures like Temple Drake, who in nihilistic desperation search for thrills, violence, even rape—anything to fill or cover their emptiness. Let me put it in extreme terms: the failure of Quentin Compson and Horace Benbow, as of the world they represent, gives Popeye the opportunity to triumph over Temple Drake.

What Faulkner sees in *Sanctuary* is beyond bearing, and his frequent immersion in sheer violence seems a way of escaping the still more dreadful void behind the violence. The book is an accumulation of horrors leaving the imagination limp, though if seen in the total Yoknapatawpha context a good many of the horrors are thematically warranted. The underlying moral fable seldom takes the form of a struggle between man and man or, as Faulkner would later say, of "the human heart in conflict with itself," for except in one or two instances the characters are bare symbols of corruption and evil. The one contrast ultimately called forth by the novel is more extreme, a contrast between man and nature. Behind the events of *Sanctuary* one glimpses bits of landscape: the spring in which Popeye spits, the birds he cannot name, the owl whose cry he fears. Even while misused and violated, the natural world alone resists reduction to the slime of what the human has become. Other than that, in *Sanctuary* there is only wasteland.

[6]

Of all the Yoknapatawpha novels *Light in August* moves in the widest social orbit and is most clearly related to distinctively "modern" themes. The past is still there, more crippling than ever in its hold upon the Yoknapatawpha characters, but the most vivid pages of the novel are devoted to the present, Jefferson in the grip of social division, the modern world as seen by so

many writers of Faulkner's generation. Hatred, alienation, martyrdom, isolation: these form the burden of
Light in August—themes worn ragged in the discourse
and writing of our time but not, thereby, at least in
Faulkner's embodiment, any the less urgent. Both the
themes and the central figure of the book suggest a
kinship with Camus' *The Stranger*—a comparison I
hesitate to press, since the surface facts seem hardly to
support it. The value in suggesting it, however, may be
to chart a progress of alienation. Joe Christmas struggles in *Light in August* with the need for discovering
his identity in an environment that is oppressively social, while Camus's Mersault is a man beyond both the
problem of identity and the kind of pressures Faulkner
masses in behalf of the problem. In a sense, Joe Christmas is a man of today, while Mersault, living in a "post-
social" vacuum, is a man of tomorrow.

Light in August is Faulkner's most sustained confrontation of modern society, but not, as it appears to me, a
confrontation fully resolved either in feeling or thought.
The novel ends with a world irremediably split between the agony of Joe Christmas, a murderer murdered, and the composure of Lena Grove, a country
girl whom evil cannot touch nor reflection trouble.
Despite Faulkner's repeated assaults upon Protestant
fundamentalism in the novel, this appalling distance
between the fates of Christmas and Lena is a *denouement* radically Protestant in spirit. At the end, as Christmas lies castrated and crucified and Lena goes off to
a new life with a husband-to-be in tow, Faulkner
offers neither the comforts of faith nor an assuaging
rationale. How can these two be reconciled—the hopeless injustice and the blithe renewal? Nothing of the
sort is possible; the race survives on the bones of the
defeated. But at least, in reading this novel which so
profoundly renders the crushing "weight" of experience,
we find a terminal point, a moment of exhausted rest,
in contemplating the outrage of two fates so disparate

that no words can provide justification. Were one to reflect very long upon the contrast between the lives of Christmas and Lena, the result would be intolerable; and so Faulkner persuades us to tolerate it through the shifting perspective of the tragi-comic. Nothing is resolved; everything continues.

The nub of the book is Faulkner's counterposition of white and Negro within the consciousness of one man, not as elements of "blood" or emotions of class, but as pure concepts of estrangement making life unbearable for a man who cannot even bear concepts. Seen this way, Joe Christmas becomes a summation of the predicament of Yoknapatawpha, his existence torn by the conflict of color as violently and wastefully as the land itself. But the tragedy of Christmas is not confined to the South, for in his mute resistance to being categorized as white or Negro—perhaps it is really a mute insistence upon being allowed to live suspended between the two, choosing whichever causes him most pain at a given moment—Joe Christmas is engaged in a torturous quest that goes far beyond the bounds of place or color. Similarly, the failure of the Reverend Hightower to sustain the moral burden lowered upon him when the life of Christmas crosses his own, is a failure that invokes our sense of the typical, not the unusual. And the pastoral strand of the plot, in which Lena Grove softly and safely winds her way through a jungle of violence that has bloodied everyone else, is the kind of appeal to the natural which the contemporary novelist, particularly if he is an American, will sooner or later make. To notice in *Light in August* elements that seem characteristic of modern fiction, is not at all to question Faulkner's originality; it is only to specify the terms of his originality.

Suggestive in most of Faulkner's books, names are particularly important in *Light in August*. Hightower, the man who retreats before the risks of human involvement and like Horace Benbow personifies the Yoknapa-

Is this a clue to the title?

tawpha tradition in its decline, is summarily realized in his name. Lena Grove, who is both the "unravished bride" and a rare prize-animal female, symbolizes the shaded serenity and fertility of life rooted in a benevolent nature; whether Faulkner also knew that the name Lena comes from the Greek Helena meaning "bright one"—and in this dark book she is the one figure of light—is something else again. The first name of Byron Bunch is a gentle play on his most unbyronic steadfastness and modesty as Lena's suitor; the second name is a hint of his role as the surviving decent everyman. The religious fanatic who adopts Christmas as a child and tries to beat the catechism into his flesh, is named Calvin McEachern.

Christmas, himself, who is thirty-three when he dies, bears a number of oblique and perhaps ironic resemblances to Christ—not the Christ of the Nativity or of the Resurrection, but of the Crucifixion. In character and conduct he is anything but Christ-like. Ignorant, benighted, brutalized, he cannot redeem himself, let alone humanity. Yet if one accepts for a moment the extreme terms in which Faulkner has conceived him— if one resists the first foolish impulse to cry "sentimentality" or "blasphemy"—even Joe Christmas, a man who at the first crucifixion might have hung at either side of Christ, seems worthy in the twentieth century of a central martyrdom. Worthy, not because of his personal qualities but simply because he exists. The arrangement of the book thus resembles an early Renaissance painting—in the foreground a bleeding martyr, far to the rear a scene of bucolic peacefulness with women quietly working in the fields.

In reading the book one is repeatedly struck by the sureness with which Faulkner distinguishes (not conceptually, but in representation) between whatever in Yoknapatawpha forms a tight coercive society and whatever still allows one to regard it as a community. Surely no distinction could be more commonplace in our time;

but in Faulkner's treatment it blazes with new meaning. It is seen in the suffering of men, so that *Light in August* stands with *Winesburg, Ohio* as one of the true renderings of American loneliness. Each of the main characters in Faulkner's novel is a man cut off. Even Percy Grimm, the ultrapatriotic murderer of Joe Christmas, has "no one to open his heart to"—a lack he shares with the very man he kills. Yet each of the characters is bound fast into his social place or function. If their obsessions and aberrations, whether in sexuality or fanatic religion, are the mark of their lostness, these are also, by the same token, the most serious evidence of their compulsive dependence upon society. In *Light in August* social, religious and sexual can be distinguished for purposes of analysis, but actually they work into one another as the materials of estrangement, the pressures that twist men apart from each other. Sitting alone on a Sunday evening just before Joe Christmas is to be lynched and imagining to himself the churchgoers now at Sunday evening prayer, Hightower, in his role of discarded priest, muses quietly and poignantly, in terms that bring together some of the dominant motifs of the novel:

The organ strains come rich and resonant through the summer night, blended, sonorous. . . . Yet even then the music has still a quality stern and implacable, deliberate and without passion so much as immolation, pleading, asking, for not love, not life, forbidding it to others, demanding in sonorous tones death as though death were the boon, like all Protestant music. . . . Listening he seemed to hear within it the apotheosis of his own history, his own land, his own environed blood. . . . Pleasure, ecstacy, they cannot seem to bear: their escape from it is in violence, in drinking and fighting and praying; catastrophe too. . . . And so why should not their religion drive them to crucifixion of them-

selves and one another? he thinks. It seems to him
that he can hear within the music the declaration
and dedication of that which they know that on
the morrow they will have to do. It seems to him
that the past week has rushed like a torrent and
that the week to come, which will begin tomorrow,
is the abyss, and that now on the brink of cataract
the stream has raised a single blended and sonorous
and austere cry, not for justification but as a dying
salute before its own plunge, and not to any god
but to the doomed man in the barred cell within
hearing of them and of the two other churches, and
in whose crucifixion they too will raise a cross. 'And
they will do it gladly,' he says in the dark window.

The sense of lostness that keeps flooding Hightower's
meditations, also marks every moment in the experience
of Joe Christmas. Child of uncertain origin, watched
over by a vengeful and half-mad grandfather, raised in
an orphan asylum where he meets neither personal love
nor personal hate, Christmas begins as an undefined
creature, a bit of palpitating and vulnerable flesh. He
learns one thing: that it is necessary to obey the rules,
and few moments in the book are more affecting than
the one in which as a little boy, after having innocently
overheard the love-making of the asylum dietician, he
stands bewildered when she tries to bribe him into silence rather than, as he expects, beating him for an
assumed infraction. This bewilderment, and the depri-
vation behind it, are to remain with Christmas until the
moment of his death.

None of Faulkner's characters has been so gro-
tesquely misunderstood as Joe Christmas; few are more
important. George Marion O'Donnell, in good Sartoris
fashion, calls Christmas a "Snopes," while Malcolm
Cowley goes even further by labeling him a "villain."
But Christmas is neither hero nor villain; he inspires
neither admiration nor loathing. He signifies the ap-

pearance, for the first time in Faulkner's work, of a type
frequent in twentieth century European literature: man
as helpless victim, a figure in whom neither good nor
evil counts nearly so much as the sheer fact of being a
victim. Though Benjy also suffers a great deal in *The
Sound and the Fury*, his idiocy provides a moat between himself and the world. Christmas, however, is entirely vulnerable, and if he were to articulate a creed—
which of course he cannot—he might say that the condition of his humanity is that he remain vulnerable.
Though incompletely realized, he is an extraordinarily
poignant image of a homeless and depressed human
being, a lost soul trapped in a limbo between brute
physicality and human consciousness. In his suffering
and his furious incomprehension before the fate he
suffers, Christmas demonstrates the truth of André Malraux's remark that "Perhaps Faulkner's true subject is
the irreparable; perhaps for him there is no question
other than that of successfully crushing man."

Before he so much as talks to anyone, before the explanatory flashbacks to his childhood, the man Christmas is defined in all his baffled aggression: working in a
sawmill he keeps "jabbing his shovel into the sawdust
slowly and steadily and hard, as though he were chop-
ping up a buried snake." With Negroes he must assert
himself as a white man, with whites as a Negro; actually
he does not know which he is, and it does not matter,
for he represents in himself the expense of our division.[4] Christmas tries to reject both roles, the white and

[4] In the fiercely written chapter which sums up the experience
of Christmas, between his boyhood with the McEacherns and
his ending at Jefferson, there is a passage embodying this perception with an unusual bluntness:

". . . he had once tricked or teased white men into calling
him a Negro in order to fight them, to beat them or be beaten;
now he fought the Negro who called him white . . . He now
lived as man and wife with a woman who resembled an ebony
carving. At night he would lie in bed beside her, sleepless, beginning to breathe deep and hard. He would do it deliberately,

the Negro, but is unable to formulate that rejection and must release it through violence even against the most neutral features of his environment. He is the most alienated figure in the Yoknapatawpha world and one of the most alienated in all modern literature: "there was something definitely rootless about him, as though no town nor city was his, no street, no walls, no square of earth his home. And . . . he carried his knowledge with him always as though it were a banner, with a quality ruthless, lonely and almost proud."

Because of his inner division, Christmas cannot endure a gesture of friendliness or an offer of affection. Hungry for days, he instinctively rejects the food— "Keep your muck"—Byron Bunch would share with him. Later, a hundred pages later, a flashback to his boyhood with the McEacherns illuminates one source of this estrangement. The boy Christmas learns quietly to accept the blows of Calvin McEachern as if they were a natural burden of life, but contemptuously refuses the damp whining affection of McEachern's wife. What that affection is he does not understand, but that there must be something better he is certain.

"*All I wanted was peace,*" he tells himself in his manhood. At times he wants "to passively commit suicide," to experience again the humiliations that have come to him since childhood. He remains forever an orphan, his world a chaotic enlargement of the asylum of his childhood. But in his dull brooding way he knows that there is something to be done and something toward which to aspire. Considering marriage

---

feeling, even watching, his white chest arch deeper and deeper within his ribcage, trying to breathe into himself the dark odor, the dark and inscrutable thinking and being of Negroes, with each suspiration trying to expel from himself the white blood and the white thinking and being. And all the while his nostrils at the odor which he was trying to make his own would whiten and tauten, his whole being writhe and strain with physical outrage and spiritual denial."

with Joanna Burden, the aging white woman who has kept him for several years, he recognizes that it would mean "*ease, security for the rest of your life. You would never have to move again.*" But he cuts himself short: "No. If I give in now, I will deny all the thirty years that I have lived to make me what I choose to be." To be categorized as either white or black is, for Christmas, to "give in," but he has chosen to be something else, perhaps what we would call a man. In his wretched and brutal way Christmas, like few other characters in Faulkner, tries to determine his identity and break through to freedom. Even his most evil act, the murder of Joanna Burden, arises in part from this desire. Since she, more than anyone else, has given him something of the manhood he desired, she must now pay heavily for ultimately failing him. In bed with Christmas she demands that their love be a pantomime of violation ("Negro, Negro, Negro," she gasps in her corrupted hunger)—she will not give him that final measure of ease, perhaps acceptance, for which he yearns. As soon as she feels he is secured, she proposes that he go to a Negro college for improvement, and again he feels the damp chilling hand of feminine philanthropy. As Hightower suggests the failure of the South toward the Negro, so Joanna Burden suggests the failure of the North.

After the murder there is only death, and Christmas meets it with sardonic ecstasy. He forces the deputies to a chase not because he intends to escape or hopes to, but simply because he wishes once more to act out his defiance. In his last extremity, when he emerges from the swamp hungry and ragged, he makes that seemingly gratuitous human gesture which, for Faulkner, is the ultimate triumph and redemption of man's life: "Can you tell me what day this is?" he asks a woman, "I just want to know what day this is." During his flight he tells himself, "*Yes I would say Here I am I am tired I am tired of running of having to carry my life like a basket of eggs.*" With awed pain he sees that the Ne-

groes "were afraid . . . of their brother afraid." And
after his death the whites know what it was about him
that "made folks so mad." It was that "he never acted
like either a nigger or a white man." Many pages
earlier, in one of his quiet moments, Christmas had
told himself *God loves me too*—it is clear in what
sense this man may be called a villain.

No one can undo Christmas' years, no one can save
him. Perhaps Lena Grove could, for she senses how
important this crucified stranger is to her. There is a
difficult and startling passage in which Lena tells Hightower that for a moment she felt Christmas to be the
father of her child—as if his martyrdom marked all life,
even the life of her infant. Christmas's death is a death
for Yoknapatawpha itself; and at the end Lena Grove,
the bovine madonna who survives as a personification
of the life principle, must leave Yoknapatawpha, the
profaned site of death.

[7]

To the portrait of modern Yoknapatawpha which
emerges from these novels Faulkner has added, in his
stories, several brilliant strokes. Most of the Yoknapatawpha stories are dependent on the novels, "That
Evening Sun," probably the best of them, being an
offshoot of *The Sound and the Fury* and "There Was
a Queen" a footnote to *Sartoris*. Two other stories,
published in the early thirties, are particularly strong in
social meanings: "Dry September," a rasping account
of a lynching, very powerful but close to stereotype in
its acceptance of the view that Southern ladies are
likely to accuse black men when they have prolonged
difficulty in finding white ones; and "A Rose for Emily,"
which can be read, with some simplification, as a caustic
parable of Southern experience.

After these novels and stories Faulkner cannot proceed much further in a direct social criticism of
Yoknapatawpha. Having seen the present for what it

is, and confirmed his sight from several perspectives, he
now attempts to wring a tentative conclusion from his
criticism. His next book, *Pylon*, is a venture beyond
Yoknapatawpha, and it finds the alien world, like the
familiar one, morally malformed. After *Pylon* comes
Absalom, Absalom!, grandest and most grandiose of
Faulkner's novels, a full-scale or perhaps overscale recapitulation of the Yoknapatawpha story notable for
major changes in outlook and stress. The recapitulation
must now be started in a new manner, for the conventional romancing of the stories later included in *The
Unvanquished* would be frivolously inadequate to so
commanding a protagonist as Thomas Sutpen, and the
realism of *Light in August* would impose on Faulkner a
need to face the past with an intolerable directness.
Both romance and realism, whatever their many differences, are too "contained" as literary modes to allow
for the mythic effects at which Faulkner aims in *Absalom, Absalom!*

The rise of Thomas Sutpen, if it were abstracted
from its highly-charged context in the novel, would be
closer to the historical actuality of pre-Civil War Mississippi than anything Faulkner has shown in his previous work. Northern Mississippi in the 1830's, the time
Sutpen first arrives in Yoknapatawpha, was a frontier
region in which only the most frail versions of the
Southern aristocracy could be transplanted or survive.
The buccaneering Sutpen comes closer to the literal
truth about the region than do the aristocratic Sartorises and Compsons, though it should be remembered
that Faulkner means Yoknapatawpha to be more than
a replica of Lafayette County, Mississippi. Yet it is interesting to note that as Faulkner gains in historical
faithfulness—in a later book, *Requiem for a Nun*, he
will stress still more the bare frontier quality of Yoknapatawpha in the 1830's—he does not relax in style or
feeling. Quite the contrary; everything now becomes
magnified in volume and pitch. The writing of *Absa-*

lom, Absalom! takes on an unprecedented ferocity, perhaps because the reality to which his probings lead him seems to Faulkner, as to Quentin Compson in the novel itself, extremely difficult to accept.

In *Absalom, Absalom!* Faulkner returns to the story of the homeland, but returns through a maze of those stylized—and thereby somewhat protective—devices which one associates with the Gothic novel. *Absalom, Absalom!* is not itself a Gothic novel, being far too serious an effort of the imagination to fall within that dubious genre. And as the story is handed from narrator to narrator, there is a gradual movement away from the heavy chiaroscuro of the Gothic: from Miss Rosa Coldfield's "demonizing" vision of Sutpen to the elder Compson's skeptical reminiscences and finally to the efforts of Quentin Compson and his Canadian friend Shreve McCannon to piece together and provide a meaning for the bits of information and surmise they have shared. Even at the end, Quentin Compson shares something of Miss Rosa's compulsive fascination before the spectacle of Sutpen's rise and fall; he too must see it in terms larger than life, full of frenzy, symbolism and melodrama. The Gothic is qualified as the story moves toward narrators decreasingly involved with its protagonists, but the effects of Gothic linger to the end.

Those effects appear in numerous ways: the fearful doomed mansion, the "shadowy miasmic" region, the driven and demonic hero, the melancholy victims of this hero's diabolism, the heavy overtones of decadence and vice. Unmistakably Gothic is the juxtaposition of Sutpen, the *demon* or *ogre*, to his wife, the *broken butterfly*—unmistakable as a version of the sadistic fantasies that often inhabit Gothic novels. Still, the crux of the novel, if only because Faulkner is seldom concerned with horror for its own sake, is to be found not in these mildewed devices but in the history of the house of Sutpen, a house which stands for the element of sheer will—the urge to expansion and perpetuation—in the traditional Southern consciousness.

Why then does Faulkner bother to use the Gothic machinery at all? Why the accumulation of horrors, the furious shrillness of tone, the Gongorism of style? Because Faulkner now conceives of the native past only in terms of excess and extravagance, as a hallucinatory spectacle, either more or less than human but seldom merely human. Even as the past is seen by him in an increasingly accurate historical perspective—perhaps because it is so seen—it ceases to be a memory of men; it is no longer a bond through blood or received feeling; it has been abstracted into a timeless pageant, ruled not by passion but by the idea or dynamic of passion. An object frozen in the defenseless mind, the past is gazed upon and mulled over with continuous amazement, and amazement, even more than horror or pity, is the response of Quentin Compson and Shreve Mc-Cannon as they unravel the Sutpen story. *Absalom, Absalom!* seems the work of a man overwhelmed by his perceptions; no, a man who has overwhelmed himself by his perceptions. And in this retelling of the Southern myth Faulkner finds that the devices of Gothic help to formalize, to "freeze," his material and, thereby, blunt its edge of feeling.

Gothic gives Faulkner distance, providing intervals when the rhetoric spins along with mechanical fury while nothing more important than a recapture of breath is actually taking place. There is so much to feel and only a limited capacity for feeling. Quentin Compson, the narrator with whom Faulkner partly identifies himself, often finds the story unbearable, and it is this discrepancy between the need for, and the possibility of, response that calls out the stage properties and stock devices of Gothic. Some novelists lack resources of feeling; others face the problem of finding an action through which to objectify their feeling; but in *Absa-*

lom, Absalom! Faulkner's major difficulty is to keep his feeling from ravaging the book. When he succeds, it is usually through the use of Gothic, through its barriers of convention between writer and material. Similarly, he establishes distance between himself and the action by employing several narrators, so that the novel is not only a story about Sutpen but also about the impact of Sutpen on Miss Rosa Coldfield and Quentin Compson, not only a review of the past but also an act of staring at it with incredulous anguish.

Finally, the Gothic, because it characteristically involves an inversion of accepted values and modes of conduct, furnishes Faulkner with a setting in which to place his by now intolerably complicated vision of the Southern past. That the action of the book should occur during "old ghosttimes" and in a world "something like the bitter purlieus of Styx" indicates how much more complex his vision is here than in the stories of Granny Rosa Millard or of "the other" Bayard Sartoris. Faulkner can now realize his values only through images of their violation, and the novel is a retelling of the Southern myth in terms of its negation, with Sutpen as the opposite of Sartoris.

But opposites can be bound together in a symbiotic knot: Sartoris and Sutpen seem to equal, in Faulkner's scheme of things, traditional Southern character. Sartoris is courage, Sutpen will; Sartoris tradition, Sutpen new energy; Sartoris chivalry, Sutpen dynastic ruthlessness. The contrast can also be put historically. Sutpen is a latecomer, an interloper who, in order to compress into his lifetime the social rise which in other families had taken generations, must act with an impersonal ruthlessness (he is not intrinsically a cruel man) which the Sartorises have learned to disguise or modulate. Just because Sutpen is not a "typical" Southern plantation owner, he expresses with terrible nakedness a central quality of the traditional South.

Of all Faulkner's characters Sutpen most closely approximates the tragic hero: he strives for large ends, actively resists his fate, and fails through an inner flaw. Less aware and more compulsive than an authentic tragic hero, he still achieves a grandeur very close to heroism. As a mountain boy from Virginia, Sutpen had once been humiliated by a liveried Negro slave at the steps of a white man's mansion, and it is this crucial moment that has impelled him to his lifelong "design" —to found a plantation as large and luxurious as any he has seen, to have "land and niggers and a fine house." His boyhood humiliation was the result of a pioneer-like innocence, for he "didn't even know there was a country all divided and fixed and neat with a people living on it all divided and fixed and neat because of what color their skins happened to be and what they happened to own." This innocence destroyed, Sutpen becomes a man possessed, and what appears to be his selfishness is really a single-minded and heedless fanaticism in behalf of his "design." He abandons his first wife, Eulalia Bon, when he learns she has a touch of Negro blood, and not because he shares the usual phobias but because he realizes that such a marriage endangers his "design." Later he marries a respectable Mississippi girl, Ellen Coldfield, to bear children who will inherit Sutpen's Hundred, the plantation he carves out of the wilderness by driving his slaves and himself.

All of Sutpen's career, all of his seemingly extravagant and incomprehensible behavior, takes on a rigid meaning once it is seen as directed toward the goal of power, the passion of the poor white boy to rise to the top of the social heap. Sutpen's refusal to recognize by so much as a nod his cultivated mulatto son, Charles Bon, which leads to Bon's murder by the white son Henry; his astonishing proposal to his sister-in-law after the Civil War that they set to work breeding and, if the issue is male, be married; his final frustrated attempt to have a son by Milly Jones, granddaughter of a plantation hanger-on—these are episodes in the triumph and self-defeat of an intransigent will. In an immediate sense, *Absalom, Absalom!* tells the story of a man straining, through work and sacrifice, to rise in a society unwilling to accept social change and fluidity. Soon, however, the novel escapes these categories and becomes a grandiose summation of the Yoknapatawpha experience, with Sutpen concentrating into his "design" all the homeland's energy and fatal obtuseness as he strives and fails, strives once again and fails, to create an invulnerable and assured dynasty. Sutpen represents the mania of ambition as it consumes all other desires; he is the will to power in its most extreme and, thereby, one likes to think, most pitiable state.

What, asks Sutpen after he has shrunk to a petty storekeeper, what in my design went wrong? "Whether it was a good or a bad design is besides the point; the question is, 'Where did I make the mistake in it?' " This is the central question of the book, twisted by Sutpen's astonishing incapacity for self-examination. One critic has declared that Faulker holds the Negro to be at fault in his symbolic role as barrier between Sutpen and the front door of the white man's mansion; but this is utterly wrong, since for Sutpen the Negro is merely a passive agent of white society: "they (the niggers) were not it, not what you wanted to hit. . . ." For other critics the cause of Sutpen's fall is what one of them calls, with latter-day Christian charity, the "sin" of miscegenation. Here, again, the work is more complex and more humane than the interpretation. It is true that precisely when Faulkner's feeling for the Negro is most generous and tender, the thought of miscegenation becomes most troublesome, evoking those ingrained phobias which are part of his inheritance. Still, the novel is distinguished by an intermittent effort to overcome such phobias. The line of Charles Bon, which degenerates into slack-mouthed idiocy, is less the instigator than the victim of Sutpen's debacle, Faulkner's attitude toward Bon being similar to his attitude toward Joe

Christmas. As for Sutpen himself, his refusal to recognize Bon is based less on a principled rejection of miscegenation—he is too obsessed by purpose to live by principle —than on the realization that his "design" would be greatly imperiled if he admitted a man with Negro blood into his family. His son, Henry, comes closer to a conventional Southern response: the prospect of miscegenation fills him with horror, and while he is ready to countenance incest between his sister and Bon he cannot agree to their marriage once he knows it would involve a mixing of blood. This curious moral distinction is bitterly questioned by Bon (*"So it's the miscegenation, not the incest, which you can't bear"*), and while Henry feels the necessity for living by it he does not try to defend it as reasonable. Later, in a brilliant section which rehearses and sharpens the main plot, Sutpen's daughter, Judith, fails her nephew, Charles Etienne St. Velery Bon, a white-skinned Negro boy. He wins her protection and perhaps even her love, but like her father in relation to Eulalia and Charles Bon, she cannot forget—now it is not so much a "design" as an inherited disease—the boy's "taint" of Negro blood. Ever more complex and involuted, the guilt passes from generation to generation, somewhat as in a Hawthorne novel.

Neither the burden of the Negro nor the "sin" of miscegenation can explain the failure of Sutpen's design. His very question allows no relevant answer, for his failure cannot be understood without judging the moral quality of his design. Sutpen's evil and heartlessness flow from his ambition to own and dominate men, and this is an ambition, we must believe, which will sooner or later fail. Faulkner says as much time and time again. Sutpen has abandoned the ethos of his frontier childhood, of the time when "the land belonged to anybody and everybody and so the man who would go to the trouble and work to fence off a piece of it and say 'This is mine' was crazy; and as for objects, nobody had any more of them than you did because everybody had just what he was strong enough or energetic enough to take and keep. . . ." In defeat, the South, like Sutpen himself, "was now paying the price for having erected its economic edifice not on the rock of stern morality but on the shifting sands of opportunism and moral brigandage." Moral brigandage— that should be plain enough.

The ideas that can be wrenched from *Absalom, Absalom!* are far less important—but this is true of most Faulkner novels—than its poignant evidence of an artist grappling with his inherited resources, struggling with and against his awareness of the wrongs in the tradition he loves, the very tradition that has also given him the capacity to see those wrongs. His surrogate-figure in the book, Quentin Compson, sees in the story of Sutpen a terrible version of his native past, and his knowledge of Sutpen's story may be regarded as a spur to his suicide in *The Sound and the Fury*. Unlike Quentin, Faulkner finds, in his later books, an escape from the dilemma of loving a past he can no longer countenance. But in the immediate anguish raised by that dilemma and the honesty with which he forces himself to look upon it, he is as one with Quentin; and in the great closing paragraph of the book, when Quentin is asked, "Why do you hate the South," his answer, we may suppose, is also the answer of Faulkner: "I dont hate it. . . . I dont hate it. . . . *I dont. I dont! I dont hate it! I dont hate it!*"

[8]

To turn from *Absalom, Absalom!* to *The Hamlet* is an experience of shock. The one is feverish, sweltering, myth-ridden; the other—even when devoted to excesses of style—is jocular, cool and somewhat like a string of tall tales. Since parts of *The Hamlet* appeared in magazines before *Absalom, Absalom!*, the difference can hardly be the result of a shift in Faulkner's outlook or temper. Usually, the development of his work proceeds not as a straight line of progress but as a complex and hesitant spiral; not as a clear movement from one social or moral attitude to another but as a variation in emphasis among several attitudes running through all his books.

Still, when one does read the Yoknapatawpha novels in their order of publication, *The Hamlet* seems a partial resolution of the dilemmas that make *Absalom, Absalom!* so tortured a book. A resolution, in that the families of the old order—Sartorises, Compsons, Sutpens—have been abandoned, and with them, the mixture of nostalgia and moral censure they aroused in Faulkner. Now, as the Snopes clan moves toward the forefront, the main opposition to its growth comes not from the old patriciate, (clearly, in Faulkner's scheme of things, drained of all energy and perspective) but from several independent farmers, men of a kind only occasionally seen in earlier Faulkner novels.

The Snopeses have always been there. No sooner did Faulkner come upon his central subject—how the corruption of the homeland, staining its best sons, left them without standards or defense—than Snopesism followed inexorably. Both as social insight and creative invention, the Snopes clan is probably Faulkner's most brilliant stroke, for no matter where one looks in the modern world, behind whichever border or curtain, there emerge the Snopeses, proliferating, powerful and, as Faulkner would say, self-progenitive. Almost anyone can detect the Snopeses—other novelists have, though not with Faulkner's intimate knowledge—but describing them is very hard. The usual reference to their "amorality," while accurate, is not sufficiently distinctive and by itself does not allow us to place them, as they should be placed, in a historical moment.

The Snopeses begin as poor whites, though they are hardly representative ones, as the Bundrens may be. Certain points of resemblance exist between Flem Snopes and Popeye, but the differences seem much larger. Flem is not a professional criminal: he quickly learns the value of respectability, he crawls through society rather than attacking it from the outside. The evil of Flem is different in kind from the evil of Popeye: the former has eyes "the color of stagnant water" while the latter recalls the "vicious depthless quality of stamped tin." For Flem, Faulkner employs images of the putrescent within nature, for Popeye, images of the cheaply mechanized. Nor can the Snopeses be considered equivalents of the city *lumpenproletariat*, since, whatever their dishonesty, they work and often work hard. None of the usual categories will do, yet they obviously represent a distinct social group. Perhaps the most important thing to be said about the Snopeses is that they are *what comes afterwards*: the creatures that emerge from the devastation, with the slime still upon their lips.

Let a world collapse, in the South or Russia, and there appear figures of coarse ambition driving their way up from beneath the social bottom, men to whom moral claims are not so much absurd as incomprehensible, sons of bushwhackers or peasants drifting in from nowhere and taking over through the sheer outrageousness of their monolithic force. They become presidents of local banks or chairmen of party sections, and later, a trifle smoother in appearance and style, they make their way into Congress or the Central Committee. Scavengers without inhibition, they need not believe in the code of their society; they need only learn to mimic its sounds.

I have suggested a comparison—far fetched, on the face of it—between the South at the time the Snopeses start to flourish and Russia after the revolution goes into decline. One need hardly be an expert in the history of either place to see where the comparison breaks down. But its value depends not on a claim to comprehensiveness; it depends on isolating one or two central aspects which, in being wrenched out of context, may, thereby, be illuminated.

In post-revolutionary Russia the traditional relationships in the countryside were destroyed, but the poverty and cultural primitivism that had been congealed in these relationships persisted. Because the revolution could not realize its egalitarian claims in the villages, there arose in place of the old landowners a new stratum of peasant leaders: uncouth and ignorant yet vigorous and ambitious, the very flesh of the Stalinist reaction. In the post-reconstruction period of Southern history, which has its points of resemblance to a counter-revolution, there also appeared a social vacuum, the result of a decay of traditional relationships and the absence of workable new ones. This vacuum the Snopeses fill, and insofar as they are its product Faulkner's description of them as "sourceless" is extremely brilliant. Uncouth yet vigorous "muzhiks" of the new South, they are, in turn, sons of the bushwhackers, source of the redneck demagogue, and tomorrow's compradors for Northern capital. They do not, to be sure, need to mouth slogans the way their Russian equivalents do; yet it is not really so hard to imagine Flem Snopes, his eye fixed on power, rising to praise some glorious leader of the party. In *The Mansion*, a later novel about the Snopes clan, State Senator Cla'ence Snopes is amusingly shown as making a political adaptation to the modern world. He begins, after the Second World War, to mimic the vocabulary of liberalism and declare himself an enemy of the Ku Klux Klan.

Though they soon invade the town, the Snopeses remain rural in speech, psychology, and manners; they could arise only in the backwoods and from the backwash of the countryside. At about the turn of the century, the clan infiltrates Frenchman's Bend, the rich river-bottom, "hill-cradled and remote," at the southern edge of Yoknapatawpha. With some reason the Snopeses are suspected of barn-burning, and it is this reputation that enables them to frighten the Varners, the family which until then had lazily dominated the economic life of Frenchman's Bend. There is a fine comic passage in which Jody Varner, uneasy about reports concerning the Snopes view of barns, tries to reason with Flem:

"I was hoping to see you," Varner said. "I hear your father has had a little trouble once or twice with landlords. Trouble that might have been serious." The other chewed. "Maybe they never treated him right; I dont know about that and I dont care. What I'm talking about is a mistake, any mistake, can be straightened out so that a man can still stay friends with the fellow he aint satisfied with. Dont you agree to that?" The other chewed, steadily. His face was as blank as a pan of uncooked dough. "So he wont have to feel that the only thing that can prove his rights is something that will make him have to pick up and leave the country next day," Varner said. "So that there wont come a time some day when he will look around and find out he has run out of new country to move to." Varner ceased. He waited so long this time that the other finally spoke, though Varner was never certain whether this was the reason or not:

"There's a right smart of country."

"Sho," Varner said, pleasantly, bulging, bland. "But a man dont want to wear it out just moving through it. . . ."

Faulkner is quick to suggest how important are the differences between the Varners and the Snopeses. In general, his eye for social gradations in the countryside and village is much keener than for social gradations in the city. At first Flem imitates slavishly, almost to parody, the dress and manners of the Varners—not merely because he wants to be like them, but also because, in ways not yet clear to him, he wants to move beyond them. He sports a tie and shirt, he walks into the Varner store "jerking his head at the men on the gallery exactly as Will Varner himself would do." But these external similarities are noted by Faulkner mainly to underscore the deeper differences. The Varners, a family of village traders and landowners, are overripe, unsystematic and relaxed in their rapacity; the Snopeses, a clan of mobile scavengers, are bloodless and calculating. Jody Varner represents a social energy gone to seed, Flem Snopes a social energy taut with purpose.

Flem becomes a clerk in Varner's store, and the chapter introducing him to the life of commerce has some lovely bits of notation:

On the Monday morning when Flem Snopes came to clerk in Varner's store, he wore a brand new white shirt. It had never even been laundered yet, the creases where the cloth had lain bolted on a shelf, and the sun-browned streaks repeated zebra-like on each successive fold, were still apparent . . . He wore (the shirt) all that week. By Saturday night it was soiled, but on the following Monday he appeared in a second one exactly like it, even to the zebra-stripes. By the second Saturday night that one was soiled too, in exactly the same places as the other . . .

He rode up on a gaunt mule, on a saddle which was recognized at once as belonging to the Varners, with a tin pail tied to it . . . He did not speak . . . a thick squat man of no establishable age between twenty and thirty, with a broad still face containing a tight seam of mouth stained slightly at the corners with tobacco, and eyes the color of stagnant water, and projecting from among the other features in startling and sudden paradox, a tiny predatory nose like the beak of a small hawk. It was as though the original nose had been left off by the original designer or craftsman and the unfinished job taken over by someone of a radically different school . . . or perhaps by one who had had only time to clap into the center of the face a frantic and desperate warning.

No sooner is Flem established than he brings his numerous relatives to the village where they form a plague-like band under his guidance. Gradually Flem gains a measure of power over the Varners, and this power is sharply increased when he consents to marry Eula Varner, a soft weight of female ripeness, who has become inconveniently pregnant after an encounter with a nearby suitor. Flem outwits and cheats the local farmers in several trades that involve everything from wild ponies to a legendary horde of gold; and, as we recall from *Sartoris* and will learn more fully in *The Town*, finally leaves for Jefferson to become vice-president of the Sartoris bank. Thus the Snopeses steadily ooze up through the village and into urban life; in *Sanctuary* Cla'ence has already become a politician and two young Snopeses have made a journey to Memphis, there to taste the enchantments of a city brothel; by *The Mansion* the energy of Snopesism seems to have reached a point of exhaustion, not so much through defeat but through being absorbed into the mainstream of American respectability. Snopesism, then, is the face of the new South as it combines the worst of the past and present—not, of course, the whole new South or even that emerging new South which, as it becomes middle class in the style of the rest of the country, may transform the Snopeses beyond recognition. And the name itself, related perhaps to Dickens' Chevy Slyme, is full of suggestion: *snoot, snot, snout, snoop.*

At the head of the clan stands Flem, a figure somewhat larger than life, Snopesism pure. Circling about him are hordes of relatives—there are always new ones, since Faulkner takes pleasure in inventing more far-fetched names and mischief for them. Each member of the clan is a mixture of Snopes and human. Ab, father of Flem, is not a complete Snopes. "He ain't naturally mean," says Ratliff, the sewing-machine agent who serves as spokesman for the farmers and choral figure in the book, "he's just soured." Though a parasite and traitor during the Civil War, Ab is in some measure a victim of the social catastrophe that has degraded everyone in Yoknapatawpha. In the story, "Barn Burning," Ab figures as a man of bitter, almost crazed, purposefulness, his taste for arson a result of social envy. His boy Sarty (curiously absent from the Snopes novels) is conceived in a vague, pathetic ambition that is suggested by his being named after Sartoris; at Ab's trial for barn burning the boy thinks to himself, *"He aims for me to lie . . . and I will have to do hit."*

No comparable sympathy for a Snopes is to be found in *The Hamlet,* a book in which a controlled distance from, and even coolness toward, the characters is necessary for producing a range of comic effects. Still, some variations are evident in Faulkner's treatment of the clan. Ike, the family idiot, loves a cow and without reserve or meanness; he stands in extreme contrast to the acquisitive cunning of Flem; and he is, accordingly, the one Snopes whose experience is rendered from within, as an extravaganza of romanticism that is meant, I would think, both as presentment and parody. Mink, the permanently enraged member of the family, is consumed by a sense of social humiliation and mangled pride, which helps explain—though not justify—his murder of the farmer, Houston; he elicits from Faulkner two of his most cherished descriptive adjectives, "indomitable and intractable." I. O. Snopes, the word-monger who mutilates proverbs with a gargantuan inventiveness—"love me, love my horse," "if wishes were horseflesh we'd all own thoroughbreds," "give a dog a good name and you don't need to hang him," "a penny on the waters pays interest when the flood turns," "all pleasure and no work might make Jack so sharp he might cut his self"—I. O. retains some relation, no matter how corrupt, to the human language. And Eck, for all his weak-mindedness, shows a touch of good nature and paternal feeling for his boy Wallstreet.

Flem, however, is in a class by himself, a figure with a marvellous energy for deceit, an almost Jonsonian monomania in pursuit of money. Cold, mean, tough, shrewd, without sentiment or visible emotion, he is not so much an evil human being as a plausible personification of evil. He embodies the commercial ethos with a grotesque purity, both as it represents the power of an undeviating will and as it appears in its ultimate flimsiness. Each step of his behavior is credible, yet his character remains an enigma. His aping of the Varners, his skill as a trader, his brutal indifference to the fate of cousin Mink, his stunning hypocrisy in offering Mrs. Armstid a few bits of candy ("a little sweetening for the chaps") after he has done her out of her last five dollars —all this is both persuasive and graphic. Such incidents bare the mechanism of Flem's character, but not the spring behind the mechanism. Flem is "there," beyond a doubt—but only on the surface. Behind his aura of demonic resourcefulness we cannot penetrate. Nor does Faulkner try to probe him as he has probed similar figures, Popeye rather poorly and Jason Compson superbly; he seems unwilling and perhaps afraid to approach Flem, preferring to regard him from a distance with a mixture of incredulity and nausea. Probably, Flem has a dimension of meaning that can be exhausted neither by his social role nor his personal traits. He is not only a personification of evil, but a sort of backwoods devil. If the sinners of Yoknapatawpha are Sartorises, the prince of their darkness is a Snopes. And a devil, however else he may be understood, is not accessible to psychology.

Now that the Snopes trilogy is complete and we can
see Faulkner's difficulties in *The Mansion* when he tries
to investigate Flem's motives, we can only conclude
that he was triumphantly right in refusing to make
Flem "human" in *The Hamlet*. He was right, that is, in
holding Flem to an extreme conception which, violating
verisimilitude, reached truth. Though Flem stands for
everything Faulkner despises, he is treated in *The Hamlet* with a comic zest, a sheer amazement that such a
monster could exist or even be imagined. The danger of
Snopesism is real, but the battlefield is still confined,
and opposed to Flem, there stands as a mature antago-
nist, if in the end a defeated one, the humane sewing-
machine agent, V. K. Ratliff.

Together with Ratliff appear a number of minor yet
extremely winning figures, a group of farmers whom the
Snopeses victimize in one way or another: Bookwright,
Tull, Houston, and others. Unpretentious, hard-working, violently and even blindly independent, these men
come through as immensely lifelike characters. They
are entirely honest: at Varner's store "customers would
enter and serve themselves and each other, putting the
price of the articles, which they knew to a penny . . .
into the cigar-box." Instinctively generous, they sense
the way in which a meal can help to bind men; Ratliff,
remarks Faulkner, could travel through the country for
six months without having once to buy his dinner. Flem,
however, carries a pail of lunch to work "which no man
had ever yet seen him eating."

These farmers possess a strong awareness of human
limit and weakness: when Ratliff plays a trick, requiring
that he appear to be taken in by Flem, he observes that
Bookwright, innocent of the stratagem, "done all he
could to warn me. He went as far and even further
than a man can let his self go in another man's trade."
With this awareness of limit goes a fierce assertion of
individuality: precisely the individuality, it must be
added, that hinders them from acting in concert against

the Snopeses. They are capable of deep and coherent feeling. Bookwright, with his sardonic sense of imperfection, consumes himself because of his failure to cope with Flem; Houston, for all his arrogance, mourns his dead wife with an awesome singleness. They are men defeated yet persistent in their integrity—and for Faulkner, a source of hope.

Speaking and acting for them, Ratliff embodies the modest virtues of rationality and humaneness. One of the few positive characters in Faulkner's novels who is utterly convincing and neither hysterical nor a windbag, Ratliff provides an aura of security for the book. His presence makes possible a sustained comic perspective upon the threat of Snopesism, for we soon learn to trust his judgment and relax with his competence. At least as he appears in *The Hamlet*, Ratliff is Faulkner's most attractive and mature spokesman for the possibilities of civilized existence, possibilities which he needs all the more intensely as he surveys the devastation that is Snopesism.

[9]

Each of the Yoknapatawpha novels seeks to recapture the experience of the homeland in one inclusive image, usually an image of polarity. *Go Down, Moses*, as it curves from civil war to social decay, is controlled by such an image: the opposed strains of blood, Negro and white, swirling through the McCaslin family in fatal mixture. Six of the book's seven stories deal with this family. Four are concerned with the ancestry, upbringing, moral testing and climactic experience of Isaac McCaslin, a central figure in the whole Yoknapatawpha saga, while the remaining two turn to the family's Negro offshoots. Behind the narrated events there looms one overwhelming and fearful fact: the curse brought down upon the family by its arrogant founder, Carothers McCaslin, when he seduced Tomey, the daughter born to him by a Negro slave. Nothing the whites can

do—neither bluster nor evasion, violence nor apology—
permits them to escape the weight of the past. As *Go
Down, Moses* unfolds the torturous family history, in
which the cycle of lust, domination and suffering is
several times repeated, it moves toward its conclusion
with astonishing moral, though not always dramatic,
force. On one side, as the book summons an almost
legendary past, the burden of injustice among men is
related to a primary violation of the land; on the other
side, as the book touches the most inflamed areas of the
present, sexual taboos among the races are shown to be
a central means for continuing the injustice of the
past.

From story to story *Go Down, Moses* reveals the
history of the McCaslin family and by indirection still
another version, blending mythic and realistic elements,
of the history of the homeland. It begins, this time,
with Carothers McCaslin, a slaveowner who wields absolute power without hesitation or guilt; it proceeds to
his sons Buck and Buddy, who live through the Civil
War enacting the motions of white domination, but in
terms that approach parody, since they no longer believe in its sacredness or use; and finally it reaches a
climax with Isaac McCaslin, son of Buck, who tries
through a gesture of expiation to break the chain of evil.

At the end of *Go Down, Moses* Isaac appears as a
man in his seventies, after more than fifty years of refusing to share in the power and profit of his white
heritage. He learns about the affair between Roth Edmonds, his young relative, and a girl who proves to be
a descendant of the Negro branch of the family—it is
almost a modern reenactment of the original story of
Carothers McCaslin and his slave Tomey. Drawn back
against his will into the risks and pain of life, Isaac sees
that the old entanglements of sexuality and power
which had shaped the lives of his ancestors are still at
work. His renunciation of the family's land and wealth,
for all its exemplary value, has not changed the social

reality of Yoknapatawpha, nor has it entirely succeeded as an act of self-purgation, since in a crucial way he remains subject to inherited phobias. But now at least he knows that they *are* phobias; he does not try to deceive himself with rhetoric about the tradition of the homeland. He knows that what keeps the races apart, tense with guilt and fear—what erects a wall between the lovers, Roth Edmonds and the Negro girl—is the same dread of a free human encounter which had first set into motion the whole cycle of violence and estrangement. He knows that as long as Negro and white remain apart, there can be neither assurance nor ease nor true affection.

The whole impetus of *Go Down, Moses* moves toward a decisive contrast: Negro and white, Lucas Beauchamp and Isaac McCaslin, a figure of enduring strength and a figure of looming conscience. Both of them descendants of Carothers McCaslin, they represent the division and self-estrangement of the homeland. Lucas, the man who refuses to bend, does not yet appear in his full power, and the story devoted to him, "The Fire and the Hearth," is one of Faulkner's more dubious experiments in mating serious material with a tone so unevenly jocular that it allows him no secure narrative point of view. Yet something of the Lucas later to be seen in *Intruder in the Dust* does come through, enough to foreshadow Faulkner's clarified and elevated response to the Yoknapatawpha experience—a response most fully developed and clearly stated in the stories about Isaac McCaslin.

"I'm a nigger," says Lucas when he demands the return of his wife from Zack Edmonds, his landlord and cousin, "but I'm a man too." Lucas is not a "modern" and certainly not a militant Negro; he is proud of his McCaslin blood, and like Ike McCaslin, he reverences the past. In no other book does Faulkner so delicately communicate the agonizing uncertainties and dimming glories to be found in the "old frail pages" of family

records. But for all his identification with the figures
of the past, Lucas knows that he is also the victim of the
past. "How to God," he tells himself, "can a black man
ask a white man to please not lay down with his black
wife? And even if he could ask it, how to God can the
white man promise he wont?" By cultivating the mask
of the curmudgeon that he has learned to use for both
self-protection and tacit aggression against white society,
Lucas triumphs over Zack Edmonds, as later in *Intruder
in the Dust* he will triumph over the entire white community. He regains his wife, but he regains her through
a demonstration of his force of character, as a personal
achievement. The principle of white domination which
had made it possible for Edmonds to take Molly Beauchamp, continues to operate. Lucas can enjoy his victory only in silence, only because he does not openly
challenge the system that had led to his humiliation.

Through the contrast between Lucas and Isaac,
Faulkner achieves his most considered and mature relation to the homeland: a balance of love and judgment,
the love surviving only because the judgment becomes
more severe. It is, he writes, "a land blessed with woods
for game and streams for fish and deep rich soil for
seed and lush springs to sprout it and long summers to
mature it and serene falls to harvest it and short mild
winters for men and animals." But it is also a land
cursed by an "old haughty ancestral pride based not on
any value but on an accident of geography, stemmed
not from courage and honor but from wrong and shame
. . ."

Faulkner now relates the exploitation of the land to
the exploitation of man, both of which he regards not
merely as active signs of evil but as violations of that
reserve and balance which a man in truly harmonious
relation to his surroundings will naturally enjoy. The
relation Faulkner sketches—it does not lend itself to
more than sketching—bears a notable resemblance to
that sense of natural piety which Martin Buber has

described as the "I-Thou" relation: a spontaneous regard and cultivated respect for the objects and creatures that surround us in both the natural and social worlds. In moving back and forth between the exploitation of the land and the exploitation of man—it hardly matters whether he establishes a causal connection between the two—Faulkner is again, as in his previous novels, concerned with a fall. But this time he is not merely concerned for a presumed state of order, which upon inspection he finds to be the very source of evil; he is also concerned for a state of innocence and poise, surely related to history but finally beyond its claims or standards.

Isaac McCaslin's recognition of the wrong and shame that corrupt his inheritance is the central moral action of *Go Down, Moses*, primarily in the superb story, "The Bear," and then, by way of confirming postscript, in the fine story "Delta Autumn." Like so many of Faulkner's novels and stories, "The Bear" turns to the past, but for once not a past of historical actuality or a mere legendary history. The retreat to the wilderness which forms this remembered past is set in a recognizable moment of the late nineteenth century, yet is somewhat apart from historical time, somewhat "timeless" in the qualities it suggests. It forms an Eden coexisting with society but never mistaken for society by those who come to it for purification and refreshment. The whole development of Isaac McCaslin consists in his effort to reconcile wilderness and society, or failing that, to decide which will allow and which frustrate the growth of moral responsibility.

During his youth Isaac McCaslin would go each year with his friends to the Yoknapatawpha forests, "not to hunt bear and deer but to keep yearly rendezvous with the bear which they did not even intend to kill. Two weeks later they would return, with no trophy, no skin." The hunt soon took on the tone of a religious retreat: away from home, from money, from women, from social distinctions and gradations. For General Compson and Major de Spain and Walter Ewell, this yearly hunting trip became a "pageant-rite"—and still more so for the sixteen-year-old Isaac and for Sam Fathers. A "taintless and incorruptible" old man of mixed Negro and Indian blood, Sam Fathers was the boy's mentor in the hunt and the acknowledged priest of the ceremony that could be held only in the forest. It was a renewal and a cleansing, a drawing of strength from a meeting with the great and totemic bear, Ben; it was a "pageant-rite" symbolizing their communion in escape from the social world. Ben was a bear "ruthless with the fierce pride of liberty and freedom, jealous and proud enough of liberty and freedom to see it threatened not with fear nor even with alarm but almost joy, seeming deliberately to put it into jeopardy in order to save it. . . ." Perhaps, too, when the men came from the town to the woods, they hoped to shed or expiate the guilt accumulated in society. And their coming was made solemn by the knowledge that the woods were doomed and the great bear also doomed. The boy Isaac, whose life rested on these unspoken verities, felt that when the bear was finally killed, "it must be [by] one of us. So it won't be until the last day." By "one of us" because none other could realize the dimensions of the loss to come on "the last day."

The boy is exposed to preliminary trials. In a hunt described—or remembered—in "Delta Autumn" he kills a buck, and Sam Fathers smears his face with the blood of the animal; the boy trembles at the thought: *I slew you: my bearing must not shame your quitting life. My conduct forever onward must become your death.* Here the hunt is a ceremony of maturing, a test of proper conduct through which Isaac ceases to be a boy; yet truly to become a man he must retain the awe before truth that is characteristic of boyhood. In "The Bear" he finally meets Ben, but only after having stripped himself of such material objects and social possessions as his watch and compass. Seeing the bear, the boy experiences an ecstasy of communion which results in his refusal to kill the animal. When the last day comes, there flows through the men a recognition that the end of an era has also come. Next morning Major de Spain breaks camp; the community is dissolved. To kill the great bear Ben is to violate a mute bond with the natural world, and the fraternity the men have felt in the hunting camp could exist only in terms of an equable relation to the natural world. Yet this is an inevitable violation, a fated part of their life, and this is why it is given to Isaac McCaslin—Isaac, the son blessed by the father—to lead in the destruction of the totem. He, alone, will keep true the memory of the totem and the tribe, not so much the rites themselves or the men who performed them but the meaning of the rites and the value of the men. Sam Fathers also knows that the death of the bear, the violation of the tabu, means the end of a way of life and the end of his own life, but he does not regret that the day has come. "For seventy years now he had had to be a negro. It was almost over now and he was glad." Ancestor of the tribe, he "saw further than them . . . further than the death of a bear."

From the hunt "The Bear" suddenly shifts to a dialogue between Isaac McCaslin, now twenty-one years old, and his cousin Edmonds; the tone changes from hieratic gravity to a surcharged oratory. Isaac has decided to relinquish the land inherited from his grandfather, Carothers McCaslin, and the cousins debate the decision, digging into the family records through which the sins of their ancestors are revealed and the meaning of Isaac's gesture understood. By surrendering the land that had been won through brigandage and held through oppression, Isaac hopes to lift the "curse" that blights the clan; an act not easily undertaken, for even as he proclaims his "repudiation" he feels it to be a "heresy." Yet he completes the

gesture by which he hopes to break the chain of inheritance and begin a new mode of life. He becomes
a carpenter, "not in mere static and hopeful emulation
of the Nazarene . . . but . . . because if the Nazarene
had found carpenting good for the life and ends He
had assumed and elected to serve, it would be all right
too for Isaac McCaslin." He hopes to find again an unstained freedom, the freedom lost to the white man
when he appropriated the land from the Indians and
enslaved the Negroes: two acts now seen as parts of
one violation. Isaac McCaslin partly repudiates his own
revered ancestors and chooses as his father the old colored man who had smeared the blood of the buck on
his face. "Sam Fathers set me free," says Isaac to his
cousin, and his recognition of his kinship to the old
man is not only an act of social choice, it is for him the
moment of truth. Thus, through the values and perceptions won in an experience approaching the condition
of myth, Isaac makes his judgment upon the world of
history: a judgment of withdrawal and what may be
called heroic passivity.

The fable of "The Bear" falls within the broad stream
of the pastoral which courses through American writing,
pastoral suggesting the conscious turn to simplicity as a
desired way of life and the nostalgia for a time which
could more fully realize that desire. Mark Twain, Melville, Cooper, Anderson, Hemingway—in these as in so
many other American writers there is a persistent looking backward to that moment in our national life
which seems sweeter and truer than the present. The
camp of Sam Fathers is a modern equivalent of Nigger
Jim's island, as Hemingway's Michigan woods are an
equivalent of Cooper's wilderness. For Faulkner this
pastoral theme has a value beyond the yearning for an
American state of innocence; it is the culmination of a
shift in social allegiance, a shift that cannot and should
not be transposed into political terms. In the sturdy
farmers of *The Hamlet*, the strong and proud Negroes

of *Go Down, Moses* and the figure of Isaac McCaslin, Faulkner has discovered new sources of hope, new possibilities of attachment. The values claimed for the tradition but denied it by the "curse," are now to be realized among "the doomed and lowly of the earth." So there occurs, as it were, a change of paradise; paradise no longer the measured historical past but the image of a pastoral and pioneer life, a life of independence, decorum and restraint. In a native version of the social contract, Faulkner writes that the earth was made by God not for man "to hold for himself and his descendants . . . but to hold the earth mutual and intact in the communal anonymity of brotherhood, and all the fee He asked was pity and humility and sufferance and endurance and the sweat of his face for bread."

That Isaac McCaslin is meant and deserves to gain our moral admiration, seems beyond doubt. Yet some of Faulkner's critics have felt that Isaac's withdrawal, for all its saintly humaneness, does not bear sufficiently upon the condition that has caused it: he leaves the world intact, still caught up in its accumulated evil, and if only for this reason—that he fails actively to engage himself—he cannot be considered an heroic figure. While generally sympathetic to this kind of argument, I doubt that it is finally decisive in relation to "The Bear." For it slights one fact: that at least intermittently Faulkner seems to believe very deeply in the intrinsic value and ultimate efficacy of passive suffering. The image of endurance, related for him both to the agony of Christ and the condition of man, evokes his deepest and sometimes uncontainable feelings. Though the twentieth century reader may have little trouble in expressing verbal admiration for this image, he cannot really credit or accept it fully, which is one reason that Faulkner, despite his modernist techniques, is a writer seriously estranged from his time. It is not merely that

he fails to share our frequent belief in social activism;
it is that he seems in most of his books to be persuaded
of the moral rightness, perhaps the invincibility, of
waiting and powerlessness. And he feels this, I would
say, not out of a commitment to doctrinal Christianity,
but out of a sense of the terribleness of history, a sense
which leads him to reach for a patience beyond hope
or despair. He supposes not that the meek will inherit
the earth, but that if they persist in their meekness they
may not need to inherit the earth. Modern readers,
whether religious or not, must find this a difficult view
to grasp; Faulkner himself finds it difficult. We are
obliged not to accept it, only to take it seriously.

"Delta Autumn" serves as a bitter epilogue to the
story of Isaac McCaslin. An old man now, he goes for
his last hunt, this time having to travel for hours before
wild country can be reached. "There was some of it
left, although now it was two hundred miles from
Jefferson, when once it had been thirty. He watched
it, not being conquered, destroyed, so much as retreat-
ing since its purpose was served now and its time an
outmoded time. . . ." Everything comes to seem a
painful contrast to the hunts of his youth: the men are
querulous, they condescend to him, none of the fraternal propriety of the early years has survived. What
had once been a ceremony is now a mere diversion.

After the others leave for the hunt, Isaac, alone in
the camp, is visited by the girl who tells him she has
had an affair with Roth Edmonds. Discovering that she
is related to him through the Negro branch of the
McCaslin family, Isaac feels as if the whole weight of
the past were again crushing him. He looks at her with
"amazement, pity and outrage," telling himself, as he
contemplates the tempting and fearful vision of a
blending of races, *"Maybe in a thousand or two thousand years in America. . . . But not now! Not now!"* He
urges the girl to marry a man of her own color, but not

because he can persuade himself that he is arguing
from justice. Not justice but evil necessity is his ground:
"We will have to wait."

To have come thus far represents an extraordinary
growth for Isaac and, in a way, for Faulkner. Nor is
that all. The girl takes the last word: "Old man, have
you lived so long, and forgotten so much that you
don't remember anything you ever knew or felt or even
heard about love?" If Isaac represents the strongest side
of Faulkner's thought, the question the girl asks Isaac—
a question he cannot answer—shows the artist triumphing over inherited limitations. But then, that is what
makes him an artist.

[10]

The sensibility which made "The Bear" possible breaks
into two discrete parts in *Intruder in the Dust*: the
political speeches of Gavin Stevens and the narrative,
half fable and half whodunit, of Lucas Beauchamp's
near-lynching. This split into ideology and imagination
suggests that Faulkner may at last have arrived at the
usual kind of commonplace sanity from which we all
suffer, a condition he is not, as a writer, particularly
equipped to deal with. Emerging from his mythical
world, he now returns to the South other Southerners
inhabit.

When Gavin Stevens launches his lectures in behalf of
Southern separatism and "homogeneity" (a term happily
left undefined), he becomes one of Faulkner's more
tedious characters. Stevens does recognize the Negro's
claim to justice: "Someday Lucas Beauchamp . . . will
vote anywhen and anywhere a white man can and send
his children to the same schools anywhere the white
man's children go and travel anywhere the white man
does as the white man does it." But he insists that the
South do the job alone: "We must expiate (the injustice) and abolish it ourselves, alone and without
help nor even (with thanks) advice." Only—and here

Faulkner crowds upon Southern apologetics—this injustice cannot be "abolished overnight by the police." He urges the Negro to be patient, and suggests that when the South has given him full justice, "together we would dominate the United States."[5]

The narrative itself, far more impressive than Stevens's oratory, centers on one event, a lynching which never quite materializes—entirely appropriate for a novel that aspires to be a fable about Southern society. (More appropriate, in fact, than an actual lynching, for the quality of Southern life, as increasingly of Northern, lies more in its possibilities than its rare climaxes.) Dominating the action is Lucas Beauchamp, a man whose silent and looming appearance makes Gavin Stevens seem a mere talkative schoolboy, as Stevens himself occasionally realizes. One part of Lucas, the lesser part, has been "trying to escape not into the best of the white race but the second best." By far the more important, Lucas is the one whom Faulkner describes as "solitary, kinless and intractable, apparently without friends in his own race and proud of it." Lucas carries a measure of white blood, yet finally belongs neither

[5] Toward what end, one wonders? To oppose those citizens whom Faulkner, in an uncharacteristic descent to meanness, calls the "coastal spew of Europe?" Perhaps he intends to say that the Southern whites and Negroes could together resist the evils of Northern commercialism, particularly its "frantic greed for money." But then he must reflect on the irony that it is the industrialization (the "Northifying") of the South which is destroying the traditional patterns of its life, including many of the Negro-white relations he would want to see destroyed. Once the South ceased to be a predominantly agrarian society, and once it removed the injustice suffered by the Negro, what claim could it then have to separateness?

I assume here that Stevens speaks at least partly for Faulkner. It is not an assumption that can be sustained through all the novels in which Stevens appears and in later ones, such as *The Mansion*, Faulkner negotiates a certain ironic distance from Stevens' conduct, if not his opinions. But the assumption would seem to hold, alas, in relation to *Intruder in the Dust*, where Stevens is so clearly admired in his role of *raisonneur*.

to the whites nor blacks as the two cohere into polar groups. He neither cringes nor defies, he refuses to live by the conventional roles open to him, he gives white society its ultimate due—he ignores it. Powerful and slow, bearing a native dignity that leaves the whites all the more sullen as they fail to mar or "place" it, carrying himself like a man whose true foci of attention are the earth and himself, Lucas Beauchamp is Faulkner's tribute to strength, suffering, patience.

As counterpoise to Lucas there is a sixteen-year-old white boy, Charles Mallison, who several years earlier had been helped by the Negro. Already tainted by the assumptions of white supremacy, Chick had tried to pay Lucas for a meal he had eaten in the latter's cabin, and Lucas refused payment. Chick had then hoped to re-establish his status through gifts, but was foiled by Lucas's prompt return with gifts of his own. He has since resented the moral debt he owes Lucas, a debt the Negro will not allow him to cancel through a conventional act of benevolence. Chick has grown up admiring Lucas' indifference to environment and unwillingness to conform to the roles white society sets out for Negroes, but the boy also feels that Lucas has dispossessed him of his racial assurance, and he is enough of a child of his society to suppose this a loss.

The story comes to dramatic focus when Lucas is accused of murdering a white man under circumstances which apparently leave no doubt as to his guilt. With quixotic stubbornness, he refuses to explain himself, refuses to talk candidly to his lawyer, Gavin Stevens, refuses to have any predictable relation to the apparatus of law in Yoknapatawpha. A lynching is momentarily expected; tension mounts in the streets of Jefferson; the Negroes crawl into hiding; the more enlightened whites are harried and disturbed; Lucas alone remains calm, stolid, almost indifferent—they can only take his life and he is an old man. For Chick, however, Lucas's imprisonment creates the most painful of moral dilemmas. He hopes that Lucas will be saved; he is appalled by the probable outcome, yet he feels a subterranean pleasure in the thought that tomorrow Lucas—no longer a man but sheer Negro—may burn in gasoline. He suffers, like so many other Faulkner characters, the conflict between a native sense of decency and a still powerful heritage.

Perhaps because he is young and, thereby, not hopelessly corrupted, Chick is "chosen" to signify the redemptive potential of the whites in Yoknapatawpha —and it is Lucas, alone in his jail, who does the choosing, since only he, the Negro, can even begin to absolve the whites of their guilt. Only to Chick will Lucas speak with a measure of candor, and on a hint from Lucas the boy goes off on a rather perilous chase, disinterring the body of the murdered white man and thereby establishing that he was not shot by Lucas. This is Chick's opportunity to pay off his debt to the Negro, and more important, to break out of the molds of conduct which Yoknapatawpha requires from him as much as it does from Lucas. Chick does not consult with or inform his uncle, Gavin Stevens, the white "liberal," for he senses that Stevens is too deeply caught up in the society of Yoknapatawpha to sympathize with his venture. Chick finds two helpers—both of them innocents, as they must be—for his mission: Aleck Sander, a Negro boy of his own age, and Miss Habersham, an elderly white woman, genteel, poor, independent. Just as Big Ben could not be hunted by the men of Yoknapatawpha until they divested themselves of material possessions and social emblems, so the mission in behalf of Lucas Beauchamp can be undertaken only by boys who have not yet been contaminated by, or old ladies who have learned to move beyond, the ordinary social world.

Intruder in the Dust can profitably be read as a modern version of the Huck Finn–Nigger Jim story, with the conscience-stricken white boy and intractable

Negro reenacting Twain's story in the harsh terms of the present. To survive, Nigger Jim has had to become crotchety old Lucas; to be just, Huck has had to become a boy in direct opposition to his society. Chick's confused feelings toward Lucas—his wish that the Negro would be a nigger *for just one minute*, Mistering white folks as if he meant it—together with his admiration for Lucas because he never will, remind one a little of Huck's feeling that if not turning in Nigger Jim as a runaway would cause him to go to hell, then that too was a price worth paying for friendship. There are significant differences, of course. Nigger Jim and Huck Finn need only escape to the raft in order to live in fraternity. Both Chick and Lucas, however, are much more socially bound; it is harder for them to reach a personal freedom that would leave behind the tokens of power and place; and at no point in the book is there any drawing together of white boy and Negro man that could resemble the idyllic moments of Huck and Nigger Jim floating down the Mississippi.

The tradition of the past now lives, not in the almost extinct Sartoris and Compson clans, but in Lucas Beauchamp; and the atonement for the past begun by Isaac McCaslin is actively continued by the white boy. Over all of Yoknapatawpha, the river-bottom of Frenchman's Bend as well as the uneasily modernized town of Jefferson, towers the figure of Lucas Beauchamp, "once the slave of any white man within range of whose notice he happened to come, now tyrant over the whole country's white conscience." And Lucas will not easily make his peace with the whites. At the end of the novel, he asserts his claim to both equality and continued recalcitrance by insisting that Gavin Stevens accept payment for legal services. For Stevens, who had doubted Lucas's innocence and done little to help him, this is clearly a defeat. Lucas will pay his own way—and thereby preserve his solitary status.

[11]

The more closely Faulkner approaches the life of Yoknapatawpha in the middle of the twentieth century,
the more vexed and insecure his work becomes. Faulkner's imagination runs toward extremes, polar oppositions and contrasts, grotesque shadowings of real situations; his world is fiercely Manichean and heavily chia-
roscuroed, a brilliant vision but not a faithful replica
of social reality; and in these respects he seems a true
sharer in one of the dominant literary traditions of
America. But during the past few decades the drift of
life in Yoknapatawpha, as elsewhere in America, has
been toward middle-class moderation, a blurring of
moral and social outlines, a softening of issues and
idiosyncrasies. Except during the 1960's there has been
less violence, less color, less excitement.

What makes this problem especially acute for Faulkner is that, either through the influence of his critics or
his growing self-consciousness as a famous writer, he
has felt obliged to become a semi-official historian for
his imaginary world, rather than the brilliant fantast
and grotesque painter that he showed himself to be
in his best work. This impulse toward soberly filling in
the nooks and crannies of his saga has led him to return, often unsuccessfully, to characters from his earlier
novels[6] and has also led him, still more unhappily, to

---

[6] It is an impulse most fully satisfied in *The Mansion*, which at
times reads like a family history brought up to date. One learns
that Jason Compson, last seen in *The Sound and the Fury*, has
recovered from his stock market losses but has lost his money
again, this time to Flem Snopes; that Benjy Compson was
brought back from the state asylum at Jackson and then burned
to death when the family mansion caught fire; that Benbow Sartoris, a child in *Sartoris*, now goes hunting with Chick Mallison . . .
    All of which has a kind of charm. A reader who cares about
Faulkner's earlier novels is likely to retain some curiosity as to

indulge his taste for heady abstractions and grand pronouncements. Shamefully undervalued in the thirties, when he was making major contributions to world literature, Faulkner was then treated in the fifties a little too much like an established institution. As a result, not enough attention was paid to the evidence that he had reached a serious impasse in his career and that the more he kept assuring us that man will "endure," the less assurance his own work showed.

Even the most sympathetic reader might find himself wondering, as the Yoknapatawpha chronicle drew to its nervous and somewhat troubled end, whether Faulkner had been distracted from his deeper interests by the buzz of controversy over the South or by his new role as spokesman for the cause of human survival. Whatever the reason, it became hard not to conclude that Faulkner was slowly emerging from his creative trance, that in his final books something had been lost of the old energy, the blazing infatuation with a world of his own making.

Nowhere do we see this more clearly than in *Intruder in the Dust*. The bare situation—Chick Mallison *vis à vis* Lucas Beauchamp—is splendidly conceived, rich with associations from the American past, easily capable of tragic expansion; it involves some of Faulkner's most intimate and persistent themes. But a good part of the

---

"what happened" to the characters in later life. And one enjoys the sight of Faulkner turning back to them, as if they were still alive for him, people he had continued to know about but had neglected to look up in recent years.

Yet there is also something disconcerting about this kind of "information." These old (and in their original contexts) marvellous characters do not really come to life again; they are merely named, discussed, ticked off. Their appearance indicates not that Faulkner is returning to old interests or enjoying a new quota of energy, but that he feels a wish for neatness, for rounding out and finishing up. And as one weighs in mind the earlier and the later novels, one is struck, painfully, by the difference between creation and annotation.

book seems designed almost wilfully to evade and hinder a mature development of these themes: as if Faulkner had lost a full conviction in the worth and reality of his world or as if, more specifically, he were driven by some need to discount, in the very manner and speech of Chick Mallison, the boy's yearning to conciliate Lucas and all that Lucas stands for. Neither the mechanics of narrative nor the intruding speeches are equal to the commanding image of Negro boy and white man which has been projected on the opening pages. The adolescent foolery about vanishing corpses is not only a strain on one's sense of plausibility, it is at harsh tonal variance with the fine scenes in which Lucas and Chick confront each other. For perhaps the first time Faulkner seems to have genuine difficulties in transforming his observations of contemporary Southern life, acute as these often are, into a fictional structure. One misses here that density of detail and grave assurance of judgment which are characteristic of the best Yoknapatawpha novels.

Similar difficulties beset *Requiem for a Nun*. This book arouses quick interest as another of Faulkner's experiments, still further evidence that he, almost alone among the older American novelists, continues to show creative restlessness. But simply as a novel it does not succeed, if only because it is very hard to accept its version of contemporary Yoknapatawpha with the full conviction one could give to Faulkner's portraits of earlier days in Yoknapatawpha. The narrative interludes of *Requiem for a Nun*, bringing together familiar stories about the legendary history of the county, are marvellously evocative; the three-act play about the current moment seems unprovisioned and thin.

Requiem for a Nun resurrects two characters from *Sanctuary*, Temple Drake and Gowan Stevens, some years after the accident which brought them to Popeye's hideout. Temple and Gowan are now respectably married, parents of two children, but still troubled by a

need to expiate their guilt and show each other grati-
tude. Wearied by her regimen of cautious goodness,
Temple decides to run off with Pete, the younger
brother of a tough for whom she had developed a
passion during her stay in the Memphis brothel. To this
plan there is but one obstacle: a Negro woman named
Nancy, a reformed prostitute whom Temple employs as
a nursemaid and confidante for an exchange of memories about their youthful sins. Nancy, in the name of
the children, begs Temple not to run off, and when re-
buffed, strangles Temple's baby in order to forestall
the greater tragedy of both children being left motherless. Condemned to die, Nancy shows no fear: she is
in the hands of God.

Simply as a play, all this is extremely weak. Faulkner
has not troubled to dramatize his story, the bulk of it
being narrated by Temple to auditors on the stage and
the point of it being ruthlessly imposed on whatever
sense of plausibility the action might convey. In a play
the familiar Faulkner strategy of spiraling back from a
troubled narrator to a troubling action—the strategy
described by Henry James in a study of Conrad as "a
prolonged hovering flight of the subjective over the
outstretched ground of the case exposed"—will not
work unless the action has first been shown. (In a novel,
even when not directly presented, the action can be
shown through its ramifications on the consciousness of
the characters; in a play this method is not available
and unless presented either directly or in terms of
visible consequences, the action tends to become a
mere topic to be discussed.) More serious is the fact
that Faulkner clearly has ideological designs upon the
reader, wishing to persuade or bludgeon one into a
large and vaporous affirmation, the nature of which remains obscure even to him and the value of which he
can but desperately affirm. And finally, what *Requiem
for a Nun* lacks but needs most is one of the major
strengths of Faulkner's earlier work: a securely-located

milieu, a sense of place as it conveys the power of
contingency over human existence.

[12]

In Faulkner's two most recent novels, *The Town* and
The Mansion, there is a richer evocation of locale,
though hardly with the overflowing zest of *The Hamlet*,
the novel to which they are formally the sequels. The
tone is now more sober, perhaps because Faulkner feels
himself to be completing a task as he rounds out both
the Snopes trilogy and the Yoknapatawpha saga, perhaps because he finds a confrontation with the present-
day world only occasionally absorbing and frequently
distasteful.

The Town brings together in predictable conflict,
though not always sufficient drama, the invading
Snopeses and the community of Jefferson, seat of Yoknapatawpha tradition, power, and respectability. It begins approximately where *The Hamlet* left off, with
Flem Snopes riding away from Frenchman's Bend in
search of new possibilities for exploitation, and it takes
the story of Snopesism triumphant into the late 1920's.
Repeating, sometimes through enlargement and sometimes depression, several of the episodes and anecdotes
which first appeared in *The Hamlet*, it charts the steady
advance of Flem Snopes toward the center of social and
economic power in Jefferson, alternately with the help
of his relatives and over their betrayed bodies. No force
in Jefferson seems able to stop Flem; hardly anyone
but Gavin Stevens, still the ruminative lawyer, and
Ratliff, still the peregrine sewing-machine agent, are
even aware that there is much need to stop him.

Faulkner is extremely shrewd in noting that Flem
Snopes comes to Jefferson not merely as an alien force
but also as an alien force which quickly adapts itself to
the colors and tones of the world it will soon dominate.
Flem starts by running a restaurant and briefly managing

the town's power plant; he becomes a petty usurer bilking tenant farmers who turn to him for quick loans; he moves into real estate, coolly manipulating relatives who act for him; and then he works his way into one of Jefferson's two banks, first as vice-president and then as president. He begins as a petty conniver (see the story "Centaur in Brass" which Faulkner later wove into *The Town*), but he ends as a banker scrupulously obeying the letter of the law and thereby invulnerable to obvious moral attack or legal prosecution. All this, so to say, is not merely predictable but ordained, not merely in the nature of Snopesism but also in the nature of the society which prepares the way for and seems almost to deserve the blows of Snopesism. Jefferson's practical and moral helplessness before Flem's assault is due not so much to its lack of resources or even his own shrewdness, but to the fact that what its leading figures do covertly, with a touch of shame or guilt, Flem does openly, without pretense, regret or self-deception. As an extreme version and caricature of economic man, Flem is able consistently to defeat those who have been somewhat softened by scruple or weakened by conscience. That is why, for all its knowledge of what Flem is and what Flem means, the town has no choice but outwardly to accept him as a solid citizen defending "civic jealousy and pride," a deacon of the Baptist church, and finally the owner of "the old de Spain house which he had remodeled into an ante-bellum Southern mansion." At least in its outlines, if not always in local presentment, Faulkner's sense of the relation between a comfortable, established community and a rapacious new social group is the equal of anything we have had in American literature since the brilliant novels of Edith Wharton on this theme.

Sharply in contrast to Flem, and ultimately a more powerful contrast then either Stevens or Ratliff, is Eula Varner Snopes, the Helen of Frenchman's Bend, whom Flem, for a proper consideration, has married when she needed to provide respectability for the baby she was carrying. In *The Town* she is still "a woman who shapes, fits herself to no environment, scorns the fixitude of environment and all the behavior patterns which had been mutually agreed on as being best for the greatest number;" but she is also transformed into an intelligent and thoughtful woman, surely the last thing any reader of *The Hamlet* might have expected. Eula's eighteen-year-long affair with Manfred de Spain, the dashing ex-mayor and president of the bank into which Flem has wormed his way, becomes a town legend: a legend admired for the lustful fidelity of its principals, enjoyed as a richly-deserved retribution for Flem and kept faithfully secret as long as it does not threaten Jefferson's respectability. But here again Faulkner shows a strong grasp of both the social nature of Snopesism and the personal psychology of Flem Snopes, for through all these eighteen cuckolded years Flem knows exactly what is happening and uses his knowledge, through a complicated series of maneuvers, to further his own ends. Eula's affair thus becomes the means by which Flem, indifferent to fine points of love or honor, rises to be president of the bank and a respected member of society. Gavin Stevens also finds himself serving as a tool of Snopes's ambition, for he is so caught up in a quixotic infatuation with the incomparable Eula that in her behalf he must soon protect Flem. It is at this point in the trilogy that Faulkner's sense of how the inadequacy of Jefferson plays into the venality of Snopesism comes through with notable force.

At the end of *The Town* Flem has won in every possible way: Stevens and Ratliff rendered almost hopeless, de Spain forced to leave town, Eula driven to breaking off her affair and then to suicide, and her daughter Linda maneuvered into a partly-felt acceptance of Flem's fatherhood. The last pages of *The Town* show Flem in a stunning evocation of social hypocrisy, as he sets up a monument for his wife:

EULA VARNER SNOPES
1889 1927
A Virtuous Wife is a Crown to Her Husband
Her Children Rise and Call Her Blessed

The monument is the final sign of Flem's triumph, for as Ratliff remarks:

. . . it was Flem's monument; dont make no mistake about that. It was Flem that paid for it, first thought of it, planned and designed it, picked out what size and what was to be wrote on it—the face and the letters—and never once mentioned price. Dont make no mistake about that. It was Flem. Because this too was a part of what he had come to Jefferson for and went through all he went through afterward to get it.

Once the monument has been raised, Flem can release his true feelings in a gesture that recalls his earlier self:

and him setting there chewing, faint and steady, and [Linda] still and straight as a post by him, not looking at nothing and them two white balls of her fists on her lap. Then he moved. He leant a little and spit out the window and then set back in the seat.

"Now you can go," he says.

Faulkner will probably return to the world of Yoknapatawpha in later books, but here it is convenient to regard *The Mansion* as if it were a conclusion for the entire saga. And so in a sense it is: for not only does it chart the destruction of Flem Snopes, it also brings the Yoknapatawpha story to the very rim of contemporary life. *The Mansion* adds little to what *The Town* has already shown about the dynamics of Flem's rise to wealth and power; if anything, Flem is reduced to a still more shadowy figure and thrust still further into the background. By now he has largely achieved his goals and as a result has been left somewhat immobile, so that our attention must be turned from his effect upon others to what others, both from within his own clan and the community at large, can do to him. This is the necessary consequence of the main theme for which *The Town* has made careful preparation: that Snopesism in its very success becomes absorbed by the world it would take over, corrupting that world yet also losing a portion of its raw energies and brute hungers. What *The Mansion* does add in regard to the destiny of the Snopeses is Faulkner's observation—but perhaps it is merely his wish—that even so consummate a devil as Flem Snopes cannot act forever with impunity; that he too must face some equivalent of Maule's curse, and face it simply because in some ultimate sense he too is prey to the weaknesses of being human; that in short, he must pay a price for having ruined the lives of Mink Snopes and Linda Varner Snopes, the two figures from within the clan who represent the retributive past and a cleansed future.

The Mansion begins with a retracing of material that had largely appeared in *The Hamlet* but treats it in radically different terms. It tells the story of Mink Snopes who had become entangled in a quarrel with his well-to-do neighbor, Houston, a farmer of overbearing temper. In *The Hamlet* Faulkner's main stress was upon Houston's grief over the death of his young wife, which had made him so violent a man; and his quarrel with Mink was seen as one of those terrible meetings which must lead to a mutual destruction, not from any objective need but simply because each is driven by an uncontainable private feeling. In *The Hamlet* Mink was venomous and wretched, almost the lowest of the Snopeses; in *The Town* Ratliff calls him "out and out mean;" but now in *The Mansion* he is viewed from a fresh perspective, the same story of Houston's murder being retold partly through his eyes, or rather, retold by Faulkner as if he were leaning over Mink's shoulder and trying to grasp the story as Mink sees it. Now we understand how intolerable Houston's arrogance must have been to Mink, and Mink himself becomes—while still wretched, still mean—a creature with a kind of bottom-dog dignity. Only formally should these two accounts be taken as what Faulkner in an introductory note to *The Mansion* has called "discrepancies." What he is really showing here is the way events shift in meaning as they are regarded through new eyes and how a consequence of a growing humaneness can be a relativism of judgment.

Imprisoned for Houston's murder, Mink assumes that cousin Flem will rescue him, since for Mink, as for all the Snopeses, Flem is the agent, the connection between their clan and the outer world. Flem, however, coldly abandons Mink, and Mink, sentenced to prison, lives only for the day he can destroy Flem. A stratagem of Flem's—through some not very persuasive manipulations of plot—lures Mink into attempting an escape; his sentence is doubled; but he waits patiently, sweating out his blood over the state's cotton.

Thirty-eight years later, when Mink is a broken man of sixty-three, his body as puny as a child's and his mind not much stronger, he is finally released from the penitentiary, mainly through the efforts of Linda Varner Snopes, who expects that he will now try to kill Flem and thereby, as she sees it, avenge her mother's suicide. The section ends with Mink's reverie:

> *Sixty-three*, he thought. *So that's how old I am.* He thought quietly *Not justice; I never asked that; jest fairness, that's all.* That was all; not to have anything for him; just not to have anything against him. That was all he wanted, and sure enough, here he was.

The scene is set for the act of retribution, but Faulkner cannot allow the retribution to come only from within the Snopes clan, for then he would fail sufficiently to connect Flem's fate with his social role and would be wasting the preparations of the two earlier novels in showing the relationships between the Snopeses and the town of Jefferson. The middle section of *The Mansion* must, therefore, be devoted to the outer world, the realm of non-Snopesdom, as it comes to grips with Flem and prepares, deliberately or not, to lend support to Mink's revenge. A great deal of new material, barely or not at all noticed in the earlier Yoknapatawpha novels, is packed into this middle section. In effect, it brings in the whole of modern urban society, trivially through some visits of Ratliff to New York, and importantly through the introduction of Linda Snopes as a grown woman who returns to Jefferson with some of the values and styles of urban society.

Linda had left Jefferson as a girl; married a Jewish sculptor in New York; gone off to the Spanish Civil War, where she suffered a puncture of her eardrums; returned to Jefferson as a member of the Communist Party (there are, it turns out, two other ineffectual members in the town); and now "meddles" with the Negroes, becomes the object of an FBI investigation, loves Gavin Stevens as vainly and hopelessly as he loves her, and shares a home with her "father," Flem, in cold silence, until her scheme for freeing Mink works out. Nothing that Faulkner has written shows, in the abstract, so large an awareness of the changes that postwar life have brought to Yoknapatawpha; but these signs of awareness remain little more than signs, inasmuch as they are not dramatically absorbed into the life of the novel. For Faulkner to cope directly or deeply with this kind of material he will have to allot it several more books, so that he can mull and brood over it, slowly making it part of his imaginative possession.

He does, however, cope with it indirectly in the final section of *The Mansion*. Mink's difficult journey homeward, from the penitentiary to Memphis to buy a gun and then back to Jefferson, becomes an occasion for noticing, often with great poignance, the changes that have occurred in the thirty-eight years between Mink's imprisonment and his release—years, as it happens, that also comprise the bulk of Faulkner's manhood. It is always the past, even the recent past, that releases in Faulkner his deepest feelings, and as Mink moves toward Jefferson his simple observations of surprise and astonishment come to seem a muted elegy. In the end, after Mink, with Linda's help, has killed Flem and made his escape, Ratliff and Stevens talk for a few moments, ruminating upon the rise and fall of Snopesism, the destruction of Flem at the very height of his apparent triumph:

> "You see?" [Stevens] said. "It's hopeless. Even when you get rid of one Snopes, there's already another one behind you even before you can turn around."

> "That's right," Ratliff said serenely. "As soon as you look, you see right away it aint nothing but jest another Snopes."

The nuances of phrasing are significant here, for they leave the fate of Yoknapatawpha in a delicate balance, with evil a recurrent growth and good a constant possibility. It is a useful place to end, for the experience which a work of fiction would enclose is always finally not to be contained, and the resolution to which the novel seems to draw never is fixed in reality.

Had Faulkner lived much beyond the moment he completed these books, he would have continued to revise his sense of the world he created. But he did not, and this lends poignance to the elegiac note in his later novels —and nowhere more so than in the rhapsodies of *Re-*

quiem for a Nun, which are perhaps the most authentic
and personal farewell that Faulkner has bid to the
world he made. One of these rhapsodies, "The Court-
house" is written in a winding breathless style which
serves for a humorous recall of Yoknapatawpha history,
partly a hymn to the vanished American wilderness
and partly an anecdote of how the loss of a lock, the
vanity of a mail rider, and the shrewdness of an early
settler led to the building of the county's first court-
house. Finer still is "The Jail," spun out in a controlled
forty-nine page "sentence," which transforms the motion of the past into the very breath of the present.
"The Jail" is a review of Faulkner's legend, touching on
most of his books and ending with an acknowledgment
that the homeland, now absorbed into "one nation,"
hardly survives as a separate region. Time caught up
with Faulkner or he with time; and for those who have
immersed themselves in his world, the impassioned
leave-taking of these rhapsodies must seem a gesture
infinitely sad.

V

Faulkner
and the Negroes

ALL OF THE TENSIONS IN FAULKNER'S WORK REACH AN
extreme in his presentment of Negro life and character.
Problems of value which in his novels emerge as problems of perception, become magnified and exacerbated
when he writes about Negroes. In saying this, I would
stress that my concern is not with Faulkner's explicit
views about the "racial question," or at least that my
concern with those views extends no further than the
way they condition the novels. In their own right,
Faulkner's opinions are usually the least interesting aspect of his work: they matter only when absorbed into
his art, there to undergo transformations of a kind that
justify our speaking of literature as a mode of creation.

Complex and ambiguous responses to the Negroes
are predictable, almost conventional among sensitive
Southern writers; they stem partly from an inheritance
of guilt and uncertainty, partly from a ripening of heart.
But in Faulkner's fiction, beneath its worried surface of

attitude and idea, there is also a remarkable steadiness
of feeling toward the Negro. His opinions change, his
early assurance melts away, his sympathies visibly enlarge; but always there is a return to one central image,
an image of memory and longing.

In *The Unvanquished* the boy, Bayard Sartoris, and
his Negro friend, Ringo, eat, play, and live together.
When the two boys and Granny Rosa Millard begin a
long journey, Bayard and Ringo, to whom Miss Rosa is
also "Granny," take turns, in simple equality, holding a
parasol over her head. "That's how Ringo and I were,"
Bayard nostalgically recalls. "We were almost the same
age, and Father always said that Ringo was a little
smarter than I was, but that didn't count with us, anymore than the difference in the color of our skins
counted. What counted was what one of us had done or
seen that the other had not, and ever since that Christmas I had been ahead of Ringo because I had seen a
railroad." Bayard is here expressing an ideal of boyhood
friendship, unaffected by social grade and resting on that
intuitive sense of scruple, that belief in "fairness," common to boys.

The same vision, or a similar one, appears in other
Faulkner novels. In *The Sound and the Fury* the only
happy memories the Compsons retain are memories of
scenes in which white and Negro children play together.
In *Absalom, Absalom!* there are no glimpses of friendship between boys of the two races, but the pioneer
innocence of young Sutpen is defined as a freedom
from both racial feeling and economic acquisitiveness.
In "The Bear" the boy, Isaac McCaslin, unconsciously
—and then deliberately—claims as his spiritual par-
ent Sam Fathers, half-Negro and half-Indian; a similar
claim determines the relationship between Chick Mallison and Lucas Beauchamp in *Intruder in the Dust*. In
the story "Go Down, Moses" an old white woman, Miss
Worsham, explains her wish to help an old Negro
woman, Mollie Beauchamp, by invoking a childhood

friendship of decades ago: "Mollie and I were born in the same month. We grew up together as sisters would." By contrast, Joe Christmas in *Light in August* seems the most deprived of Faulkner's characters precisely because he has no childhood memories to fall back on.

The most dramatic rendering of this theme occurs in the story, "The Fire and the Hearth." For the white man Roth Edmonds, Mollie Beauchamp is "the only mother he ever knew, who had not only delivered him on that night of rain and flood . . . but moved into the very house, bringing her own child, the white child and the black one sleeping in the same room with her so that she could suckle them both." As a boy, Roth feels that his home and the home of his Negro friend Henry Beauchamp have "become interchangeable: himself and his foster-brother sleeping on the same pallet in the white man's house or in the same bed in the negro's and eating of the same food at the table in either, actually preferring the negro house. . . ." And then the moment of pride: Roth refuses to share his bed with Henry and lies alone "in a rigid fury of the grief he could not explain, the shame he would not admit." Later he knew "it was grief and was ready to admit it was shame also, wanted to admit it only it was too late then, forever and forever." Forever and forever—the terribleness of this estrangement recurs in Faulkner's work, not simply as a theme, but as a cry of loss and bafflement.

Beneath the white man's racial uneasiness there often beats an impatience with the devices by which men keep themselves apart. Ultimately the whole apparatus of separation must seem too wearisome in its constant call to alertness, too costly in its tax on the emotions, and simply tedious as a brake on spontaneous life. The white man is repeatedly tempted by a memory playing on the rim of his consciousness: a memory of boyhood, when he could live as a brother with his Ringo or Henry

Beauchamp—his Nigger Jim or Queequeg—and not yet wince under the needle of self-consciousness. The memory—or a longing in the guise of memory—can be downed by the will and blunted by convention, but it is too lovely and in some final sense too real to be discarded entirely. Beneath the pretense to superiority, the white man reaches for what is true: the time when he could compare bits of knowledge about locomotives with Ringo, share food with Henry Beauchamp, not in equality or out of it—for the mere knowledge of either is a poison—but in a chaste companionship. This is what the white man has lost, forever and forever; and the Negro need not remind him of it, he need only walk past him on the street.

It is a memory fed by guilt. As a confession of failure within society, it shows that status has brought not satisfaction but grief and shame. By questioning the entirety of adult relations, it reveals a hidden weight of despair. Because it glances at the possibilities of life beyond society, the writer can imagine it only in a setting of pastoral simplicity or childhood affection. It is a plea to be forgiven for what is and perhaps—but here Faulkner is uncertain—must be. And it is a yearning to find release, to fall away from the burden of one's whiteness.

Touching as this vision of lost fraternity is, it also involves an outrageous naïveté. As Leslie Fielder has remarked, the white man "dreams of his acceptance at the breast he has most utterly offended. It is a dream so sentimental, so outrageous, so desperate that it redeems our concept of boyhood from nostalgia to tragedy." Miss Worsham says of Mollie Beauchamp, "We grew up together as sisters would"—but how many decades of distance have intervened she does not add. It is as though she and Roth Edmonds and all the other whites unconsciously hoped they need but turn again to their childhood companions to find in undiminished purity the love destroyed by caste. How the Negroes themselves might look upon this violated dream they do not think—perhaps they do not dare—to ask.

This image of the white man's longing is not, of course, unique to Faulkner; it appears with astonishing frequency in American writing, and often together with that pastoral impulse so strong among our novelists and poets. Faulkner has rendered it with a particular urgency and sadness, in a setting where at best the races live in quiet rancor. That he has repeatedly turned to this image may be considered a triumph of instinct, but the shape and weight he has given it are a triumph of art.

No such singleness or steadiness can be found in Faulkner's more conscious depiction of the Negro. One finds, instead, a progression from Southern stereotype to personal vision, interrupted by occasional retreats to inherited phobias and to an ideology that is morally inadequate to the vision. These shifting attitudes may be broken into three stages, each symbolized by a major Negro character: Dilsey, Joe Christmas and Lucas Beauchamp.

In *Soldiers' Pay*, Faulkner's first novel, a Negro (George the train porter) briefly appears as a conventional accessory. In *Sartoris* the Negro servants are regarded with truculent condescension, Joby and Simon, the old family retainers who are mere comic stereotypes. When Joby lights a fire on Christmas Day, Faulkner assures us that he feels "the grave and simple pleasures of his race." And when Simon visits some Negro ladies, there follows an uncomfortable moment of low comedy:

"Ef it ain't Brother Strother," they said in unison.
"Come in, Brother Strother. How is you?"
"Po'ly, ladies; po'ly," Simon replied. He doffed his hat and unclamped his cigar stub and stowed

it away in the hat. "I'se had a right smart mis'ry
in de back."

". . . . Whut you gwine eat, Brother Strother?"
the cook demanded hospitably. "Dey's party fixin's,
en day's some col' greens en a little sof' ice cream
lef fum dinner."

"I reckon I'll have a little ice cream en some of
dem greens, Sis Rachel," Simon replied. "My teef
ain't so much on party doin's no mo'. . . ."

Faulkner does this sort of thing skilfully enough, and
since the speech of some Negroes may well verge on
self-burlesque, the passage cannot simply be dismissed
as "unreal." But its reality is of a superficial order, dis-
playing a gift for condescending mimicry rather than the
moral sympathy and perception we may expect from a
novelist of the first rank.

In *The Unvanquished* a similar stereotyped response
to the Negro soon gives way to an awareness that his
psychology is not quite so accessible to the white man
as the latter would like to believe. Faulkner stresses the
free-and-easy relations between white master and Negro
slave in the Old South, the peculiar intimacy between
a man sure of his command and another who sees no
possibility or feels no desire to challenge it; and we
know from historical record that, together with brutality,
such relationships did once exist. But new voices appear now, particularly the voice of Loosh, a discontented Negro who deserts the Sartoris manor for the
Northern lines. "I done been freed," says Loosh,
"God's own angel proclamated me free and gonter general me to Jordan. I don't belong to John Sartoris now;
I belong to me and God." When asked why he has
spirited the Sartoris silver to the Yankees, Loosh replies
with vehemence and point: "You ax me that? . . .
Where John Sartoris? Whyn't he come and ax me that?
Let God ax John Sartoris who the man name that give

me to him. Let the man that buried me in the black
dark ax that of the man what dug me free."

Loosh's pregnant questions are repeated, in *Sartoris,*
by a Negro of a later era. Caspey, home from the First
World War, announces: "I don't take nothin' fum no
white folks no mo' . . . War done changed all dat. If
us cullud folks is good enough ter save France fum de
Germans, den us is good enough ter have de same
rights de Germans is. French folks think so, anyhow,
and ef America don't, dey's ways of learnin' 'um." For
such "sullen insolence" Caspey is knocked down by
Bayard Sartoris with a stick of stove wood and told by
Simon, his father, to "save dat nigger freedom talk fer
town-folks."

Neither Loosh nor Caspey is conceived in warmth
or developed in depth. Both are singled out for an
uneasy kind of ridicule, and their rebelliousness is
hardly taken seriously. What is damaging here is not so
much Faulkner's laziness of statement as the assumption, throughout his early treatment of Negroes, that
they are easily "knowable," particularly by disen-
chanted Southerners with experience in handling them.
Since Faulkner at his weakest, however, remains a writer
of some consequence, overtones of doubt and uneasiness
shade his portraiture of Negroes even in the minor
novels. The discontented ones are seen as loutish or
absurd, but this impression is undercut by the power
with which their discontent is now and again rendered. One of Faulkner's most admirable qualities as a
writer is that even when he wishes to settle into some
conventional or trite assumption, a whole side of himself—committed forever to restless inquiry—keeps resisting this desire.

In *Sartoris* there is also a glimpse of another kind of
feeling toward the Negro. Visiting the MacCallums,
young Bayard instinctively—out of a natural courtesy
in abiding by the manners of his hosts—treats their
Negro cook with the same rough easiness that the hills-

men do. Bayard does not stop to reflect upon the meaning of this companionship, nor does Faulkner stop to
give it any special emphasis: it comes through in a
brief ceremony of shaking hands. But in an unfinished
way, it points toward a strong motif in Faulkner's work:
his conviction that fraternity is morally finer than
equality, a fraternity which in his early novels makes
the demand for equality seem irrelevant but which in
his later ones can come only after equality has been so
long secured as to be forgotten.

A gifted artist can salvage significant images of life
from the most familiar notions: witness Dilsey in *The
Sound and the Fury*. Dilsey is a figure remarkable for
her poise, her hard realism, her ability to maintain her
selfhood under humiliating conditions. Yet the conception behind Dilsey does not seriously clash with the
view of the Negro that could be held by a white man
vaguely committed to a benevolent racial superiority.
Accepting her inferior status and surviving as a human
being despite that acceptance, Dilsey is the last of
Faulkner's major Negro characters who can still feel
that the South is a "natural" community to which they
entirely belong. No sensitive reader would care to deny
her strength and moral beauty, but I should like to
register a dissent from the effort of certain critics to
apotheosize her as the embodiment of Christian resignation and endurance. The terms in which Dilsey is conceived are thoroughly historical, and by their nature become increasingly unavailable to us: a fact which if it
does not lessen our admiration for her as a figure in a
novel, does limit our capacity to regard her as a moral
archetype or model.[7]

[7] But is not Don Quixote, surely a moral archetype, also conceived in historical terms unavailable to us? Yes, he is. Don Quixote, however, survives as a figure "beyond" history, we no longer
care about his historical genesis or purpose; while Dilsey, we cannot but remember, is a woman caught up in the recent historical
condition of the Southern Negro. Whether time will do for Dilsey what it has done for Don Quixote, no one can say.

In *The Sound and the Fury* there is an important modulation of attitude toward the Negro. While Dilsey's strength and goodness may be acceptable to traditional paternalism, she gradually assumes a role not quite traditional for the Southern Negro; she becomes, toward the end of the book, an articulate moral critic, the observer with whom the action of the novel is registered and through whom its meanings are amplified. She is not merely the old darky in the kitchen champing at the absurd and evil ways of the folks up front; at the climax of the novel she rises beyond that role, to a concern with universal problems of justice. This is not to suggest that Dilsey is in any way a rebel against the old order of Southern life. She regards most of the Compsons with contempt not because they are white or representative of the ruling social group but because they do not fulfill the obligations that have accrued to their status. Judging the whites in terms of their own proclaimed values, she criticizes not their exploitation of Negroes but their moral mistreatment of each other. This judgment, held with force and purity, leads Dilsey to a principled respect for the human person as such. When the name of the idiot Compson child is changed from Maury to Benjy, she snaps: "He *aint wore out the name he was born with yet, is he.*" When her daughter whines that "people talk" because Dilsey brings Benjy to the Negro church, the old woman replies: "Tell um the good Lawd don't keer whether he smart or not. Dont nobody but poor white trash keer dat." This sense of honor toward every person in her orbit, this absolute security in her own judgment, is Dilsey's most admirable trait, and a sign, as well, of the more complex treatment of Negroes that is to appear in Faulkner's books.

From traditional paternalism to an awareness of the injustice suffered by the Negro in Southern society— this, one could say, is the change that now occurs in the Yoknapatawpha novels. But the change is more complicated still, for the growing concern with injustice as a problem flows from an expansion of paternalism to its widest human limits. Dilsey and Joe Christmas are very different kinds of people, but Christmas is possible only because Dilsey already exists.

With *Light in August* the Negro assumes a new role in Faulkner's work. If Dilsey is characterized by an unbreakable sense of "belonging" in a world she knows to be falling apart, Joe Christmas feels that he has no home, that he always has been and must always remain homeless. If in the earlier work the focus of attention is on the white man's feelings toward the Negro, now there is a shock of discovery, a discovery of the Negro "as Negro."

The Faulkner to whom the Looshes and Caspeys and even Dilseys had seemed so accessible now emphasizes that for the whites the Negro often exists not as a distinct person but as a specter or phantasm. He writes brilliantly of what might be called the fetishism of false perception, the kind of false perception that has become systematic and has acquired both a pseudo-religious sanction and an intense emotional stake. Joanna Burden, daughter of abolitionists raised in the South, confesses that "I had seen and known Negroes since I could remember. I just looked at them as I did at rain, or furniture, or food or sleep. But after that I seemed to see them for the first time not as people, but as a thing, a shadow in which I lived, we lived, all white people, all other people. I thought of all the children coming forever and ever into the world, white, with the black shadow falling already upon them before they drew breath. And I seemed to see the black shadow in the shape of a cross." What is so remarkable about this passage—and it seems to me one of the most remarkable in all of Faulkner—is that here the false perception comes from a mixture of humaneness and fright, the two no longer separable but bound together in an apocalyptic image of violation and martyrdom.

In *Light in August* a lynch mob "believed aloud that it was an anonymous negro crime committed not by a negro but by Negro . . . and some of them with pistols already in pockets began to canvass about for someone to crucify." The phrase "not by a negro but by Negro" reflects a deepened understanding; the reference to men canvassing "for someone to crucify" suggests that Faulkner has been thinking hard about the role of frustration in shaping white behavior. In Percy Grimm, the small-town boy who has absorbed sadism from the very air, Faulkner gives form to his pained awareness that a society of inequality can lead only to abuse of status and arbitrary violence. This idea is expressed more abstractly in *The Wild Palms* when Faulkner describes the "indelible mark of ten thousand Southern deputy sheriffs, urban and suburban—the snapped hatbrim, the sadist's eyes, the slightly and unmistakably bulged coat, the air not swaggering exactly but of a formally pre-absolved brutality." Precise in each detail, this description opens to brilliance in the final phrase, "a formally pre-absolved brutality"—a phrase that epitomizes a vision of society.

That the white man has been calloused by status and the fear and guilt inevitable to status is not a novel insight; but to a writer wrestling with the pieties of the Southern tradition the price of such knowledge can hardly come low. For it is not, after all, the "South," that convenient abstraction of geography or history, about which Faulkner sees this; it is his own immediate cut of land, the place where he will spend his remaining time and die. Consider, then, the significance of the scene in *Light in August* where a sheriff, preparing to sweat some information out of a Negro, tells his deputy, "Get me a nigger"—get me a nigger, no matter which, they are indistinguishable.

We witness in Faulkner's novels a quick and steep ascent: from benevolence to recognition of injustice, from amusement over idiosyncrasies to a principled concern with status, from cozy familiarity to a discovery of the estrangement of the races. Realizing that despite their physical nearness Negroes must coil large parts of themselves beyond the vision of white society, Faulkner remarks in the story "The Old People" upon "that impenetrable wall of ready and easy mirth which negroes sustain between themselves and white men." Instead of being easily reached, the Negro is now locked behind suspicion; and while he may be, as Quentin Compson has said, "a form of behavior . . . [an] obverse reflection of the white people he lives among," he is also and more importantly something else: a human being whom the whites can seldom know. (One of Faulkner's later stories, "Pantaloon in Black," dramatizes this idea: after the death of his wife, a Negro runs berserk with grief while the whites, blind to the way he expresses it, sneer at his apparent insensitivity.) As Faulkner discovers the difficulty of approaching Negroes, he also develops an admirable sense of reserve, a blend of shyness and respect; trusting few of his preconceptions he must look at everything afresh.

A curious result of this growth in perception is, occasionally, a loss of concreteness in the presentation of character. Faulkner's discovery of the power of abstraction as it corrupts the dealings men have with one another, can lead him to portray Negroes in abstract terms. If the mob in *Light in August* looks upon black men as "Negro" in order to brutalize them, Faulkner sometimes looks upon them as "Negro" in order to release his sympathy. Joe Christmas and Charles Bon are sharply individualized figures, but there also hangs over them a racial aura, a halo of cursed blackness. In an early story, "Dry September," this tendency toward the abstraction of character is still clearer; like a paradigm of all lynching stories, it is populated not with men but with Murderer and Victim.

Nor is it accidental that those Negroes whom Faulkner most readily imagines in the posture of the victim should be mulattoes. Trapped between the demarcated races, the mulatto is an unavoidable candidate for the role of victim. Velery Bon in *Absalom, Absalom!* is a man adrift. The Negroes "thought he was a white man and believed it only the more strongly when he denied it," while the whites, "when he said he was a negro, believed that he lied in order to save his skin." Joe Christmas is cursed by "that stain on his white blood or his black blood, whichever you will." Whether he actually has Negro blood is never clear, and this uncertainty points a finger of irony at the whole racial scheme.

Such symbolic uses of the mulatto do not exhaust the reasons for his prominence in Faulkner's novels. Mulattoes are living agents of the "threat" of miscegenation, a "threat" which seems most to disturb Faulkner whenever he is most sympathetic to the Negro. All rationalizations for prejudice having crumbled, there remains only an inherited fear of blood-mixture. The more Faulkner abandons the "ideas" of the folk mind in relation to Negroes, the more does he find himself struggling with the deeper phobias of the folk mind. In two of the novels where miscegenation is a major theme, *Light in August* and *Absalom, Absalom!*, it arouses a painfully twisted response. Miscegenation releases the fears of the white unconscious but also suggests, as Faulkner will hint in a later book, an ultimate solution to the racial problem. Even as it excites a last defense for the dogma of superiority, the thought of miscegenation opens a vision of a distant time when distinctions of blood and barriers of caste will be removed. In *Absalom, Absalom!* there is a whole range of responses to miscegenation, from the strongly-articulated sympathy for its victims to the conventional prophecy that it will lead to a corruption of the races; and it is quite impossible to say with any assurance where Faulkner's final sympathy, or the final stress of the novel itself, lies. Because of this ambivalent response, the mulatto occasions some of

Faulkner's most intense, involuted and hysterical writing. As a victim the mulatto must be shown in all his suffering, and as a reminder of the ancestral phobia, must be made once or twice to suffer extravagantly. But since Faulkner is trying to free himself from both phobia and the injustice it sustains, the mulatto also excites in him his greatest pity, a pity so extreme as often to break past the limits of speech. On the mulatto's frail being descends the whole crushing weight of Faulkner's world.

With the appearance of Lucas Beauchamp, most of Faulkner's previous attitudes toward the Negro are transcended. Lucas is neither at home in the South, like Dilsey, nor homeless, like Joe Christmas; he exists in himself. He is well enough aware of white society and he knows exactly what it is; in "The Fire and the Hearth" he does not hesitate to express his bitterness. But as he strides into sight in *Intruder in the Dust*, powerful and complete, he is entirely on his own: he has put society behind him. Too proud to acquiesce in submission, too self-contained to be either outcast or rebel, Lucas has transformed the stigma of alienation into a mark of dignity and assurance. He is truly a character who has "made" himself, who has worked through to his own kind of authenticity. The gain is high, so too the price; for Lucas is friendless, and his grandeur is a crotchety grandeur. Apparently meant by Faulkner as a tribute to the strength and endurance of the Negroes, Lucas is something better still: a member of an oppressed group who appears not as a catalogue of disabilities or even virtues, but as a human being in his own right. He is not a form of behavior but a person, not "Negro" but a Negro.

Occasionally Faulkner lets him slip into the stubborn old nigger who grumbles and bumbles his way to domination over the delightfully helpless whites. This may be justifiable, for, to an extent difficult to specify, the "stubborn old nigger" is Lucas' social mask—and

Faulkner realizes now that in white society Negroes must often use a social mask. Because he is so aware that they can seldom risk spontaneity in the company of whites, Faulkner, like the boy Chick Mallison, circles about Lucas with humor and a shy respect, never daring to come too close lest the old Negro growl at him. He feels about Lucas somewhat as Chick and Stevens do, sharing the boy's irritated awe and the man's uneasy admiration. Toward no other character in any of his books does Faulkner show quite the same uncomfortable deference; of none other can it be said that Faulkner looks up to him with so boyish and pleading an air, as if he wishes to gain from the old man a measure of forgiveness or acceptance, perhaps finally even love.

By indirection, Lucas challenges a good many of the notions Faulkner has previously expressed about the Negroes. In the final scene of *Intruder in the Dust* Lucas shows himself unyielding and unforgiving; he insists upon taking the white man's gesture of equality as if it came from condescension—and who will dare bluntly to contradict him? In an earlier scene Lucas stares up at Stevens from his jail cell, refusing to speak to him openly because he senses that the white lawyer believes him guilty. Completely dramatized and without any intruding comment, this scene suggests the insight that even the best whites are full of ambiguous feelings toward the Negroes and hence not quite to be trusted by them.

This insight acknowledged, one is tempted to speculate about certain of Faulkner's attitudes toward the Negroes. Throughout his work there is an admiring emphasis on their patience and "endurance." Negroes are "better than we" because "they will endure." In the Appendix to *The Sound and the Fury* Faulkner honors Dilsey and her kin with a bare sentence, "They endured." Such sentiments, fondly quoted by traditionalist critics, have their obvious bearing when advanced as statements about the past; but if, as Faulkner intimates, they are also meant as prescription and prediction, they invite a measure of doubt.

How Negroes "really" feel about Southern, or American, society is terribly hard for any white man to say. Serious whites, as they learn more about the hidden, the true life of Negroes, grow hesitant to generalize: they discover how little they know. Yet one may wonder whether Negroes are quite as ready to "endure" as Faulkner suggests—a question that has a decided relevance to his work, since a fixed idea about Negro "endurance" can limit his capacity to see Negro life freshly.

Faulkner wishes to dramatize his admiration for their ability to survive injustice, and he is right to do so. Nor is his respect for the power and virtues of passivity confined to his treatment of Negro figures; it comes through with great assurance in his portraits of Lena Grove and Ike McCaslin; and indeed, it forms one of his deepest personal feelings toward human existence. But it may still be suggested that Faulkner, like any other man of his color, has less "right" to admire the posture of passivity in the Negroes than he does in the whites. And we must also suppose that those human beings, like the Negroes, who have long been subjected to humiliation will probably resent it, no matter how much they may be required to veil their more intimate responses. Is this not exactly what Faulkner begins so brilliantly to show in his treatment of Lucas Beauchamp, a man whose irascible desire for justice—he demands nothing else from white society—is quite distant from the style of "endurance"? May it not be that the patient willingness to "endure," far from being a root attitude among Negroes, is another of the masks they assume in order to find their way through a hostile world? Again I add that this is not merely a question concerning the social order of the South: it arises repeatedly and with growing urgency in some of Faulkner's later novels.

Though he has given us a wider range and taken a

deeper sounding of Negro character than most other American writers, Faulkner has not presented in his novels an articulate Negro who speaks for his people. No one has the right to demand that he do so, but it is a legitimate problem in literary criticism to ask why he has not. That such a Negro may not be within Faulkner's range of personal experience is unimportant, unless one accepts the naïve assumption that fictional characters must always be drawn from a writer's immediate knowledge. Faulkner's honesty, his continuous moral growth, but above all, the inner logic of his own work—all these would seem to require that he confront the kind of Negro who is in serious rebellion, open or hidden, against the structure of the South.

To present such a character, Faulkner would have to take the risk of examining Negro consciousness from within, rather than as it is seen or surmised by white characters. It may be said that precisely Faulkner's awareness of the distance between the races and of the ultimate inaccessibility of the Negroes makes him hesitate to use a Negro as his center of consciousness. Such scruples deserve to be honored, yet the fact is that great writers, including Faulkner himself, are always coming up with characters "they do not know"—surely this must be part of what is meant when we say they are using their imagination. To portray Negro consciousness from the inside would be a hazard for Faulkner, as it must be for any white novelist, but the possibility, perhaps the need, for such an attempt arises from his own achievement. And he has never been a writer to avoid risks.

All such speculations apart, Faulkner's later books testify to the almost obsessive role the Negro continues to play in his imaginative life. *Requiem for a Nun* casts a Negro prostitute and dope addict, Nancy, as scourge and saviour of white society. Nancy's murder of a white child is traced back to the earlier guilt of the child's parents; and even as she prepares to die in her repentance and piety, she becomes a nemesis calling them back to their moral obligations. In assigning this role to Nancy, Faulkner is perhaps placing too heavy a weight of responsibility on the Negroes, and in a way opposite to the harangues of *Intruder in the Dust* he may even be doing them a certain injustice. For it is a little unreasonable—though surely also desperate—to burden the Negroes with the salvation of the whites. Whatever the whites will be able to manage in this latter department, they will have to do for themselves.

One suspects that the difficulties behind the creation of Nancy reflect a charge of emotion, a surging mixture of guilt and impatience, which Faulkner cannot objectify in conduct or character and which, therefore, forces him toward a kind of Dostoevskian apocalypse. Because of this ideological weight, Nancy figures in the novel more as an abstract intention than as a blooded human being. Lacking the rich particularity of a Lucas Beauchamp, she is "Negro" rather than a Negro, and "Negro" put to very special and unclarified uses. Still, the novel shows that Faulkner continues to brood over the Negroes, passionately and erratically; and as long as these questions remained alive for him, there was reason to hope they would take on fresh embodiment in future novels.

The shift of response toward the Negro forms a moral history, a record of growth from early work to last. But it would be a grave distortion to suppose that this history is entirely reckoned once attitudes and underlying themes have been traced—these are only the raw materials from which literature is made or, perhaps more accurately, the abstractions critics like to draw from or impose upon literature. Despite the ideological passages in *Intruder in the Dust*, Faulkner is not, and should not be considered, a systematic thinker; he has no strictly formulated views on the "Negro question," and as a novelist he is under no obligation to have them.

In the more than two decades of his literary career he has taken a painful journey of self-education, beginning with an almost uncritical acceptance of the more benevolent Southern notions and ending with a brooding sympathy and humane respect for the Negroes. His recent books indicate that no other social problem troubles him so greatly, and that his mind is constantly driven to confront it. What counts in his work is not the occasional splinter of program that can be scratched out of it—whoever wants a precise platform or a coherent sociology for the Negroes had better look elsewhere. Faulkner's triumph is of another kind, the novelist's triumph: a body of dramatic actions, a group of realized characters. No other American novelist has watched the Negroes so carefully and patiently; none other has listened with such fidelity to the nuances of their speech and recorded them with such skill; none other has exposed his imagination so freely, to discover, at whatever pain or discomfort, their meaning for American life.

In the end, Faulkner's great homage to the Negroes is that one need only hear and see. There is the sermon ("I got de ricklickshun en de blood of de Lamb!") delivered by the visiting St. Louis preacher in the Negro church at the close of *The Sound and the Fury*, as magnificent in its way as the sermons of Father Mapple in *Moby Dick*, Dinah Morris in *Adam Bede* and the Jesuit father in *Portrait of the Artist as a Young Man*. Since the St. Louis preacher speaks at length, listen instead to the shorter movement of Negro dialogue, the ripples of accent and meaning, at the beginning of *The Sound and the Fury*:

"Is you all seen anything of a quarter down here."
Luster said.

"What quarter."

"The one I had here this morning." Luster said. "I lost it somewhere. It fell through this here hole in my pocket. If I dont find it, I cant go to the show tonight."

"Where'd you get a quarter, boy. Find it in white folks' pocket while they aint looking."

"Got it at the getting place." Luster said. "Plenty more where that one comes from. Only I got to find that one. Is you all found it yet."

"I aint studying no quarter. I got my own business to tend to."

"Come on here." Luster said. "Help me look for it."

"He wouldn't know a quarter if he was to see it, would he."

"He can help look just the same." Luster said. "You all going to the show tonight."

"Dont talk to me about no show. Time I get done over this here tub I be too tired to lift my hand to do nothing."

"I bet you be there." Luster said. "I bet you was there last night. I bet you all be right there when that tent open."

"Be enough niggers there without me. Was last night."

"Niggers money good as white folks, I reckon."

"White folks give niggers money because know first white man comes along with a band going to get it all back, so nigger can go to work for some more."

Or listen to Jason Compson as he reports an exchange with a Negro:

And then a Yankee will talk your head off about niggers getting ahead. Get them ahead, what I say. Get them so far ahead you cant find one south of Louisville with a blood hound. Because when I told him about how they'd pick up Saturday night, and carry off at least a thousand dollars out of the country, he says,

"I don't begrudge um. I kin sho afford my two bits."

"Two bits hell," I says. "That dont begin it. How about the dime or fifteen cents you'll spend for a damn two cent box of candy or something. How about the time you're wasting right now, listening to that band."

"Dat's de troof," he says. "Well, ef I lives twell night hit's gwine to be two bits mo dey takin out of town, dat's sho."

"Then you're a fool," I says.

"Well," he says, "I dont spute dat neither. Ef dat uz a crime, all chain-gangs wouldn't be black."

And finally to the cadences of the passage in "Red Leaves" where an escaped Negro slave is captured by his Indian masters, a passage which forms an elegy for all human effort, all defeat:

Two Indians entered the swamp, their movements noisy. Before they reached the Negro they stopped, because he began to sing. They could see him, naked and mud-caked, sitting on a log, singing. They squatted silently a short distance away, until he finished. He was chanting something in his own language, his face lifted to the rising sun. His voice was clear, full, with a quality wild and sad. "Let him have time," the Indians said, squatting, patient, waiting. He ceased and they approached. He looked back and up at them through the cracked mud mask. His eyes were bloodshot, his lips cracked upon his square short teeth. The mask of mud appeared to be loose on his face, as if he might have lost flesh since he put it there: he held his left arm close to his breast. From the elbow down it was caked and shapeless with black mud. They could smell him, a rank smell. He watched them quietly until one touched him on the arm. "Come," the Indian said. "You ran well. Do not be ashamed."

VI

The Moral Vision

In the beginning was the wilderness. "Almost pathless," the earth was marked only "by the tracks of unalien shapes—bear and deer and panthers and bison and wolves and alligators and the myriad smaller beasts. And unalien men to name them too." America was a paradise: the last paradise.

A firm presence in most of Faulkner's work, the natural scene serves as more than literary ornament or sensuous refreshment. Occasionally, and then not too happily, the plenitude of nature stirs Faulkner to philosophic reverie in the manner of Thomas Hardy; equally infrequent is that delight in well-cultivated farm land, a delight in orderliness and harmony, which fills the novels of George Eliot. For Faulkner there is a radical disjunction between social man and the natural world, and in most instances the two can be yoked together only by an act of force. The wilderness is primal, source and scene of mobility, freedom, innocence; society, soon after it appears, begins to hollow out these values. And not one or the other form of society but the very idea of society is regarded with skepticism.

This myth is lent imaginative credence by the hold

of the frontier on our national life. A myth of space, it recalls a time when men could measure their independence by their distance from each other, when "personal liberty and freedom were almost physical conditions like fire and flood." In magnified volume but steady pitch, it records the secret voice of a society regretting its own existence.

Inescapably, the settling of the wilderness was a violation. For a short time afterward it was still possible to establish a precarious balance between the natural and the social—a balance which might have preserved a vestige of paradise. In those pioneer days, the first Yoknapatawpha settlement was "a meager huddle of crude cabins set without order and every one a little awry to every other and all dwarfed to doll-houses by the vast loom of the woods which enclosed them. . . ." You could shoot "a bear or deer or wild turkey simply by standing for a while in your kitchen door." [8]

The pioneer equilibrium could not survive for long. Several of Faulkner's loveliest stories, remarkable for their stylistic poise and elevation, anticipate the death of the wilderness—notably "Red Leaves," in which a change of society is reflected in the absurdity of an Indian tribe being burdened with unwanted Negro slaves. The earth is no longer held in that communal anonymity to which Faulkner looks back; and Isaac McCaslin, examining the waste of the homeland, says of the American white man: "The woods and the fields he ravages and the game he devastates will be the consequence and the signature of his crime and guilt, and his punishment."

The forest line recedes. In "The Bear," set in the late nineteenth century, there is still a frequent return to the wilderness, and within its narrowed precincts something of the original freedom can still be enjoyed. But by "Delta Autumn," a story of the present day, one

[8] This quotation, as the others preceding it in this section, comes from *Requiem for a Nun*.

must drive for hours to reach the woods, "the territory in which game still existed drawing yearly inward. . . ." As an integral part of American experience, the wilderness is gone—and with it the possibility for an independent and self-sustained life.

Tamed and plotted as it now is, the natural world remains with man, and in moments of stress exerts a primordial force. But in daily life the grandeur of natural things is lost—they are put aside in preserves to be visited; and the men of Yoknapatawpha can claim little of the power that comes from a close instinctual tie to the wilderness. The farmers of *The Hamlet* do retain some of this feeling for natural life, as in this dialogue on birds and trees:

. . . . . A bird, a shadow, fleet and dark and swift, curved across the moonlight, upward into the pear tree, and began to sing; a mockingbird.

"First one I've noticed this year," Freeman said.

"You can hear them along Whiteleaf every night," the first man said. "I heard one in February. In that snow. Singing in a gum."

"Gum is the first tree to put out," the third said. "That was why. It made it feel like singing, fixing to put out that way. That was why it taken a gum."

"Gum first to put out?" Quick said. "What about willow?"

"Willow aint a tree," Freeman said. "It's a weed."

Respectful familiarity, humorous fondness, neat observation—all these characterize the relation of the farmers to nature; but while the natural world may yield them food and shelter and mild fugitive pleasures, it can seldom be a metaphor, as once it was, for life itself. A fine anthology of nature passages could be gathered from Faulkner's books, but it would fail to make clear what can be seen only through a reading in context: that above and beyond the satisfactions nature provides the senses—satisfactions entirely real and desirable—it is important to Faulkner as recalling the era of pastoral manners and the dream of pioneer life. This dream society violates, and one important agent of violation is woman.

Now it cannot be charged against Faulkner, as John Jay Chapman did against Emerson, that a visitor from Mars would never learn from him what even the Italian opera makes clear: that there are two sexes in the world. Faulkner is all too willing to proclaim the subtle and insidious powers of women, to evoke a sense of their dizzying attractions, even to speculate, in the style of legend, on female malevolence as one of the root terrors of existence. At least as serious as Chapman's complaint against Emerson is the fact that seldom in Faulkner's work do we find a mature recognition of the possibilities in the relations between men and women —possibilities, I might specify, of fulfilled love and tragic complication. And a writer unable to summon the first of these is likely to have troubles in reaching the second.

Such splendid old ladies as Miss Rosa Millard, Aunt Jenny Du Pre and Dilsey, all conspicuously beyond the age of sexual distraction, gain Faulkner's admiration. They neither threaten nor attract; they give household orders and provide intuitive wisdom; they are beyond the magical powers of sexuality. But there is hardly a young woman in Faulkner's novels—one notable exception is Linda Snopes in *The Mansion*—who does not provoke quantities of bitterness and bile; and so persistent is this distaste for the doings of "woman-flesh" that it cannot be dismissed as a vagary of either Faulkner or the characters who convey it.

Few writers have trained such ferocity on the young American bitch: Cecily the "papier-mache Virgin" of *Soldiers' Pay*, Patricia the "sexless yet somehow troubling" flapper of *Mosquitoes*, and that abomination of castrating femaleness, Temple Drake. With her "cool, predatory and discreet" eyes, Temple anticipates the kind of modern woman about whom it is hard to say which is more alarming: her coldness or her availability. At the moment she flourishes in Manhattan, but any American town with a claim to sophistication can provide examples: smoother, more "cultured" and self-contained than the Temple Drake of *Sanctuary*.[9] To have noticed and rendered her with such deadly accuracy, is surely one of Faulkner's triumphs; yet she rouses currents of disturbance that cannot be understood or justified strictly in terms of the novel itself. Again and again, the thought—or sight—of her drives Faulkner to a pitch of hysteria and nausea, as if in her compulsive negation of the feminine she were also its evil apotheosis.

A similar ferocity is directed against Belle Mitchell of *Sanctuary*, the kind of woman who consciously uses her body to certify her domination over men. The same ferocity is directed against that gorgeous lump of fertility called Eula Varner in *The Hamlet*, and against those young women, like Charlotte Rittenmeyer in *The Wild Palms* and Laverne Schumann in *Pylon*, who sin not through personal malice but through the impersonal mechanics of their sex. Even Lena Grove, for all her appearance of submissiveness, digs iron claws into her man with a serene possessiveness of instinct; the affection she draws from Faulkner depends on a humorous belief that it is pointless to resist her.

Nor does Faulkner hesitate to state these feelings explicitly. In *Absalom, Absalom!* Charles Bon learns "you cant beat women anyhow and that if you are wise or dislike trouble and uproar you dont even try to"—a lesson Faulkner never tires of repeating, though always with the certainty that men, being victims of

---

[9] Faulkner realized as much when he tried to create an older version of Temple Drake in *Requiem for a Nun*.

themselves, must prove incapable of learning it. Quentin Compson goes further than Bon; "women," he says "are like that . . . they have an affinity for evil." The Reverend Hightower, urging Byron Bunch not to marry Lena Grove, remarks, "No woman who has a child is ever betrayed; the husband of a mother, whether he be the father or not, is already a cuckold. . . . There have been good women who were martyrs to brutes. . . . But what woman, good or bad, has ever suffered from any brute as men have suffered from good women?" And in the story "Was" these notions are given a droll color when a hardened bachelor who has accidentally wandered into an old maid's bedroom is told he will now have to marry her: "You come into bear-country of your own free will and accord. All right; you were a grown man and you knew it was bear-country and you knew the way back out like you knew the way in and you had your chance to take it. But no. You had to crawl into the den and lay down by the bear. And whether you did or didn't know the bear was in it dont make any difference."

Exceptions to this treatment of the sexes can be found: Houston and his young wife in *The Hamlet*, like the unfortunate poor white Goodwins in *Sanctuary*, do love each other with a measure of happiness and meaning. Between Gavin Stevens and Linda Snopes in *The Mansion* there is a troubled incoherent love which at least escapes Faulkner's usual formulas. So slight a weight, however, do these exceptions carry in Faulkner's world, that they cannot set up a counterpoise to the dominant attitudes felt and expressed toward women. This inclination toward misogyny need not always be taken too literally or solemnly; the passage from "Was" reflects the wry folk view that if people live long enough they are likely to stumble into some traps, usually those they have spent their lives avoiding. Much of Faulkner's talk about women suggests the timbre of folk humor, the sort of playful and deliberately inflated grumbling that might once have been heard on a Saturday afternoon in country stores. But so persistent a devotion to popular attitudes, in both their humorous surface and earnest core, must be related to some governing personal bias, some obscure uneasiness before these victims of "periodic filth."

Faulkner's inability to achieve moral depth in his portraiture of young women clearly indicates a major failing as a novelist. It is an instance where his reliance on the folk imagination, fruitful though it usually is, plays him false. But even as it leads to a tedious sameness and predictability of characterization, the distrust of women serves a symbolic function in the unfolding of his work. Women are the this-worldly sex, the child-bearers who chain men to possessions and embody the indestructible urge to racial survival. As the personification of the reality principle, they contrive to perpetuate the species no matter what dreams or destruction men indulge in. Faulkner's men, like Melville's, are happiest when they "get away," escaping to the woods for a few weeks of female-less companionship. His women are happiest—or, since Faulkner might say that to them happiness does not matter, they are most content—when men are subdued to their social tasks.

Nature and society, freedom and women, form the opening terms of Faulkner's moral dialectic. It is this inescapable clash between polar elements of human experience that releases much of the Faulkner drama and the violence accompanying the drama. Far from relishing violence for its own sake, Faulkner is a fastidious romantic who shrinks from all that is malformed and vicious; the horror into which his books erupt is a sign of over-reaction, of nerves torn loose. As it flames into violence, this conflict between the dream evoked by nature and the reality personified by society gives rise to Faulkner's moral position, his distinctive way of looking upon life.

When he steps forth to "talk philosophy," often in

disrespect to the rhythm of his novels, Faulkner is somewhat less than impressive. In explicit statement he
shows an alarming fondness for platitude, a fondness
that lures him to portentous capitalizations; and it does
him little good, either as novelist or moralist. Still, in
creating his fictions he enjoys the advantage of being
able to work on the one assumption that frees morality
from the barrenness of abstract moralizing—the assumption that moral judgments, to be valuable, must
be specific, delimited, concrete. Faulkner's insights into
human conduct finally evade the grasp of formula; they
inhere in, are the very stuff of, his dramatic actions; and
as a rule, he does not successfully abstract them into
statement. My point, I had better add, is not the familiar objection to an author's "intrusion" with reflective
or speculative passages. I am remarking only on the
local quality and structural relevance of such passages.

The Faulkner who likes to ruminate on the Significance of Life is present in the early poems, a little too
quick and easy at striking the pose of the world-weary,
life-sated skeptic: "He now with Solomon all things
knows; / That lastly, breath is to a man / But to want
and fret a span." Human life, he announces in *Mosquitoes*, springs from "the old miasmic womb of a
nothingness latent and dreadful." Man, declares the
elder Compson in *The Sound and the Fury*, is "conceived by accident and his every breath is a fresh cast
with dice already loaded. . . ." And in *Light in August* Faulkner observes, without visible embarrassment,
that "the faces of old men are lined by that sheer accumulation of frustration and doubt which is so often
the other side of the picture of hale and respected full
years."

Reflections of this kind occur in many of Faulkner's
books; the cruel "Player" or heartless "Cosmic Joker"
in command of the universe is indicted for his uncon-
cern with human hopes and needs. The language of
such passages, often elaborate and tortured, seems in-

congruous beside the flat and pedestrian thought; indeed, the very straining of the language betrays the inadequacies of the thought. One looks for, but seldom finds, some tinge of irony or saving humor, some anxiety that the philosophic kite may be perilously high.

This side of Faulkner, fortunately a minor side in all but his more recent novels, suggests an odd blend of native and literary influences. One is struck by the image of a provincial intellectual dipping into the treasures of folk wisdom and salvaging bits of cracker-barrel pessimism—for a sensitive mind exposed to the drone of American optimism may find something bracing in a defiant assertion of its opposite. In some of these passages there is also a distressing "literary" quality, acquired through hard, misdirected reading. The ghosts of Swinburne, Omar Khayyam and Housman wander about the premises, mooning in soft alliteration; the lesser Conrad is also in sight, meditating the vicissitudes of fate as he strains adjective after adjective. Faulkner's facile version of stoicism ("we must just stay awake and see evil done for a little while its not always," says the elder Compson) is peculiarly a mark of late romanticism; and late romanticism is a temptation Southern writers cannot always forgo. Too complacent in their weariness, Faulkner's stoical pronouncements often seem unearned, statements drawn from other books and voices rather than authentic to his own.

This Faulkner—the self-conscious philosopher who will some day have to answer for the creation of Gavin Stevens—is much occupied with the notion of honor. Frequently invoked in his books, particularly the early ones, it is a notion that proves strangely elusive, and in its elusiveness, increasingly cut off from moral issues.[1]

---

[1] Perhaps those of us raised in a culture where the concept of honor is no longer central—which is to say, any urban or industrial culture—are disqualified from appreciating its full import. If so, that would suggest how precarious the concept has become for modern man; indeed, my speaking of it as a "concept" reveals pre-

It allows some of Faulkner's characters a gamut of theatrical display, as also, at times, a release of more substantial values, such as their readiness to stake everything on a personal act defined not so much through its intrinsic meaning as through the fullness of passion that is brought to it. But the concept of honor remains hard to define, just as the code of honor proves hard to embody and justify in experience.

In *The Unvanquished*, which records the decay of the Southern code of honor, it is invoked for "the deed done not for the end but for the sake of doing"—and insofar as this refers to the "Southern cause," it may indicate uncertainty or guilt about the rightness of that cause. In the Appendix to *The Sound and the Fury* there is a passage which seems both a defiant assertion of the code of honor and a backhanded recognition that, for a mature mind, it must come to be inadequate as a principle of conduct. General Andrew Jackson, writes Faulkner, "set the well-being of the nation above the White House and the health of his new political party above either and above them all set not his wife's honor but the principle that it must be defended whether it was or not because defended it was whether or not." To find such declarations a little strained is not to disparage the principle of honor, but to suggest that when removed from a context of tested moral judgment it must sooner or later turn stiff and, thereby, impoverish human conduct. Honor remains a value to which Faulkner is ready to grant admiration, and never more so than when it seems quixotic or absurd; but there is also a growing recognition in his work that ultimately it is somewhat hollow—more show than substance—and unable to satisfy a mature moral sensibility.

As Faulkner's work develops there is a gradual shift in

cisely that. Yet there is also, I think, much to be said for the modern belief that other, "inner" values are both more estimable and serious than that of honor.

emphasis from honor to integrity, a shift found not so much in explicit statement as in the deeper bias of his work. It is through this process of imaginative growth, far more than through his philosophical pretensions, that the genuine moralist in Faulkner emerges. Optimism, pessimism, stoicism, honor—such fixed and familiar categories give way to a sympathetic concern for the fate of the individual person as he struggles within the world and within himself, seeking, if never quite managing, to validate himself as a human being. Honor points to what one is in the world, integrity to what one is in oneself. Honor involves a public relation to others, a standard of pride and dignity, a level of status and reputation; integrity an ease of being and security of conscience. Honor requires an act of the will, integrity is a condition that cannot be summoned. Honor depends upon an assertion of one's worth, integrity upon a readiness to face the full burden of one's existence. Many of the whites in Faulkner's novels are eager to preserve their honor; the more impressive among the Negroes, though not they alone, exemplify the life of integrity.

Some attempts have been made—with small success, I think—to read Faulkner as a Christian traditionalist. His distinctive moral position has a number of sources, and among these one of the more important is surely an imperiled version of Christianity. The South in which Faulkner grew up was perhaps more concerned with Christian belief than most other areas of American life, but the quality of that concern was hardly such as to win the impassioned adherence of a sensitive young writer. Faulkner encountered Christianity more closely than most other American novelists of his generation, but encountered it mainly in a state of decay. For him, as for so many other modern writers, the idea of Christianity can survive only when wrenched from its institutional and perhaps historical context: that is, it survives as an extreme possibility or vision of personal saintliness.

Like the Southern past, Christianity is felt mainly and most poignantly through its absence. Easter week forms a backdrop for the Compson tragedy; the crucifixion, for the murder of Joe Christmas. Christianity appears as an occasional standard of judgment, a force to resist, a memory that troubles, a principle of contrast; but not as a secure inheritance. Faulkner struggles to define his moral outlook against the backdrop of a dissolution of traditional beliefs, and what matters in his work is not so much the backdrop, which is familiar, as the struggle, which is unique. For only a prolonged examination of modern reality could lead him from the debris of religious and regional feeling to the active morality of his best novels.

His work, to be sure, is full of symbols, references, echoes drawn from Christian drama, theology and tradition. The recurrent figures of simple purity—Dilsey, Byron Bunch, Isaac McCaslin—may be seen as embodiments of primitive Christian virtues, and Faulkner's commitment to these virtues as rooted in a sympathy for the uncontaminated Christianity which has flourished mostly among rural Negroes in the South. At the other extreme there are figures and emblems of crucifixion which show how deeply the story of Jesus and the doctrines of Protestantism have left their marks upon his imagination. But if we are serious about this matter and not merely indulging in a game of symbol-netting, then we must conclude that neither Faulkner's admiration for the primitive virtues nor the hold of the crucifixion upon his imagination is sufficient to warrant calling him a Christian traditionalist. Only a certain relation between the two would enable us to do that, for either of them alone, or even both together, can characterize non-believers. In moral outlook and technique Faulkner is a writer capable of moving between the far extremes of simplicity and sophistication, but he does this as a modern man caught up in the problematic nature of modern life: its restlessness, insecurity, and uncertainty.

Part of Faulkner's skill as a novelist is that, in the main, such moral affirmations as he does offer are imbedded in his materials and cannot finally be separated from them: dramatic gestures, not theoretic statements, characters seen in motion, not comment released in stasis. Accessible to people of every social grade, if only they reach and suffer, integrity is placed in a wide variety of situations—though Faulkner inclines to extreme situations from a wish to submit all that is "indomitable" and "intractable" in human character to the most urgent pressures. Dramatically, this test occurs in the clash of antithetical forces of freedom and necessity in the Yoknapatawpha world. Cursed by the tragic need to compromise their freedom, men can still redeem themselves through a gesture which, if it does not mitigate their defeat, can declare their humanity in defeat.

Sometimes the curse is named or pointed to. For Quentin Compson, who tells his sister "there's a curse on us its not our fault," it is the agonizing weight of family relations, as felt in the contradiction between proclaimed ethic and daily defeat; it is the destroying friction of body against body, soul against soul. For Joe Christmas and Joanna Burden the curse is nothing less than the entanglement and pain and cruelty that comes —must come—when two human beings draw close: the entanglement that leads Hightower to reflect, "Too much happens. That's it. Man performs, engenders, so much more than he can or should have to bear. That's how he finds that he can bear anything." For Isaac McCaslin the curse is the whole fabric of the society in which he lives, the inheritance of "a ravaged patrimony, the dark and ravaged fatherland still prone and panting from its etherless operation." For the reporter in *Pylon* it is a metaphysical conviction that nothing suffocates hope more than the necessary passage of ordinary events, the certainty that you "walk the earth with your arm crooked over your head to dodge until you finally get the old blackjack at last and can lay back down again." For Harry Wilbourne and the river convict of *The Wild Palms* it is the passion for movement which each knows will not suffice but must be continued. And sometimes the curse is named in humor, it is that final touch of excess which breaks suffering into fragments of self-ridicule, as when Jason Compson, his money stolen, his search for the thieves disappointed, his body bruised, finds that "I had my hand right on a bunch of poison oak. . . . So I didn't even bother to move it." Or excess of feeling can spill over into silence, as when Ratliff becomes so furious with the Snopeses that he talks "himself wordless, mute into baffled and aghast outrage."

Always larger and more compelling than anything that can be said about it, the curse is the inescapable mold of life for Faulkner's characters: Joe Christmas struggling against both his whiteness and his blackness; the Reverend Hightower unable to mediate between dream and reality; Bayard Sartoris wondering what purpose can sustain breath; Harry Wilbourne infatuated with his own weakness; Thomas Sutpen compelled to die in a squalor of exploitation; Quentin Compson driven to suicide by the pain of consciousness; even Mink Snopes waiting his lifetime to kill the cousin he knows he must kill. Whatever is burden in life—be it the consequence of society or character, exploitation or sin, injustice or evil—constitutes the curse. Faulkner's key word is "outrage," a word he places with great strategic force throughout his books and which for him signifies an essence of the human response. The curse, in short, is a great part of what we mean by the human condition.

Du Homme, the old Indian chief had been called in

the story, "The Old People." And then they shortened his name to Doom.

There remains available to each man the gesture, striking or subdued, by which he declares himself. Lucas Beauchamp demands his receipt from the white lawyer, refusing to compromise his need for justice. Harry Wilbourne, choosing to spend his life in jail, declares that *"between grief and nothing I will take grief."* Cash Bundren, making a coffin for his mother, bevels it as neatly as he can, for the perfection of the work is a mode of filial love. When Lena Grove, big in belly, walks through the Mississippi farm land, her very posture speaks of her sureness of self. Paying an installment on the boots he has wanted, Jiggs insists they be taken out of the store window—to examine them?—"No, I just want to see them come out of that window." Aunt Mollie Beauchamp, after her grandson has been executed in Chicago for murder, *"wanted him home, but she wanted him to come home right. She wanted that casket and those flowers and the hearse. . . ."* The unnamed little girl who follows Quentin Compson will not put down her bread so that she may eat her ice cream in comfort, and for no reason—it is simply her way of eating ice cream. Riding his mule up a hill, Byron Bunch suddenly bursts into speech, justifying his gesture: "I can bear a hill, a man can. It seems like a man can just about bear anything. He can even bear what he never done. He can even bear the thinking how some things is just more than he can bear."

And the two extremes: Joe Christmas, out of the swamps and ready for death, politely inquires, what day is it—and in the knowledge that it is Tuesday, a wholly ordinary Tuesday, he has at least one tie with the human; Popeye, least concerned of all Faulkner's characters to retain a tie with the human, whispers to the sheriff a moment before his execution, "Pssst! . . . . Fix my hair, Jack!"

This, in response to the curse, is the Faulkner gesture. It can be a gesture of rebellion or submission; it can signify adherence to ritual or the need to accept defeat in total loneliness; it can be an arbitrary sign of self-hood or a final assertion of indifference. But always it is the mark of distinct being, the way a man establishes and defines himself. An affirmation of human capacity or a paltry insistence on human limitation, the gesture marks each man in his singularity.

The opposition of curse and gesture forms the dramatic and moral pattern of Faulkner's work, and within that opposition he declares the items of his moral bias: his respect before suffering, his contempt for deceit, his belief in the rightness of self-trust, his enlarging compassion for the defeated. At its greatest, the gesture shows that for Faulkner heroism signifies exposure, the taking and enduring and resisting of everything which comes between birth and death. At its smallest, the gesture is an assurance given by each man to himself, that in some ultimate and indestructible way he too is a sentient human creature, capable of pain and, therefore, perhaps of joy. For Faulkner's characters the gesture becomes the outer shape of their integrity; it is their way of trying to accept the full weight of experience, so that at the end nothing will have been left undone or unfelt. Even when inarticulate, they are committed in their own way to the life of consciousness: to knowing and taking whatever comes, to recognizing the simultaneous presence of all one's experience at any moment of one's life. It is a kind of freedom.

(PART 2)

An Achievement
Considered

The world of William Faulkner is so enticing as a locale of the imagination that one is tempted to forget that the individual novels must themselves be the final object of criticism. In the following pages, Faulkner's more important books are considered separately, in their own right. Rather than pretend to a series of "comprehensive" analyses, I have chosen in each section to concentrate on one or two problems central to the novel under consideration. Of such minor works as *Sartoris* and *The Unvanquished* enough has perhaps been said in earlier pages; of books like *Mosquitoes* and *Knight's Gambit* not much needs to be said.

I

The Sound
and the Fury

IT WOULD BE IMPOSSIBLE TO SAY HOW LONG *The Sound and the Fury* had been germinating in Faulkner's mind when he began to write. The writing itself took three years, a long time for a novelist who, from impulse and perhaps on principle, has often composed rapidly. An immense outlay of creative labor, the book is one of those rare efforts in which an artist breaks through to the core of his matter. Faulkner himself recognized as much. Asked by a group of Mississippi students which of his novels he considered best, he replied: "*As I Lay Dying* was easier and more interesting. *The Sound and the Fury* still continues to move me." Faulkner's judgment is correct: these are his best novels, *The Sound and the Fury* is his masterpiece.

It is a difficult masterpiece. The Benjy section, one of the few original efforts at experimental writing ever undertaken in America, places some formidable barriers in the way of an unprepared reader; and those critics who feel, as does Malcolm Cowley, that "we can't be sure . . . the four sections of the novel are presented in the most effective order" raise an important question, one which the later school of Faulkner exegetes too often ignores. Why, indeed, since the problem is of far more than "technical" interest, does Faulkner begin with a narrator who is an idiot?

Since the collapse of the Compson family is to be shown as a completed history, Faulkner can forgo the orderly accumulation of suspense that might be had from a conventional narrative. Beginning near the end of his story, he must employ as his first perceiving mind a Compson who has managed to survive until Easter 1928. Mrs. Compson is too silly and Jason too warped to preserve, let alone present, the family history. Quentin is dead, Caddy gone, and Dilsey must be saved for her role as chorus of lament. Only Benjy remains—and this, far from being accidental, is a symbolic token of the book.

Of all the Compsons, Benjy alone is able to retain the past; he alone has not suffered it in conscious experience. Being an idiot he is exempt from the main course of action and untainted by self-interest. Because he cannot color or shape his memories, his mind serves the novel as an entirely faithful glass. Unable to order events in sequence, he must grope for fragments, stumbling over stray chips from the quarry of the past. All these effects of perspective Faulkner might have gained from a narrator of superior intelligence who would look upon the Compsons from a distance—all but the poignant immediacy that only Benjy can provide. In *Absalom, Absalom!* the Sutpen history ricochets off the consciousness of Quentin Compson; in *The Sound and the Fury* the Compson history is already "in" Benjy's mind. Where Quentin, as introductory or perceiving mind, makes for distance and historical summation, Benjy creates disordered closeness and, perhaps, identification.

But can one identify with an idiot? If Benjy's memories were tightly locked in the shell of his mind, if their quality were determined by his idiocy, it would clearly be impossible. Benjy does not act or talk or reflect; his only function is to lead directly and without comment into the past. He brings no sharply formulated point of view to his memories, in the sense that Quentin and Jason will; his remembering does not organize or condition that which he remembers. To "identify" with Benjy is, therefore, to abandon him as a person and yield oneself to the Compson experience. Yet this abandonment becomes a way of learning to appreciate his role and value. We gain our experience of the Compsons mainly from the materials coursing through his mind, and it is these materials alone that enable us to see that behind his fixed rituals there are genuine meanings, half-forgotten tokens of the past which survive for him as realities of the present. Whenever Benjy has to change the motions of his routine—going around the town square toward the left rather than the right, for example—he is stricken with agony, and he registers it in the only way he can, by bellowing. The pattern of order to which he is so attached may signify nothing in itself, nor need the pain consequent on its disruption signify anything—unless there are those present who understand and can remember what Benjy clings to. Without knowing observers, Benjy is simply the past forsaken. None of the Compsons has remained to care and only Jason so much as remembers; soon it is we, the alien readers, who together with Dilsey must take the burden on ourselves. Only then can we understand Benjy.

Lacking any sense of time, Benjy feels the reality of 1902 or 1912 as closely as that of 1928, the death of grandmother as sharply as Luster's "projecking" with his graveyard. Only through a mind such as his could the past be raised to a plane of equality with the present and the two dissolved in a stream of chaotic impression. Were either Quentin or Jason to open the novel, an apparent order would be imposed on the past, but an order reflecting their private interests. An external observer, used somewhat like Captain Marlow in Conrad's novels, might provide breadth and balance of judgment, but with some loss in immediacy. Such an observer might report the Compson history but could not present it; his very role as commentator would change the shape of the book. But Benjy, precisely because he lacks formed personality and has no need for detachment, can reveal the Compsons in both intimacy and distance, completeness and chaos.

The Benjy section forces the reader to participate in the novel, to become, as it were, a surreptitious narrator; otherwise he cannot read it at all. Given the material of the past, or at least a shrewdly formed simulation of its chaos, he is then required to do the work which in an ordinary novel is done by the writer or narrator. This method exacts from the reader an increment of attention, prodding him to compose in his mind a conventional narrative which accompanies, registers, but finally submits to the narrative of the book. The bewilderment, produced by Benjy's flow of memory, sharpens one's responses, teaches one to look for clues, parallels and anticipations.

Though the last section contains a few incidents not anticipated in the earlier ones, these are merely bitter footnotes to a text of disaster; almost everything else is foreshadowed by Benjy. *The Sound and the Fury* does not launch an action through a smooth passage of time; it reconstructs a history through a suspension—or several suspensions—of time. In the water-splashing incident to which Benjy so persistently returns, the behavior of the Compson children is an innocent anticipation of their destinies; each shows himself as he will later become. The Benjy section thus forms not merely one part or one movement among four, but the hard nucleus of the novel. Later sections will add to the pathos of Quentin's reflections and the treachery of Jason's conduct, but merely as variations or extensions of what has already been present from the beginning.

Of greater specific weight than the others, the Benjy section is ultimately clearer in its perceptions and more delicate in sensibility; from it there begins an emotional decline which graphs the novel's meaning. Benjy is the past recaptured; Quentin, imprisoned in his own consciousness, cannot hold the past with the purity Benjy can; Jason violently breaks from the past; and the concluding section completes the book's movement from a claustrophic private world to a sterile public world, from the subjective heart of Compson life to a cold record of its death. Each of the first two sections is primarily a retrospect, yet both manage to carry the story forward to clarity and resolution. When he wishes to create an atmosphere of closeness and involvement Faulkner depends on stream-of-consciousness; but toward the end, except when describing the Negro revival meeting, he writes in a style of clipped notation, a style —later to be harshened in *Sanctuary*—signifying distance and revulsion. Coming, as it must, at the beginning of the book and shortly before the visible collapse of the Compsons, the Benjy section is a last reminder of what their world once was.

Benjy is a risk. His section could easily become sentimental or incoherent or a pointless flaunting of ingenuity; it is saved from such failings by the fact that he never ceases to be an idiot, never becomes aware of his enormous pathos, never falls into mere shrewdness or saintliness. The material flowing through his mind may form a complex pattern of significance, but he is not the one to know it. He embodies a kind of purity that is very much this side of good and evil, yet he never presumes, for he has not even learned, to judge or reject. A failure in tact would be disastrous here: let Benjy once show himself coyly aware of his role, let him once slip into the oracular mode, and the illusion would be shattered. The slip does not occur; Faulkner is never in greater command of his material than in the Benjy section, nor more devoted to the classical principles of rigor, impersonality, and austerity than in this most experimental of his writings. Admiring it, one remembers Virginia Woolf's remark comparing Jane Austen to the Greek dramatists: "she too . . . chose the dangerous art whereby one slip means death."

That Benjy's flow of memory must be accepted as a convention rather than as "real" makes Faulkner's success all the more remarkable. The reflections of Quentin Compson can be attributed to an actual man, and Jason's too; but not those of Benjy. Little is known of idiots, and the little that is known suggests that their "thoughts" are a good deal more fragmented and incoherent than Benjy's. For all its complexity, the Benjy section is an extreme simplification, probably difficult to justify by any standard of strict verisimilitude. It hardly matters. Faulkner is concerned not with the mental life of an actual idiot, but with rendering a plausible effect: a flow of disturbed memory which, in the absence of contrary knowledge, can be associated with an idiot.

To picture this disturbed flow of memory one must assume that it makes sense, that an order inheres in it or can profitably be drawn from it. The impression Faulkner seeks to establish, at least the first one, is that Benjy's memories are formless; yet only through precise form can this impression take root and thrive in the reader's mind. Satisfying the needs of both character and author, a simulation of disorder comes to convey an order of significance.

Toward this end Faulkner drafts all his ingenuity, and refrains, moreover, from the rhetorical bombardments that mar a number of his other books. Self-effacing and rigidly disciplined, he directs his language to the uses of his subject, and the result is that his writing is more delicate and controlled than anywhere else in his work. He stakes everything on elemental presentation. He avoids complex sentence structures explicitly involving logic, sequence, and qualification. In place of an elaborate syntax, there is a march of short declarative sentences and balanced compounds following the journey of Benjy's senses. Monotony is the obvious risk of this grammatical stripping, but it is escaped in several ways: frequent time shifts in Benjy's memories, a richness of concrete pictorial imagery, and an abundance of sharply inflected voices. The internal regularity of individual sentences is thus played off against the subtle pacing and tonal variety of the sequence as a whole— the sentences invoking Benjy and the sequence that which exists beyond Benjy. Though the rhythm and shape of the sentences vary but little, there is a wide range of speed. Beginning with relatively large units, Benjy's memories break into increasingly small fragments until, at the climax,[1] brief sentences of recalled incident whirl feverishly about one another, mixing events from 1898, 1910, and 1928. And then the agitated spinning of Benjy's mind comes to an abrupt stop, resting in memories of childhood.

No elaborate similes or metaphors, no hyperbole or euphuism; the few symbols are worked with niggardly concentration, and, thereby, with all the greater effectiveness. Pared and precise, eluding abstraction and reverie, the writing absorbs its color from the life it appropriates, the pictures of behavior and accents of speech. It favors concreteness and spareness, particularly nouns naming common objects, and adjectives specifying blunt sensations.

Through such nouns and adjectives Faulkner manages his transitions in time. Places, names, smells, feelings—these are the chance stimuli that switch Benjy from one track of memory to another. As they impress themselves on him, jolting his mind backward or forward in time, they seem mere accidental distractions, and it is important for the credibility of the section that they continue to seem so; but they are also carefully spaced and arranged so as to intensify Faulkner's mean-

1 Pages 87 to 92 in the Modern Library Edition.

ings by effects of association, incongruity and, above all, juxtaposition.

Juxtaposition is here both method and advantage. Through it we gain sudden insights and shocks which, in small symbolic presentiments or recapitulations, crystallize the meanings of the sequence—insights of the kind a man may have when he looks back upon a life's work and knows, indisputably, that it is waste, or shocks of the kind a man may feel when he looks upon his child and considers the blows to which it is certain to be exposed. By making the past seem simultaneous with the present, Faulkner gains remarkable moments of pathos, moments sounding the irrevocable sadness that comes from a recognition of decline and failure. And remarkable, one must add, for the way small incidents and contrasts, little more than the slurred minutiae of life, suggest the largest issues in human conduct.

In a fragment that may roughly date 1902, Mrs. Compson chides Caddy for proposing to take the seven-year-old Benjy into the winter cold without overshoes: "Do you want to make him sick, with the house full of company?" Formal sentiment followed by actual motive, the sentence reveals Mrs. Compson to her marrow. As if aware that she may have betrayed herself, she then takes the idiot boy's face into her hands and calls him "My poor baby." A page beyond, in a scene set eleven years later, the neurasthenic Mrs. Compson is still calling Benjy "the baby." But when this "baby" starts moaning during a trip to the family graveyard, she is helpless and it is Dilsey who knows how to placate him: "Give him a flower to hold."

At the climax of the Benjy section, fragments from 1900 and 1928 alternate. The strands from 1900 show Caddy feeding her little idiot brother with kindness and care, those from 1928 show Caddy's daughter, Quentin, asking at a family meal: *Has he got to keep that dirty old slipper on the table. . . . Why dont you feed him in the kitchen. It's like eating with a pig.*

A few pages earlier there occurs a similar contrast between Caddy and her daughter. In 1909 Caddy and a
boy are making love on a swing in the Compson back-
yard. Discovering them, Benjy "cried and pulled Caddy's dress." Caddy tries to break away from her lover
and when he remarks that Benjy "can't talk," she replies in agitation, "He can see." Running into the house
and holding each other in the dark, Caddy and Benjy
weep together. "I won't anymore, ever," the girl whispers. A few lines below, in a fragment from 1928, the
girl, Quentin, is sitting on the same swing with a circus
man. Scolding Luster for letting Benjy follow her, she
cries out, "*You old crazy loon. . . . I'm going to tell
Dilsey about the way you let him follow everywhere I
go. I'm going to make her whip you good.*"

Shortly after Caddy's wedding Benjy stands at the
gate of the Compson house, crying loudly. His Negro
keeper explains, "Aint nothing going to quiet him.
. . . He thinks if he down to the gate, Miss Caddy
come back." To which Mrs. Compson, with her usual
sensitiveness, replies, "Nonsense." On the following
page, in a passage set two or three years later, Jason and
Mrs. Compson are discussing how Benjy managed to
get out of the yard and "attack" some little girls coming
home from school. "*How did he get out, Father said.
Did you leave the gate unlatched when you came in,
Jason.*"

In each of these juxtapositions, the whole Compson
story is enacted: in Mrs. Compson's whining over her
"baby," in the treatment of Benjy by his sister and
niece, in the varying significance the gate has for Benjy.
Such contrasts reveal the family's history in all its vul-
nerability, and the result is not an account but a picture
of experience, a series of stripped exposures. When
Benjy's mind comes to rest, the final effect of these
juxtapositions is overwhelming. To specify that effect
accurately requires a somewhat startling comparison. In
Jane Austen's *Persuasion* the writing forms a highly

polished and frequently trivial surface of small talk, and only toward the end does one fully realize that beneath this surface has occurred a romance of exquisite refinement. In the Benjy sequence, the writing forms a surface that is rough, broken, and forbidding, and only toward the end does one fully realize that beneath it Faulkner has retrieved a social history of exquisite pathos. At opposite poles of technique, the two pieces have in common an essential trait of art: they reveal more than they say.

If the Benjy section can be viewed as an opening movement in which the dominant motifs have been introduced, it should be followed by a reflective andante, an unfolding of consciousness and comment. This is the kind of writing that tempts Faulkner to his more sententious postures, but in the Quentin section, notable for its high seriousness and restraint, such temptations are largely resisted. When one considers how fine a consciousness is now required to maintain the purity and candor achieved in the Benjy section, the wonder is not that Quentin's reverie sometimes fails, but that it succeeds at all.

It succeeds in those passages where Quentin, having surrendered himself to the voices of memory, is least in evidence as either person or problem. Few pages in American writing have the corrosive fierceness of those in which Quentin recalls the simpering, maddeningly genteel tone of his mother's voice as she tries to ingratiate herself with Caddy's fiance. Between Quentin's memory and the associations it evokes there is a deeply affecting interplay:

> . . . . We have sold Benjy's *He lay on the ground under the window, bellowing. We have sold Ben-jy's pasture so that Quentin may go to Harvard* a brother to you. Your little brother.

These distraught phrases, Mrs. Compson's in roman and Quentin's in italic, build toward a sum of irony and sadness. Mrs. Compson is telling Caddy's loutish fiance to regard Quentin as his brother, and that is irony enough. In Quentin's memory it is quickened, and saddened, by Benjy's bellowing, which passes judgment on Caddy's wedding. Irony and sadness merge when Mrs. Compson tells Herbert to look upon Quentin as "Your little brother," for the phrase can only recall the image of the true little brother, the idiot beneath the window.

Nor can there be too great praise for the scene in which Quentin, walking through Cambridge, is obstinately followed by a silent little girl, and then accused of assaulting her. The shadowy child, whom Quentin calls "sister," stirs memories of Caddy; the charge against Quentin, of which he is not guilty, rakes those ambiguous desires, bordering on a wish for incest, he has always felt toward his sister. Invoking guilt of conscience through innocence of behavior, this play of symbolic action reflects Quentin's problem in ironic reverse.

[handwritten margin note: Personally, I regard the scene as too long.]

It is credible enough, this problem; it solicits our sympathy; but it cannot carry the weight in the novel that Faulkner intends. The Benjy section, by picturing a disintegration specific to one family yet common to our age, gains its strength from a largeness of reference. The Quentin section abruptly reduces the scope of the novel to a problem that is "special" in a clinical sense and not necessarily an equivalent or derivative of the Compson history. Where Benjy recalls a world, Quentin nurses an obsession. The exact nature of this obsession is not easy to determine: it is partly a problem of his sexual life and partly a problem in family or caste pride. Between the crumbling Compson world and Quentin's obsession there is unquestionably a relation, and Faulkner's effort to fortify that relation is nothing short of heroic; but as we engross ourselves in Quentin's reverie we should remember that the novel's frame of reference, if not changed, has been excessively narrowed. Benjy mourns the loss of love; Quentin is troubled, he thinks, by the neglect of chastity. They are hardly the same problem.

Quentin's obsession with virginity, it may be claimed, reflects the crisis attendant on a denial or collapse of Christian values. Perhaps; but an obsession is not of a piece with a rational moral concern, and Quentin's worry about virginity follows at least as much from his private condition as from a wish to defend traditional values. Even if taken as a defense of those values, the Quentin sequence must seem unsatisfactory, for Quentin can summon only a threadbare and unglorious version of Christianity. Too much rests, for Quentin, on "the minute fragile membrane of Caddy's maidenhead." I doubt that even the strictest Christian moralist could suppose Quentin's chastity neurosis a satisfactory embodiment of the tragic themes announced and developed in the Benjy section. I would also doubt that Quentin can sustain the weight some critics have thrust upon him: the weight of a search for standards of conduct and value in a world that has not only lost them but no longer cares about the loss. In his own pitiable way Quentin is engaged in such a quest; some hunger for an informing sense of principle surely lies behind his lostness; but to say this, unfortunately, is not to reconcile us to his part in the novel, for too often his quest shrinks disastrously to mere nostalgia, forcing us to notice the discrepancy between what he is and what he is supposed to signify.

Perhaps, however, Quentin is intended merely as a "case," a victim, like his little brother, of the family debacle? Were such a reading possible, there could be no complaint about the presentation of Quentin's character. But then another, more serious problem would emerge: the book would list too heavily—as indeed it

may in any case—toward a documentation of the abnormal. The whole section, and particularly the running
debate between Quentin and his father, requires us to
assume that he is meant as a center of intelligence, an
ethical agent and critic. The one character who struggles toward an inclusive view of his family history,
Quentin must in some way be seen as a morally aware
person, not merely a psychological case. That Popeye is
presented in terms of pathology need not trouble us at
all, for whatever else he may do in *Sanctuary* he is not
called upon to register its moral implications. But Quentin is supposed to take everything in, to perceive and reflect and comment. He tries hard and the effort is frequently touching, but his obsession finally bars him
from understanding fully the nature and dimension of
the Compson tragedy. Quentin is too weak, too passive,
too bewildered for the role of sensitive hero. Benjy,
though an idiot, reveals the family situation more faithfully than Quentin, for the events Benjy remembers tell
us more than the efforts of Quentin to comprehend
them. Or to put it another way, Quentin does not add
enough to what the Benjy section has already provided.

This comparison may be reinforced by a glance at the
symbolic patterns of the two sections. Because the few
symbols in the Benjy section are imbedded within or
arise from the action itself, they seem organic and
spontaneous, while the far more numerous symbols of
the Quentin section are often arbitrary, scattered in
effect and literary in source. It is a difference between
craftsmanship and literary self-consciousness, between
symbols unobtrusively working on the reader's sensibility and symbols aggressively thrust before his eyes.

At several points in the Quentin section Faulkner inserts references to Hamlet. Were he employing these as
a form of irony, they might enrich the section. But, so
far as I can tell, there is no warrant for such a reading
and every reason for supposing that Faulkner wishes us
to take Quentin as a modern, if lesser, Hamlet figure—

thoughtful, melancholy, troubled by the ways of women. A poor bewildered boy who has a certain mournful credibility, Quentin lacks anything that might resemble the dash and intellect of Shakespeare's character; it is surely no kindness to press upon him comparisons beyond his capacity to bear.

Equally questionable is Faulkner's use of the clock symbol in the Quentin section. One expects that this section will abound with references to time, and throughout it there can be heard a steady ominous ticking—which forms a setting appropriate enough for a mind that knows its time to be running out. All this comes through well enough in the Quentin section, but Faulkner, either from a troubled identification with Quentin or a fondness for experiment, feels obliged to proliferate a multitude of symbols and to employ them as heavy didactic pointers. After a while, one follows the symbolic patterns as if they were an end in themselves, rather than a means for validating the narrative. The passage in which Quentin visits a watchmaker illustrates just how factitious the symbolism can become. Entering the watchmaker's store, Quentin asks whether any of the watches in the window is correct. "No," replies the man, "they haven't been regulated and set yet."

> There were about a dozen watches in the window, a dozen different hours and each with the same assertive and contradictory assurance that mine had, without any hands at all. Contradicting one another. I could hear mine, ticking away inside my pocket, even though nobody could see it, even though it could tell nothing if anyone could.

The trouble with this passage is that it contains almost nothing but symbolism. Imposed in order to draw a parallel, and rather pointless if taken literally, the incident does not follow significantly from the previous action; Faulkner, not Quentin, needs the visit to the

watchmaker. The symbolism is, therefore, little more
than a tricky duplication of what the novel presents in
direct dramatic terms: that Quentin is beset by a confusion of values and lives in a time that is out of joint.

Those symbols which seem obtrusive have usually
been thrust into the text as clever improvements on the
decor. Others, arising organically from the setting and
action, are both entirely right in relation to that which
they symbolize and arresting in their own qualities.
As Quentin walks through Cambridge, chaotically re-
viewing his past, he thinks of Caddy's sexual looseness,
and the honeysuckle, a flower sweet and cloying, gets
"all mixed up in it." Recurring through the section as a
signal for memory, the flower takes Quentin back to his
rebuke of Caddy for running about with a "town
squirt," her hysterical rejoinder, their adolescent decision to commit suicide—an entire scene edged with
incestuous implication. The flower is also a token of
home, of what was for Quentin the softness and sweet-
ness of the South. In Cambridge "there were vines and
creepers where at home would be honeysuckle. Coming
and coming especially in the dusk when it rained, getting honeysuckle all mixed up in it as though it were
not enough without that, not unbearable enough."
Sexual reminder and signal for nostalgia, the flower
evokes a meaning private to Quentin. In his mind it
stands, ultimately, for Caddy and his troubled feelings
toward her; whereas, for Benjy, Caddy "smelled like
trees." In this contrast the significance of the two sections is condensed.

Equally cogent are the numerous references to money
that wind through the Jason section. Jason fears Benjy
will bellow so much at the nearby golf course, "they're
going to begin charging me golf dues, then Mother and
Dilsey'll have to get a couple of china door knobs and a
walking stick and work it out, unless I play at night
with a lantern." In April he recalls that last September
he gave the girl Quentin money for schoolbooks, ex-

actly $11.65. In a dialogue with a drummer, he curses those "damn eastern jews" who "produce nothing" and "sit up there in New York and trim the sucker gamblers." So it runs through the section: cotton market quotations, sums taken and lent, sums stolen, sums lost, Negro extravagance, the possibility of renting Benjy as a sideshow since "there must be folks somewhere who would pay a dime to see him."

It is the Benjy section, however, that unfolds the most finely controlled symbols in the novel. As a lesser motif, a number of death notes are struck: Benjy moans in memory, holds his private graveyard of flowers, smells the death of father and grandmother. The Negroes, expressing their social sensitiveness in symbols of superstition, also wait for death: T.P. hears the hooting of a squinch owl and the howling of the Compson dog; Roskus sees "the sign"; Dilsey tells the children, "You'll know in the Lawd's own time." Muted at the beginning and then largely withheld in the Quentin and Jason sections, these voices of foreboding and judgment suddenly come forward at the end, reaching their climax in the Negro preacher's sermon.

But the dominant symbol in the Benjy section is grim and homely: a golf ball. Its use is entirely apposite, unstrained, and woven into the behavior of the characters. That Benjy's beloved pasture has had to be sold we soon discover; that it should then be transformed into a golf course is bitterly appropriate. There follows a play of symbolic incident which lights up and intensifies the meaning of the novel: being an idiot Benjy is fascinated by the flight of the golf balls on the nearby links; the cries of "caddie" remind him of his absent sister and prompt his rush of memory; the caddies search for balls; when Luster asks a Negro woman, "You all found any balls yet," he is rebuked, "aint you talking biggity"; "Naw, sir," says Luster to Benjy, "you cant have it. . . . What business you got with it. You cant play no ball"; and, adds Luster in a later passage, "they'll knock your head clean off with one of them balls"; finally Benjy "got undressed and I looked at myself, and I began to cry. Hush, Luster said. Looking for them aint going to do no good. They're gone."

More could be said about Faulkner's use of symbols; it may be better to say that they are often a mare's nest for critics. The contemporary eagerness to interpret works of literature as symbolic patterns is often due to a fear or distaste of direct experience—sometimes, of direct literary experience. It is supposed that a symbol is always deeper or more profound than the object or condition it symbolizes, hence the kind of readings we have recently had, in which virtually every noun in *The Sound and the Fury* is elevated to symbolic significance. When hardened into critical dogma, this mode of interpretation supports the assumption that truth or reality is always "behind" what we see and sense—that an essence lurks in the phenomenon, a ghost in the machine, a spirit in the tree. This view reflects a hesitation before the rough surface of experience, a wish, perhaps, to relegate it to metaphysical category. Yet what would the symbols of *The Sound and the Fury* matter, how could they stir our emotions, were they not subordinate to Faulkner's power in rendering pictures and recording voices? Symbolic patterns certainly appear in the novel, and important ones; but their importance depends on the primary presence of represented objects and people. As an instance of this pictorial mastery, here is Dilsey, an old woman on a Sunday morning:

She wore a stiff black straw hat perched upon her turban, and a maroon velvet cape with a border of mangy and anonymous fur above a dress of purple silk, and she stood in the door for awhile with her myriad and sunken face lifted to the weather, and one gaunt hand flac-soled as the belly of a fish, then she moved the cape aside and examined the bosom of her gown.

In another typical paragraph there is a similar grasp of gesture and thing:

> Dilsey prepared to make biscuit. As she ground the sifter steadily above the bread board, she sang, to herself at first, something without particular tune or words, repetitive, mournful and plaintive, austere, as she ground a faint, steady snowing of flour onto the breadboard. The stove had begun to heat the room and to fill it with murmurous minors of the fire, and presently she was singing louder, as if her voice too had been thawed out by the growing warmth, and then Mrs. Compson called her name again from within the house. Dilsey raised her face as if her eyes could and did penetrate the walls and ceiling and saw the old woman in her quilted dressing gown at the head of the stairs, calling her name with machine-like regularity.
>
> "Oh Lawd," Dilsey said. . . .

To speak of greatness with regard to one's contemporaries is dangerous. But if there are any American novels of the present century which may be called great, which bear serious comparison with the achievements of twentieth-century European literature, then surely *The Sound and the Fury* is among them. It is one of the three or four American works of prose fiction written since the turn of the century in which the impact of tragedy is felt and sustained. Seized by his materials, Faulkner keeps, for once, within his esthetic means. *The Sound and the Fury* is the one novel in which his vision and technique are almost in complete harmony, and the vision itself whole and major. Whether taken as a study of the potential for human self-destruction, or as a rendering of the social disorder particular to our time, the novel projects a radical image of man against the wall.

II

As I Lay Dying

A STORY OF A JOURNEY, AN ACCOUNT OF ADVENTURES ON the road—this may be the outward form of the novel, but the journey proves exceedingly curious and the adventures disconcert. Having died while a son sawed her coffin beneath her window, Addie Bundren is carted away in the family wagon through the back roads of Yoknapatawpha. The family thereby honors, with an absurd literalness, her reiterated wish that she be buried in the Jefferson cemetery. Unwilling adventurers, the Bundrens can do nothing well; their journey, like their life, is wasteful and erratic. Prompted by awe for the dead, but also by a cluster of private motives, they plod through mishaps both terrible and comic: fire and flood, suffering and stupidity. When they reach the town, the putrescent corpse is buried, the daughter fails in her effort to get an abortion, one son is badly injured, another has gone mad, and at the very end, in a stroke of harsh comedy, the father suddenly remarries.

Crossing farce with anguish, As I Lay Dying is a story of misfortunes fabulously multiplied. Anse is certainly right, though hardly for the reasons he supposes, when he declares himself a "misfortunate man." All the Bundrens are "misfortunate"; it is their special talent. There is a kind of story, like Leskov's *The Enchanted Wanderer*, which heaps so many troubles on the back of its hero that the final effect is perversely comic; to this family of fiction *As I Lay Dying* is related. Recalling also the Dostoevskian novel in its coarse mixture of emotions, the book stumbles from catastrophe to catastrophe, a marathon of troubles. Suspense is maintained by the likelihood that still greater troubles are to come, while the ability of some characters to survive with equanimity becomes both an assurance of the comic tone and a wry celebration of mankind.

That *As I Lay Dying* is something more than a record of peregrine disaster we soon discover. As it circles over a journey in space, the novel also plunges into the secret life of the journeyers. Each of them conducts the action a little way while reciting the burden of his mind; the novel resembles a cantata in which a theme is developed and varied through a succession of voices. In *As I Lay Dying* the theme is death, death as it shapes life. The outer action, never to be neglected and always fearsomely and absurdly spectacular, is a journey in a wagon; the inner action is the attempt of the Bundrens to define themselves as members of a family at the moment the family is perishing.

Neither fire nor flood is the crux of the novel, nor any physical action at all; it is Addie Bundren's soliloquy, her thoughts as she lay dying. This soliloquy is one of Faulkner's most brilliant rhetorical set-pieces, placed about two-thirds of the way through the novel and establishing an intense moment of stillness which overpowers, so to speak, the noise of the Bundren journey. Until that moment in the book, Faulkner lightly traces the tangled relationships among the Bundrens—the father, the daughter, Dewey Dell, the sons, Cash, Darl, Jewel and, Vardaman. It seems at first that Darl, the most introspective of the sons, is the cause and catalyst of family tensions. He guesses Dewey Dell's pregnancy and silently taunts her with his knowledge; he hovers over Jewel with eager attentiveness and broods upon the rivalry between them. But Addie's soliloquy makes clear that the conflicts among the children are rooted in the lives of their parents, in the failure of a marriage. It is Addie who dominates the book, thrusting her sons against each other as if they were warring elements of her own character. From her soliloquy until the end of the novel, the action is a physical resolution of the Bundrens' inner troubles, a resolution which must be achieved if the body is to be buried in some sort of peace.

Dying, Addie remembers her youth. Always she had searched for a relation with people by which to impress her will; at no point did her energy find full release. The search for meaning was for her a search for impact, a fierce desire that not all her desires be dissipated in words. Hard, single-minded, intolerant, Addie is one of these Faulknerian characters concerning whom one finds little to admire except their utter insistence upon taking and struggling with life until the end. As a schoolteacher she "would look forward to the times when they faulted, so I could whip them. When the switch fell I could feel it upon my flesh; when it welted and ridged it was my blood that ran, and I would think with each blow of the switch: Now you are aware of me! Now I am something in your secret and selfish life. . . ." But when she married Anse she learned that, for all her fierce willfulness, she would never penetrate to his secret and selfish life.

First came Cash and then "I knew that living was terrible. . . . That was when I learned that words are no good; that words don't ever fit even what they are trying to say at. . . . Love, Anse called it. But I had been used to words for a long time. I knew that word was like the others: a shape to fill a lack. . . ." Cash she cherished, for through his birth she reached understanding, both of Anse and herself. But when Darl

came, "At first I would not believe it. Then I believed I
would kill Anse. It was as though he had tricked me,
hidden within a word like within a paper screen and
struck me in the back through it." After Darl's birth,
Anse seemed to die for her, though "He did not know
he was dead, then. Sometimes I would lie by him in
the dark, hearing the land that was now of my blood
and flesh, and I would think: Anse. Why Anse. Why
are you Anse." And then her moment of ecstasy: "I
believed that I had found it . . . that the reason was
the duty to the alive, to the terrible blood. . . ." Sin-
ning with preacher Whitfield, she bore Jewel. What
came after that seemed unimportant: "I gave Anse
Dewey Dell to negative Jewel . . . Vardaman to replace the child I had robbed him of. And now he had
three children that are his and not mine. And then I
could get ready to die."

The way in which the Bundren children are born,
remarks Olga Vickery in a suggestive study of *As I Lay
Dying*, establishes the "level of their awareness of Addie and the mode of their participation in her burial."
Cash, the earnest and admirable carpenter, is—or is to
become—the moral head of the family. Reflecting Addie's strength and self-possession at the moment she
first realized that "living was terrible," he is free of the
furies that torment his brothers. Too free, perhaps; his
imagination limps behind his conscience, and he is so
absorbed in the coffin that he does not notice a family
crisis darkening about him.

Unlike Cash, Darl is capable of projecting himself
into the feelings of his brothers; but he cannot establish a firm and distinct personality, one with which they
could come to terms. This poor-white farm boy resembles one of those characters who prowl through Henry
James's later novels, all flittering consciousness but no
core of self. His eyes lighting constantly on the family
wounds, Darl speaks more frequently and in many more
scenes than the other Bundrens; the wanderings of his

mind become an important means for moving the narrative. His somewhat disembodied consciousness is not that of an external observer but, so to speak, of the family itself: the secret hovering Bundren voice, often unwelcome to the Bundrens themselves. He senses that Jewel is the truly beloved son despite the fact that he, Darl, proffers and receives the gestures of love; and he knows, too, that the horse on which Jewel bestows such fierce care serves as surrogate for Addie. Darl even hints he has discovered the reason for Addie's violent attachment to Jewel:

> She would fix him special things to eat and hide them for him. And that may have been when I first found it out, that Addie Bundren should be hiding anything she did, who had tried to teach us that deceit was such that, in a world where it was, nothing else could be very bad or very important, not even poverty. And at times when I went in to go to bed she would be sitting in the dark by Jewel where he was asleep. And I knew that she was hating herself for that deceit and hating Jewel because she had to love him so that she had to act the deceit.

It now becomes clear what Darl meant when he said, somewhat earlier, "I cannot love my mother because I have no mother. Jewel's mother is a horse." The motherless Darl must acknowledge, "I don't know what I am."

Jewel speaks only once, and then in a fantasy which aligns mother and himself against the Bundrens: "It would just be me and her on a high hill and me rolling the rocks down the hill at their faces . . . by God until she was quiet. . . ." Dewey Dell and Vardaman, both the issue of Addie's indifference, are female vegetable and frightened, perhaps deranged child, the one concerned only with her ease and the other pure in feeling but unable to distinguish between dead mother and the fish he carries in his hand. The ineffectual Anse de-

claims in self-pity: "It's a trial. . . . But I don't begrudge her it. No man can say I begrudge her it." Addie
is right: in some fundamental sense her husband is
dead, though proper sentiments still come out of him,
like hair from a corpse.

Softened and dulled, Addie's emotional yearnings reappear among her children, as indeed they suffuse the
entire novel. Though it contains a group of figures who
in all the obvious ways are among the least conscious in
Faulkner's work, the book is, nonetheless, devoted—almost as if it were a Jamesian novel—to the effort of
several characters to achieve a break-through in consciousness. They brush against each other for friction
and light; the very irritation one produces in another
forces all of them to some glimmer of awareness; and
the climax of the mother's death, herding them into a
brief closeness, serves to intensify this discovery through
pain. Not the least of Faulkner's achievements is that
he locates the striving for a fine consciousness in a
family like the Bundrens, realizes the incongruity of
this, and then transforms the incongruity into the very
terms of his triumph.

Addie's sons, in their struggle toward self-definition,
discover that to answer the question, *Who am I?*, they
must first consider, *What was my mother and how did
she shape me?* The rivalry between Darl and Jewel,
which recurs through the book like an underground
tremor, is a rivalry in sonship, and it is Darl's sense of
being unwanted which drives him to his obsessive ques-
tionings and finally his collapse. As the children try,
each in his fumbling or inarticulate way, to learn the
meaning of living as son or brother, Addie's authority
persists and grows; indeed, her power is never greater
than during the moment after her death, when the
Bundrens realize how thoroughly the dead live on, ty-
rants from the past. In their search for selfhood the
Bundrens demonstrate their mother's conviction that

language is vanity while action is the test of life: "I would think how words go straight up in a thin line, quick and harmless, and how terribly doing goes along the earth, clinging to it." The sentence prefigures the Bundren history and announces the theme of the book —though not the entire theme. For at the end Cash is able to reach toward that harmonious relation between word and action which none of the Bundrens, not even Addie, sees enough to desire.

Tyrannical in its edict of love and rejection, the will of the mother triumphs through the fate of her children. Cash, the accepted son, endures a preposterous excess of pain largely because of his own inattention and the stupidity of the others. He thereby learns the meaning of kinship, his brothers impinging on him through the torment they cause him; and at the end he takes his place as the mature witness of the wreckage of the family. Jewel, by breaking from his violent obsession, fulfills his mother's prophecy: "He is my cross and he will be my salvation. He will save me from the water and the fire." Literally, that is what Jewel does, and when he parts from his horse in order to speed Addie's burial he achieves a direct expression of filial love. Dewey Dell, munching her banana, continues to move in an orbit of egoism; Vardaman remains pathetic and troubled; and Anse gets himself another wife, "duck-shaped" and with "hard-looking pop eyes."

Darl is the family sacrifice. An unwanted son, he seeks continually to find a place in the family. The pressures of his secret knowledge, the pain of observing the journey, the realization that he can never act upon what he knows—these drive Darl close to madness. Now he dares taunt Jewel: "Whose son are you? . . . . Your mother was a horse; but who was your father, Jewel?" From the sobriety of Cash, Darl moves to the derangement of Vardaman; in a brilliant passage he and Vardaman "listen" to their mother in the coffin:

She was under the apple tree and Darl and I go across the moon and the cat jumps down and runs and we can hear her inside the wood. "Hear?" Darl says. "Put your ear close."

I put my ear close and I can hear her. Only I can't tell what she is saying.

"What is she saying, Darl?" I say. "Who is she talking to?"

"She's talking to God," Darl says. "She is calling on Him to help her."

"What does she want Him to do?" I say.

"She wants Him to hide her away from the sight of man," Darl says.

"Why does she want to hide her away from the sight of man, Darl?"

"So she can lay down her life," Darl says.

Betrayed by Dewey Dell and assaulted by Jewel, Darl is taken away to the asylum. Only Cash understands him; only Cash and Vardaman pity him. Speaking of himself in the third person, a sign of extreme self-estrangement, Darl says: "Darl is our brother, our brother Darl. Our brother Darl is in a cage in Jackson where, his grimed hands lying light in the quiet interstices, looking out he foams, 'Yes yes yes yes yes yes yes yes.' " To the end it is a search for kinship that obsesses Darl, and his cryptic row of affirmatives may signify a last, pathetic effort to proclaim his brotherhood.

Upon this investigation of a family's inner history, Faulkner has lavished his most dazzling virtuosity. Like *The Sound and the Fury*, *As I Lay Dying* stakes everything on the awareness of its characters. There is neither omniscient narrator nor disinterested observer at the rim of the story; nothing being told, all must be

shown. But where *The Sound and the Fury* is divided
into four long sections, of which three convey distinct
and sustained points of view, *As I Lay Dying* is broken
into sixty fragments in which fifteen characters speak or
reflect at various turns of the action and on numerous
levels of consciousness. The prolonged surrender to a
few memories in *The Sound and the Fury* permits a
full dramatic recall; the nervous and jumpy transitions
in *As I Lay Dying* encourage a sensitive recording of
character change. It would be difficult to exaggerate the
complexity of *As I Lay Dying*, or the skill with which
Faulkner manipulates its diverse points of view. So remarkable is this skill, the critic runs a danger of regarding the novel mainly as a fascinating exercise in dexterity.

Once it is agreed that in a final estimate the emphasis
belongs elsewhere, this dexterity is a thing to enjoy and
admire—particularly the way each Bundren, speaking
in his own behalf, comes to illuminate the others. The
first word of the book, uttered by Darl, is "Jewel," and
it announces a major theme: Darl's fitful preoccupation
with his brother. On the same page Darl quickly
sketches Jewel: "Still staring straight ahead, his pale
eyes like wood set into his wooden face, he crosses the
floor in four strides with the rigid gravity of a cigar-
store Indian dressed in patched overalls and endued
with life from the hips down. . . ." Several pages later
Darl speaks again, describing Jewel as the latter caresses
his horse with obscene ferocity. After these introductory
glimpses, Jewel comes forward for one page, a page of
fantasy concerning his frozen love for his mother. The
perspective shifts to Cora Tull, a comically righteous
neighbor who sees much yet not really enough, and
from her we learn that Jewel has been favored by years
of Addie's "self-denial and downright perversity."
Speaking for the first time, Dewey Dell remarks that
"Jewel don't care about anything he is not kin to us in
caring, not care-kin." When Darl learns his mother is

dead, he thinks immediately of Jewel: "*I say, she is dead, Jewel, Addie Bundren is dead.*"

Jewel has now been seen from several points of view, each different yet complementary to the other, and he has spoken once; but he is to be fully understood only when we reach the Addie section and discover the condition of his birth. "With Jewel—I lay by the lamp, holding up my own head, watching him cap and suture it before he breathed—the wild blood boiled away and the sound of it ceased." We can now surmise why it is he, and none of his brothers, who saves Addie from water and fire, why he consents to sell his horse, why he pummels Darl when they reach Jefferson. From a multitude of slanted and crossing impressions, an image of Jewel is slowly composed; but any final interpretation must be our own, for there is no detached observer who speaks for Faulkner, not even to the extent that Dilsey does in *The Sound and the Fury*. The secondary characters surrounding the Bundrens as a chorus of comment and comedy never achieve more than partial understanding. Faulkner presents; the reader must conclude.

The method of *As I Lay Dying* brings with it the danger that the frequent breaks in point of view will interfere with the flow of narrative. In a few scenes this does happen, particularly in those of Darl's reflections which become so densely "poetic" they claim more attention than their place in the narrative seems to warrant. But once Addie's soliloquy is reached, the physical journey in the wagon and the psychological journey through the family closely parallel each other; and each gains dramatic relevance and lucidity from the other.

Each character provides a line of action and impression, but not, of course, with the same sureness and plausibility. Picturesque as they may be, Dewey Dell and Vardaman are hardly bold originals; they serve well enough as foils and accessories, but they seem to have been borrowed from the common store of Southern fiction rather than created in their own right. One minds less their being measured from a ready-made pattern than the neatness and predictability of the measure —their very idiosyncrasies prove neat and predictable. Still, a distinction is to be made even among stereotypes; Vardaman has a kind of stock vividness, while Dewey Dell is the one Bundren who fails to emerge clearly.

Similar strictures might be made against the father but not, I think, with equal justice. Faulkner's critics have been very severe on Anse, cracking the whips of morality over his frail back. Poor Anse, he is hardly the man to support judgment. He is merely a figure to be watched and enjoyed, resourceful in exploiting his laziness, gifted at proclaiming the proper generalities at not quite the proper time, and in a shuffling sort of way, diffident and almost humble. It is just possible that in drawing Anse Faulkner wished to impress on us one or another moral lesson, but far more likely that he struck upon a universal comic type, the tyrannically inept *schlemiehl* whose bumbling is so unrelieved and sloth so unalloyed that he ends by evoking an impatient and irritated sympathy.

Darl raises problems. Because we quickly concern ourselves with him and eagerly respond to his restless search for self-knowledge, his sudden crackup comes too much as a surprise. Faulkner's motives for introducing it may easily be inferred and even accepted, but to say this is not to assume that he has sufficiently prepared for the crackup in the immediately preceding sections. Darl's part of the novel is an instance of a "misplaced middle," the introductory presentation bulking so large, particularly because of Darl's role as an observing eye, that there remains little space in which to prepare and justify his own denouement. Given the large demands made on his vision, Darl's later collapse could be accepted only if Faulkner devoted more attention than he

does to showing the boy's drop from sanity to madness.
There are hints, of course, and it is only fair to add that
many readers find them quite sufficient: hints that come
when Darl dares taunt Jewel openly and Vardaman al-
ludes to his knowledge that it is Darl who has fired the
barn in which Addie's coffin lies. But these intimations
merely span a gap that needs to be filled. Darl's madness does not follow strictly or "inevitably" enough
from what has preceded it; and, if only because our
identification with him has been too sharply punctured,
we are left with a surplus of unused sympathy.

Often as excessive as Darl's fate is the burden of
language Faulkner thrusts upon him. Between author
and character there seems to be an unfortunate entanglement, certainly a lack of ironic distance—and in
a way that recalls Faulkner's relation to Quentin Compson in *The Sound and the Fury*. When Darl is used
merely to observe the other Bundrens, as in the splendid
scene in which he remembers Jewel's sacrifice to buy
his horse, the closeness between author and protagonist
does not disturb, for then Darl himself is largely removed from our vision. But when he turns toward his
inner life, exploring his disturbed consciousness, Darl is
assigned reflections sharply out of character. That he occasionally abandons Southern idiom for a poetic reverie
is in itself unexceptionable, a heightened style being as
good a way as any to simulate the life of the inner
mind. Nor is the difficulty merely that these reflections
do not seem appropriate to Darl; they would be quite as
pretentious from a philosopher as from a farm boy:

The river itself is not a hundred yards across, and
pa and Vernon and Vardaman and Dewey Dell
are the only things in sight not of that single
monotony of desolation leaning with that terrific
quality a little from right to left, as though we had
reached the place where the motion of the wasted
world accelerates just before the final precipice. Yet

they appear dwarfed. It is as though the space between us were time: an irrevocable quality. It is
as though time, no longer running straight before
us in a diminishing line, now runs parallel between
us like a looping string, the distance being the dou-
bling accretion of the thread and not the interval
between.

About the remaining Bundrens there can be no
qualms. Jewel is done with harsh, rapid strokes, seldom
brushed as delicately as in the portrait of Darl; but for
a figure whose behavior forms a ballet of turbulence,
the harshness and rapidity are exactly right. Addie
Bundren is a remarkable image of a passionate woman
who, except for an illicit interval, has known only
barrenness. Driven dark into herself, unable to express
her love for her favorite son, and ending with a realism
of attitude more stringent than her husband can
imagine, Addie spends her years in loneliness and can
bequeath her sons nothing but unfulfilled passion and
a refusal to accept easy assuagements. In her desperation to preserve her family and to raise her children
properly, she seems classically American. Have we not
met this harassed, angular and fervent woman in Willa
Cather's novels of pioneer life and Sherwood Anderson's memoirs of his childhood? Long before we reach
Addie's soliloquy we see her overbearing effect upon
the children; and when she does speak, it comes as an
explosion of ecstasy—a piece of writing that for emotional intensity may justly be compared with the great
forest scene of *The Scarlet Letter*.

It is on Cash, however, that Faulkner bestows his
most admirable touches. Lacking the intensity of Jewel
or the moody restlessness of Darl, he comes through
with greater resonance and richness than the other
Bundrens; he alone among the brothers is neither
delusional nor obsessed; and he is one of the few
Faulkner characters who are not merely revealed but

also grow as a consequence of their experience. At the beginning he is lightly sketched into the story, with an affectionate mockery that hardly suggests his later importance. How far did you fall, Cash, that time you slipped off the church roof? "Twenty eight foot, four and a half inches, about," he solemnly replies. And when he speaks directly for the first time, it is to explain in thirteen marvelously adduced reasons why he made the coffin on the bevel. "1. There is more surface for the nails to grip. . . . 13. It makes a neater job."

Throughout the journey Cash says very little and suffers in quiet; but he is now watching the drama within his family, almost as if he were seeing it for the first time. He thereby gains an understanding of the journey, implicitly taking it as a test of character and integrity. He matures in his feelings and in his power to express them. Sometimes, he says about Darl,

". . . . I ain't so sho who's got ere a right to say when a man is crazy and when he ain't. Sometimes I think it ain't none of us pure crazy and ain't none of us pure sane until the balance of us talks him that-a-way. It's like it ain't so much what a fellow does, but it's the way the majority of folks is looking at him when he does it."

This growth from unimaginative self-containment to humane concern appears again in Cash's musings over a phonograph:

"I reckon it's a good thing we ain't got ere a one of them. I reckon I wouldn't never get no work done a-tall for listening to it. I don't know if a little music ain't the nicest thing a fellow can have. Seems like when he comes in tired of a night, it ain't nothing could rest him like having a little music played and him resting."

But surely the final emphasis belongs not to the novel's subject or technique; its claim to our affection

rests on more than its study of family relations or its
brilliance in handling points of view. Such things matter only insofar as they bring us closer to the book's
essential insight or vision, its moral tone. Of all Faulkner's novels, *As I Lay Dying* is the warmest, the kind-
liest and most affectionate. The notion that Faulkner
is a misanthrope wallowing in horrors is possible only
to those who have not read the book or have read it
with willful obtuseness. In no other work is he so
receptive to people, so ready to take and love them, to
hear them out and record their turns of idiom, their
melodies of speech. Smaller in scope than Faulkner's
other important novels, *As I Lay Dying* lacks the tragic
consistency of *The Sound and the Fury*, the grandeur
of *Absalom, Absalom!*, the power of *Light in August*.
But it shines with virtues distinctly its own: a superb
sympathy for the lowly and incoherent, an implicit
belief that the spiritual life of a Darl Bundren can be
as important as the spiritual life of a Lambert Strether,
a readiness on Faulkner's part to immerse himself in
people radically unlike himself. Look—he seems to be
saying—look at the capacity for suffering and dignity
which human beings have, even the most absurdly
wretched of them! The book is a triumph of fraternal
feeling, and because it is that, a triumph, as well, in the
use of idiom. No finer example of American lyricism,
that indigenous style stemming from *Huckleberry Finn*,
could be found in twentieth-century writing than this
passage in which Darl remembers . . .

> When I was a boy I first learned how much better
> water tastes when it has set a while in a cedar
> bucket. Warmish-cool, with a faint taste like the
> hot July wind in cedar trees smells. It has to set at
> least six hours, and be drunk from a gourd. Water
> should never be drunk from metal.
>
> And at night it is better still. I used to lie on the
> pallet in the hall, waiting until I could hear them

all asleep, so I could get up and go back to the bucket. It would be black, the shelf black, the still surface of the water a round orifice in nothingness, where before I stirred it awake with the dipper I could see maybe a star or two in the bucket, and maybe in the dipper a star or two before I drank. After that I was bigger, older. Then I would wait until they all went to sleep so I could lie with my shirt-tail up, hearing them asleep, feeling myself without touching myself, feeling the cool silence blowing upon my parts and wondering if Cash was yonder in the darkness doing it too, had been doing it perhaps for the last two years before I could have wanted to or could have.

Or this passage in which Darl describes Addie's coffin being carried into the house:

It is light, yet they move slowly; empty, yet they carry it carefully; lifeless, yet they move with hushed precautionary words to one another, speaking of it as though, complete, it now slumbered lightly alive, waiting to come awake. On the dark floor their feet clump awkwardly, as though for a long time they have not walked on floors.

And almost as vivid is Jewel thinking of his mother as she dies:

. . . her hands laying on the quilt like two of them roots dug up and tried to wash and you couldn't get them clean. I can see the fan and Dewey Dell's arm. I said if you'd just let her alone. Sawing and knocking, and keeping the air always moving so fast on her face that when you're tired you can't breathe it, and that goddamn adze going One lick less. One lick less. . . .

Because he writes of the Bundrens with a comely and tactful gravity, a deep underlying respect, Faulkner is able to blend extreme and incongruous effects—the sublime and the trivial, anguish and absurdity, a wretched journey through the sun and a pathetic journey toward kinship. An American epic, *As I Lay Dying* is human tragedy and country farce. The marvel is, that to be one it had to be the other.

Sanctuary

PERHAPS BECAUSE IT SEEMS TOO GROSS AND IMPERVIOUS to qualification, the novelist's power to shock is seldom rated highly by modern critics. This view is as limited to certain phases in the history of taste as it is honorable, intelligent, and not quite adequate. Whoever turns an eye to the novels of Dickens and Dostoevsky must be aware of the extent to which they depend on the power to shock: the power to release that single thrust of action which can excite the reader's intense horror or revulsion. Many great writers have enjoyed crass and violent effects, and without hesitation assaulted delicacy.

In its own lesser way *Sanctuary* depends on this power to shock. Apart from some first-rate comic diversion, it drives brutally toward two climaxes, the corncob violation of Temple and her later account of it to Benbow. And no matter what complaint is proposed about their use in the novel, these moments of shock are necessary to its organizing scheme; the notion that *Sanctuary* merely offers cheap thrills, a notion for which Faulkner himself is in part responsible, deserves short shrift. Most of Faulkner's work, good or bad, exhibits his moral intent, an extreme aversion from the horrors he is compelled to notice.

The trouble lies elsewhere. Shock in *Sanctuary* derives not from a lack but from an excess of moral feeling—a feeling often uncontrolled and without an adequate object of attack. Written with unmodulated fervor, the novel resembles a polemic run wild; its thematic line moves with a stringent clarity but is neither contained nor reinforced by a quite credible human context. Its dominant emotions stain the prose a shade too lurid for anything which even the violent and melodramatic plot might require. Indeed, Faulkner is so possessed by his hatred for the world of Popeye that it is precisely his moral sensibility, outraged and baffled, which prompts his wish to shock. Given the magnitude of his revulsion, what other recourse does he have? For the materials of the novel are neither complex nor resilient enough to serve the purpose behind it; the feelings which drove Faulkner to write do not find a satisfactory equivalent in the work itself. Perhaps the problem is unavoidable, perhaps such extreme traumas of revulsion cannot be embodied in a coherent action.

What one misses is the resistance every writer must erect against his own intentions, that moral flexibility which comes from a willingness to assume that in a work of art, even if not in real life, no issue is quite settled in advance. As regards *Sanctuary*, this means that human effort need not always be seen as hurtling to bleak disaster—at least not with such mechanical and almost pleasurable assurance. From the very beginning Benbow's futility is so unqualified that his side of the novel suffers a quick prolapse, and one wonders whether in all of Yoknapatawpha there might not be a sturdier agent of justice than this sadly henpecked lawyer. The helplessness of Ruby Goodwin is apparent almost as quickly; and only they, Benbow and Ruby, so much as care to oppose Popeye. Without a greater resistance than these two can muster, the novel is reduced to a staccato of incidents which lack the quality of drama even when they are exciting. The final effect resembles the aggravation of a wound a good deal more than the release or cleansing of an emotion.

All surface turbulence, brilliant surface at times, *Sanctuary* seldom strikes a fully-articulated or complex meaning. The suspicion that its violent motions conceal a void may result from Faulkner's fastidious distance from his material, an unwillingness to breathe the foul air of Temple and Popeye. It is somewhat perplexing that a writer who excels in works of radical subjectivity should now confine himself to an approach that can only be called behaviorist; apart from his eagerness to try new techniques, the change seems a consequence of his hatred for the world of his own novel. *Sanctuary* concentrates on sheer events, seldom examining the sources of conduct; and in several crucial sections, particularly the rape scene, displays an opacity which comes from a crowding of action, a blurred jam of scurrying and commotion.

It is this behaviorist bias which prompts critics to read *Sanctuary* as an allegory, for a bare sequence of events lends itself to schematic interpretation far more easily than does a complex imitation of experience. Faulkner dwells on details of appearance and behavior with a hard, sometimes overfocussed intensity, so much so that the novel, breaking past the aim of faithful representation, moves toward an autonomous realm of grotesque emblems and events. Naturalism pushed to its extreme limit becomes something other than itself, a kind of expressionist nightmare. The scene in which the virile punk Red is buried, offers a good illustration:

> The floral offerings flew; the coffin teetered. "Catch it!" a voice shouted. They sprang forward, but the coffin crashed heavily to the floor, coming

open. The corpse tumbled slowly and sedately out and came to rest with its face in the center of a wreath.

"Play something!" the proprietor bawled, waving his arms, "Play! Play!"

When they raised the corpse the wreath came too, attached to him by a hidden end of a wire driven into his cheek. He had worn a cap which, tumbling off, exposed a small blue hole in the center of his forehead. It had been neatly plugged with wax and was painted, but the wax had been jarred out and lost. They couldn't find it. . . .

In creating such expressionist nightmares Faulkner evokes a sense of fatality beyond meaning or purpose, a sense of fatality quite without the grandeur which sometimes accompanies it in the work of Hardy and Conrad. The doom summoned in this book is petty and absurd; here, as André Malraux has remarked, "the figure of destiny stands alone behind all these similar and diverse beings, like Death in a hospital ward of incurables. . . ."

A book resembling a ward of incurables can hardly be expected to provide a copious display of human character; what it does yield is several brilliant gargoyles and caricatures. To the extent that the main figures of *Sanctuary* need merely satisfy the requirements of a bizarre action, they are superbly done. To the extent that they have to convey a body of implication somewhat more complex than is possible in allegory—which is to say, the extent that we are invited to consider their inner motives—they do not entirely suffice.

Horace Benbow's weakness is comprehensible and often precisely rendered: no one, certainly no man, is likely to forget the serio-comic business about the dripping box of shrimp. But Temple's depravity and Popeye's viciousness, though we never doubt their "existence" in the world of the novel, require stronger motivation than they receive. It may be argued in behalf of Temple that she anticipates a kind of woman who has become very important in American life and literature: the trembling, sexless, ferocious bitch. This claim is true, and Faulkner deserves credit for his observation. But in celebrating Temple as a cultural phenomenon it is too easy to neglect her limitations as a character in a novel. Even as a symbolic figure she is too frail and "special"—too frail and "special" in her very bitchiness—to signify quite as much as Faulkner would have us assume; she falls too easily from the possibility of archetype into the misery of pathology. Taken as an individual, she is pitiable but not, finally, interesting enough. We tend to see her as a series of distraught and compulsive gestures, a blurred outline of expressionist notation. Only at moments does she spring to full life, as in the half-dozen pages which record her pleasure and pain at finding herself in Miss Reba's house, or in the ending where Temple and her daddy ("My father is a judge") sit in the Luxembourg Gardens, listening to Massenet and Scriabin, and she feels "sullen and discontented and sad." Remarkable things certainly happen to Temple, yet she herself usually remains indistinct and remote, perhaps because Faulkner's contempt for her values is so extreme he cannot stop to illuminate her motives.

To be sure, Temple is accurately done in a clinical sense. Dr. Lawrence Kubie, in his psychoanalytical study of *Sanctuary*, remarks on the expertness with which Faulkner has conceived Temple's fantasying. "In the face of danger," he writes, "Temple had a momentary hallucination that her body had changed into that of a boy. The rude awakening from this dream, and the shocking rediscovery of her unchanged anatomy gave rise to a secondary phantasy . . . in which there was a fusion of the idea of rape, castration and death. . . ." For Temple the rape is like a nightmare, a half-desired nightmare; and Faulkner observes, with admirable precision, how this nightmare disorders her sense of time, intolerably prolonged periods alternating with urgent compressions. His skill in handling dream materials would be of great use to the novel if it were in the service of a sustained characterization or if, alternately, Temple had been approached primarily through images of unconscious life.

By contrast, Popeye is a triumph of vividness. Nor is this vividness affected by the terms in which he is conceived: as a depraved gangster, as the projection of a fear of impotence, or as an inclusive symbol of evil. In his stiff hat and tight suit, his rubbery eyes, his fear of all animals and readiness to kill any man, Popeye is indisputably present. And what is the point of caviling about him when no one can forget him? Only in the last chapter, a perfunctory summary of Popeye's early life, does Faulkner stumble. The failure, I would emphasize, is in the perfunctoriness, the sudden drop of interest and evident eagerness to be done with the book, rather than the assumption that Popeye's past, if known, could illuminate his present. One school of criticism frowns upon this last chapter since it shows Popeye to have been "merely" sick. Mr. W. H. Frohock, for example, contends that characters like Popeye should be portrayed as "evil without being abnormal," but this is a view which, as a rule, can be defended only if some belief about Original Sin is preferred to, or regarded as "more profound" than, a view of evil as conditioned by social and psychological experience.

Faulkner's occasional clumsiness in handling shock and his failure to provide dimension for his characters, trouble the shape of the book. *Sanctuary* is either too long or too short. Adequate preparation for its few critical incidents would require a book considerably longer than the present one; confined attention to those incidents would require no more than a long story. Several chapters—the visit of the Snopes boys to Memphis, Miss Reba's memorable tea party, Red's funeral—

are not essential to the theme of the novel. Yet these chapters are the finest in the book. Wild burlesques, they exploit such stock elements of folk humor as the absurd adventures of small-town boys during their first visit to the big city and the fondness of brothel madams for respectable talk during slack hours. Though apparently meant as relief from the narrative, these interludes compress more reality than the realistic passages, signify more than the scenes obviously meant to be significant. Together with the passages dominated by Popeye and the one or two in which Temple acquires a flicker of animation, they go far toward redeeming the book—as well as reminding us once again of Faulkner's gift for seizing on critical moments of life even in those novels that do not fully satisfy us as representations of life.

"Far toward redeeming . . . not fully satisfy. . . ." Are these cool and cautious phrases what one really wants to say about this novel?

If the question seems odd, perhaps it is because modern criticism does not fully encourage one to rely upon personal feelings when discussing a book. And in regard to a work like *Sanctuary*, the question is a particularly difficult one. *Sanctuary* raises no great problems of interpretation: most literate readers are likely to share a common view of its meaning. By now its impact is also a matter of common knowledge, those who detest the novel offering evidence as forceful as those who admire it. But when it comes to estimating the value of *Sanctuary*, a notorious silence overcomes Faulkner's critics, perhaps becaue they sense that here neither approval nor dismissal matters as much as recording faithfully one's primary response.

Sanctuary is a remarkable book, not to be forgotten. It is a modern book, assaulting the reader rather than delighting him, stirring his discontent and disgust rather than softening him in the ways of the world. It is surely not the cheap shocker it once was supposed to be, nor does it quite warrant the philosophic expansion it has suffered at the hands of Frenchmen and exegetes.

Sanctuary lives in memory after a first reading, but neither deepens nor grows after a second. No new pleasures, no discoveries of hidden values and resources come to one upon returning to the book. On a second reading one is struck mainly by the reasons for having been struck by *Sanctuary* the first time. But not by very much else: the shock remains, yet no surprise follows, for the book is compulsively fervent, wilfully monolithic, rigid in purpose, tone and effect. It is too feverishly transparent in its intentions, too much at the mercy of its own stringencies—which, if not a radical criticism, may at least point toward a significant limitation.

Sanctuary lives for us because it presents an extreme situation in extreme terms, thereby satisfying the expectations that "modern" literature uniquely excites. It is caught up with our sense of a major cultural event: the collapse of order, the loss of morale, whatever it may be that leads us to think of society as mechanical and inhumane. *Sanctuary* is a book of the historical moment, not so much in theme or statement as in deepest qualities—its raw fascination with violence, its closeness to nihilism. Perhaps the book is excessively of the moment: too thoroughly, even abjectly in the grip of its hateful and hated subject.

About a novel that raises such irksome problems of involvement, there may be no immediate need or possibility for a "definitive" judgment. That, we can leave to posterity. For us *Sanctuary* is like a hard and painful blow: the ache lingers in memory, the shock cannot be dismissed. Yet we might also remember that for all its uses, a blow is not the profoundest way of transforming human consciousness.

IV

Light in August

MODERN CRITICISM IS TOO READY TO ASSUME A DEEP CON-
gruence between form and content in a work of fiction,
thereby neglecting to ask whether the sheer persistence
of these terms may indicate that they point to necessary distinctions. There is, to be sure, something valuable in a stress upon the intimacy between form and
content in a successful work of literature—provided one
bears in mind that this unity is never complete and the
relation among its elements is somewhat less than perfect. But modern criticism, in its passion for "structural
analysis," too often forgets this qualification. Too often
it proposes *ad hoc* rationalizations for adjusting mishaps
of form to supposed needs of content, or indulgence
of content to presumed requirements of form. And in
practice this means to ignore the fact that in the novel,
that most impure of literary genres, the actual relation between form and content is almost always unfinished and improvisatory, rarely as neat as critics like
to suppose. Accepting this fact may at least allow us to
trace the varying relationships between thematic content and embodying form: where the two really fuse,

where they draw apart, and where a clash breaks out between them.

In *Light in August* a central concern is with the relation between a man's social role and private being: Hightower as a failed minister who rots in quiet neglect and Hightower as a ruminative observer of human folly, Joe Christmas as a harried mulatto who starts life without even a name and Joe Christmas as a bewildered man struggling toward the rudiments of consciousness. The one character, Lena Grove, in whom the distance between social role and private being is slight, necessarily emerges as a comic figure. She stands for the outrageous possibility that the assumption shared by Faulkner and his cultivated readers may be false:—the assumption that suffering finds a justification in the growth of human consciousness. For Lena is and does "right" with a remarkably small amount of consciousness or suffering, neither of which she apparently needs very much; she is Faulkner's wry tribute to his own fallibility, a tribute both persuasive and not meant completely to persuade.

The split between social role and private being wounds us in ourselves, but we feel the pain most sharply when facing other people. It is in moments of confrontation that one is most troubled by a sense of self-estrangement, as in moments of loneliness that one learns to reckon the exhaustion that comes from human relationships. These are the facts—so, for the purposes of the novel, Faulkner invites us to regard them— which shape the design of *Light in August*.

The book is focused on a series of confrontations: Lena-Burch, Lena-Bunch, Lena-Christmas, and then another series: Bunch-Hightower, Christmas-Hightower Grimm-Christmas. These meetings, mostly between strangers and some of them mere suggestions of possibility, form the spinal column of the book. If, as I have been saying, Faulkner means to dramatize both the terrors of isolation and the erosion of relationships, it is appropriate that several characters, each breaking out of his own obscurity, should collide, cause pain and then part. There are large possibilities for drama in such a pattern, if only because it virtually insures strong climaxes; and Faulkner has mined these possibilities to their limits. There are also troublesome problems of organization—for one, how to avoid a split of the narrative into several divergent lines. It would be excessive to claim that Faulkner has quite solved these problems.

The necessary meetings take place: the chords of dissonance are struck. A link is established between each of the three major characters, though a rather tenuous one between Lena and Christmas, forced upon them more by Faulkner's desire to weight the book with symbolic richness than by an inherent necessity of the action. For we cannot assume that a relationship in a novel has been established simply because an author indicates his wish that it be there or a critic obligingly infers its necessity. The problem is not how to rationalize in one's mind the several strands of action, but what Faulkner makes of them in the book. Put another way, it is a problem in economy and waste: How much is gained for Christmas by his juxtaposition to Lena? How bright an illumination does the mind of Hightower cast on the conduct of the other characters? What value follows from the contrast between the stillness of Lena and the restlessness of everyone else?

Light in August moves on two levels of time: the dramatic present, shaped almost entirely into terse and powerful scenes, and the recalled past, worked up through discursive summaries and flashbacks. In the main, those sections of the novel set in the present command greater vividness and authority than those falling back into the past. The sections set in the present are there because we must see them; the sections set in the past are there because we need the information they provide. The numerous cinematic flashbacks come to appear too conspicuously "functional," several of

them occurring whenever the source or meaning of a
scene requires more material than Faulkner can provide
within it. Between the requirements of the theme and
the rhythm of the action there is thus a certain conflict,
and it is not always happily resolved. Two of the flashbacks, those for Joanna Burden and Doc Hines, are in
excess of what the narrative requires or their intrinsic
value might justify; the grotesque Hines episode, coming at a point where the reader's emotional resources
have already been engaged by the tragedy of Christmas,
has a distracting rather than intensifying effect. Faulkner solicits too wide a variety of emotions, and the
reader, to conserve his powers of response for the climax
he knows is yet to come, must begrudge the flashbacks
the attention they might deserve. This is especially true
in the second half of the novel, where there is a wasteful scattering of effects among subordinate characters.

So rich a novel as *Light in August* might easily absorb
this waste were it not a symptom of a more important
weakness. The novel proposes a triad of actions: Christmas carries the burden of the book, Lena a sub-plot idyllic in itself but significantly ironic in regard to Christmas, and Hightower, as participant and observer, has a
dual function. He must fail Christmas in his moment
of crisis and must provide a reflective consciousness
upon which the conduct of the surrounding characters,
most notably Lena and Christmas, can register. Necessarily, these actions involve a complex shifting in point
of view. No single character can comprehend all that is
happening; the meanings must beat against each other
as do the actions themselves—when, that is, they beat
in time.

Like all of Faulkner's Negroes, Christmas is seen
mainly from the outside, but he is so graphic a figure
that for a good portion of the book this limitation is entirely satisfactory. Observed in moments of characteristic conduct—reading a pulp magazine from cover to
cover "as though it were a novel," somberly shaving

during his flight—Christmas seems immediately and indisputably real. We know about him all that we need to know, and perhaps more than we can fully absorb. But midway through the book, in the chapter where he murders Joanna Burden, one comes to feel that an interior view, an intimate record of what his experience signifies to him, may now be necessary. For the development of the novel leads one to expect that we will now see directly and fully what it is—the "it" is in his mind—that leads him to kill his mistress. My criticism is based not on any general notions about novels or Negroes, but on the inner logic of *Light in August* itself. Like a camera sighting its object from a distance and then edging its way toward close-up, the book moves in, warily, toward Christmas—but not to the point of entering his inner life, not to the point of providing the "flash-in" that we are led to desire. As a result, the murder of Joanna Burden, while explicable through several hints placed by Faulkner, does not acquire the tragic scope and intensity it should have. It remains too much an event in the story, not enough an experience of Joe Christmas. In the final reckoning, to be sure, the failure to work into Christmas' mind does not seriously detract from his total impact; nothing could. But it does cause the novel's weight of consciousness to be lowered upon another character—not, happily, upon Lena Grove.

Beyond a doubt Lena is the most harmoniously conceived and drawn figure in the book, reflecting one of Faulkner's most benign moods: a relaxed whimsical affection for simple life and a readiness to grant major virtues to passivity as a moral style. In writing about Lena, Faulkner never strains, as with Hightower, or becomes feverishly troubled, as with Christmas. Yet she is decidedly less interesting than Hightower or Christmas, and one should resist the desire of certain complex critics to romanticize her simplicity, for then she would be less interesting still. She is surely not to be compared,

as one Christian-minded critic has, to the primitive
saints, if only because she has never known the life of
trouble, the ordeal of surmounting, which is usually
taken as a prerequisite for sainthood. She may indeed
possess, as another critic writes, a "holistic" consciousness which shields her from the suffering of the other
characters, but it necessarily remains a very limited sort
of consciousness. So meager and self-contained an intelligence as Lena's must limit, though not eliminate,
our feelings for her.

Those who see in Lena a triumph of healthy tradi-
tionalism and in Christmas the self-destructiveness of
"modernism"—who see this and nothing else—do not
really grant Faulkner's mind its due. They take an important step with him, but fail to follow his later turn-
ings. It is true enough in a way that Lena is healthy (it
is the health of pre-consciousness) and Christmas sick,
but surely Faulkner has not written so troubled and
complex a book merely to tell us that. Is he not rather
suggesting that Christmas and Hightower are destroyed
because each, in his own inadequate way, does try to
accept the challenge of his humanity, the first by seeking selfhood and the second by a deluded immersion in
history, while Lena, the good unruffled vegetable Lena,
survives them all in her impervious detachment? Lena's
story frames the agonies of the book, at the beginning as
she walks, blithe and pregnant, toward Jefferson, and
at the end as she and Byron Bunch go off, watching
her child and seemingly unscarred by all that has happened. There is something utterly outrageous and in-
furiating in her capacity to move through and past this
accumulation of miseries—so outrageous and infuriat-
ing that one must acknowledge the final effect of the
novel to be perversely comic: a comedy that underscores
the tragic incommensurability between the fates of Joe
Christmas and herself. That, Faulkner seems to be saying, is the way things are: the Joe Christmases get
lynched, the Lena Groveses get husbands, and anyone

who would seek moralities of reconciliation in all this must be a bit of a fool.

That the Lena I have been sketching should so completely triumph is something we do not find easy to accept, for it hardly assuages our self-esteem as cultivated persons; and so there is naturally an inclination to elevate her into a kind of moral heroine or earth goddess or even a putative saint. But for the sake of the novel, we should decline this temptation. The point and the power of it all rests on the fact that Lena is just a good healthy amiable country-girl, and to conclude anything else is not only to dissolve the tensions of the book but to transform Faulkner into the simpleminded moralist which in his inferior books he is.

The reading I have suggested here not only allows the novel a well-earned complication of irony, it also invokes an observable truth: the price of consciousness often is self-destruction, and equally often the reward for animal calm is safety. One may be fond of Lena, but one identifies with Hightower or, in a somewhat different way, with Christmas. To regard Lena as an agent of morality and let it go at that, is to graze the notion that goodness is contingent upon a noble paucity of intelligence.

Because of Lena's inherent limitations and the failure to enter Christmas's mind, a great burden falls upon Hightower. Although he moves us again and again, although he is unforgettable as the young minister preaching a kind of martial godliness and his characterization is poignant as the old man lacerating himself on the tasks Byron Bunch brings him, Hightower will not quite do. Alfred Kazin is right in saying that Hightower is "too vague, too drooping, too formless, in a word too much the creature of defeat and of obsession, to compel our interest or our belief. . . . Hightower, acting in various sections of the book as a foreground observer, brings to them not merely a stillness but a deadness which intervenes between us and the other characters."

To register the full meaning of Christmas's tragedy, Hightower must command an active mind and fresh sensibility. Yet, insofar as he is an actor in the story rather than its somewhat detached observer, he must fail Christmas, and fail him because of his fear of human involvement and his need for protective routine. Here Hightower becomes what Sherwood Anderson called a "grotesque," the shell of a once ardent man, reminiscent of the twisted creatures who wander through *Winesburg, Ohio*. This mustiness of character, though persuasive enough in its own right, seriously qualifies Hightower's usefulness as the moral "reverberator" of the novel. Fully to absorb the significance of all he sees, fully to grasp the meaning of Christmas's death, Hightower would have to be less delusional than in fact he is; and if less delusional he might more actively have tried to prevent Christmas's death. Yet the theme and working-out of the novel require that Christmas die and no one be able to prevent it.

Now, between the role of actor and the role of observer in a novel there is no necessary conflict; both can be performed by the same character. Nor is it difficult to see that such a character might have a large capacity for understanding and a small one for action. But some conflict is clearly present between the kind of behavior allotted Hightower and the qualities of observation he is presumed to possess. In a somewhat different way Richard Chase has noticed the same problem:

In the case of Hightower there seems to be a failure of consciousness precisely at the point where we should understand the quality of the association between Hightower and his own history. Hightower has projected his sexual and spiritual impo-

tence back upon a myth of his grandfather. Faulkner goes along with Hightower on this point, assuming too much that a fantasy projected from
some center of real causation is the cause itself. He
nearly allows Hightower to determine the quality of
his [Faulkner's] consciousness.

Faulkner is almost always uncertain in his treatment
of those characters who serve both as chorus and center
of intelligence. The claims he makes for his intellectuals
he can rarely validate; Hightower, Benbow, and Gavin
Stevens are not nearly such impressive thinkers as he
would have us suppose. And it is only occasionally that
he has managed to solve—or skirt—this problem. In
The Hamlet the sewing-machine agent, Ratliff, is credible in both roles simply because he performs them not
as a sophisticated intellectual or what passes for one in
Faulkner's mind, but as a Yoknapatawpha man completely at home in his world. In *The Sound and the
Fury* the roles are split, Quentin Compson providing a
center of intelligence and Dilsey a magnificent chorus.
Neither so flaccid as Benbow nor so pretentious as
Stevens, Hightower is easier to accept than both of
them; but he is still taken too much at his own valuation. One is reminded of T. S. Eliot's remark about a
character in *Roderick Hudson:* "He [James] too much
identifies himself with Rowland, does not see through
the solemnity he has created in that character, commits
the cardinal sin of failing to 'detect' one of his own
characters." Faulkner's failure is more complex: he
does "detect" Hightower's weakness and delusion, but
tries to endow them with a tragic grandeur they cannot
possibly sustain. Between Faulkner and Hightower, as
between Faulkner and most of his reflective figures,
there is insufficient distance. Exactly right in his relation to Lena and at one or two points perhaps a trifle
remote from Christmas, Faulkner is certainly much too
close to Hightower—too close, particularly, in his fan-

tasying about the Southern past, a fantasying Faulkner
sometimes accepts and more often grows impatient and
irritated with, but which nevertheless creates problems
of involvement. It is a sign of this excessive involvement
that while many fine passages are granted Hightower,
few of these passages have the sustained scenic thickness,
the absolute immersion in the flow of experience, that
one finds in the chapters devoted to Christmas: notably
the remarkable figure of the wheel rushing through his
mind at the end of the novel ("As he sits in the window, leaning forward above his motionless hands, sweat
begins to pour from him, springing out like blood, and
pouring. Out of the instant the sandclutched wheel of
thinking turns on. . . .").

That *Light in August* suffers a certain structural incoherence, an occasional imbalance between matter
and form, seems clear; and this may be the reason it fails
to achieve the classic economy of *The Sound and the
Fury*. Yet one can only hope that such strictures, whatever their usefulness, will not be taken too solemnly.
The "looseness" of representation which roused Henry
James to severity is here an evident flaw; but surely
this novel, if only because of its reliance on the scenic
method and its enviable portion of creative energy,
would have attracted the eye of the James who wrote the
preface to *The Awkward Age*. Few American novels are
so lavish in dramatic incident, so infused with images of
sensation, so precisely fixed in place and weather. The
most stringent criticism—too stringent, I should think—
to be made of *Light in August* is that Faulkner's clumsiness in transitional stitching and narrative preparation,
particularly his lame summary of Christmas's young
manhood, reduces the book to a series of brilliant tableaux. But even then, the tableaux remain in all their
solidity, the rich scenic substance of the novel.

Obvious though it might seem, this point requires a
kind of special presentation at the moment. American
criticism, fascinated by mechanics and ingenuity, is

ready to honor everything in a novel—ingenuity of structure, schemes of imagery, deeply inlaid symbolism, weighty moral implications—everything but the immediate rendering of life, the picture itself, which *is* the novel and without which there would be little cause to read, let alone interpret, works of fiction. It is this abundance of representation, this copiousness of postures observed and manners poetically evoked, that makes *Light in August* so splendid a novel.

The picture, not the deliberate symbol, is the source of this excellence. In most of the instances in *Light in August* where Faulkner employs symbolic devices they are poorly and often half-heartedly done. Remove the several cloudy suggestions that Christmas is some sort of Christ figure, and it would hardly matter: Christmas affects us as a vulnerable man, not as a religious token. When the boy Christmas discovers that women are "victims of periodic filth," and soaks his hands in the warm blood of a sheep he has slaughtered, this symbolic incident adds little to what we already know about Christmas. A rather showy display of parallels, it merely raises a problem in credibility. By contrast, the symbol of the wheel of thought which turns in Hightower's mind "with the slow implacability of a medieval torture instrument, beneath the wrenched and broken sockets of his spirit," is a remarkable soaring of the imagination. Here the first requirement for a symbol is entirely satisfied: that it enlarge the meaning of the object to which it refers and enforce attention in its own right. No mere arbitrary sign or pale duplicate, the symbol acquires a color and momentum of its own, referring back to its object—the fate of Hightower—but also enriching the book with new associations. Seldom do the other symbols in *Light in August* fit so well, and none plays nearly so important a role in sustaining the book as do the dramatic scenes themselves. Finally, it is the sheer power of representation, the power of apprehending and then taking a full unflinching measure of an experience, which makes *Light in August* so remarkable a book.

Power in a successful work of fiction is recognized easily enough; accounting for its sources is another matter. In *Light in August* one may point to Faulkner's absolute sureness of locale, equalled only in *As I Lay Dying* and *The Hamlet*. More than mere pleasant landscape or inert backdrop, the locale is quickened to a force visibly shaping and opposing the characters. As in Hardy, the locale becomes a "character," a sentient presence with qualities of its own. On the first page of the book Lena is placed through a few exact details: "six or eight times a year she went to town on Saturday, in the wagon, in a mail-order dress and her bare feet flat in the wagon bed and her shoes wrapped in a piece of paper beside her on the seat." Lifting the sentence to precise rightness are two details, evidence of intimate knowledge: the feet flat in the wagon bed and the shoes wrapped in a piece of paper.

The farmer, Armstid, who befriends Lena is defined by the words "humped" and "bleacheyed," the first noting his condition as a poor farmer and the second his mildness as a submissive man. In a few sentences describing Lena's offer to share food with another farmer, a distinctive style of behavior is perceived and rendered:

> 'I wouldn't care for none,' he says.
> 'I'd take it kind for you to share.'
> 'I wouldn't care to. You go ahead and eat.'

Partly, too, the power of the novel derives from Faulkner's awareness of the recalcitrance of the social world. *Light in August* is the most socially inflected of Faulkner's novels, sensitive to the limitations and distortions society imposes on human conduct. In none of his other books is there such a full rendering of the force of dead institutions and dead matter as they exact their tyranny upon men. That men are not free to choose

their world and their selves, that past and present con-
spire to defeat the eager will, is a common notion in
Faulkner's books, usually explained by references to a
flaw in character or an arbitrary blow of fate. In *Light
in August*, however, the limits of freedom are defined
primarily through social co-ordinates, Christmas, in one
important sense, being simply a function of his society,
and Hightower a relic of his. The entire experience of
Christmas is that of dashing himself blindly against a
series of walls which contain his movements and frustrate his desires. He has no abstract conception of society whatever, but he learns through the most bitter
lessons that it confines and breaks the will. Aware of
how refractory his environment can be, Christmas often
reacts with a wry anticipation of suffering, an almost
comic bewilderment before the terrors of social existence.

The power of the novel has other, perhaps deeper
sources. Faulkner is never better, never more fully committed to the grandeur and misery of the human lot,
than when showing the entanglements between men,
their gift for draining one another of all strength, ex-
hausting one another of all hope and yet thereby living out their destinies. Chapter twelve of the novel, in
which the affair between Christmas and Joanna Burden
reaches its climax, is surely one of the most powerful
pieces of writing ever done by an American: a narrative which leaves one not so much with the sense of
having witnessed an ordeal as having participated in it.
All of the straining and heaving of Faulkner's prose, the
reaching out after improbable tropes, the magnification
of rhetorical effects, is justified here by the fury with
which Faulkner sets out to subject the reader to the full
weight of a human experience, driving further and further, relentlessly, to its very marrow. One can quote almost at random, though never with anything like the
power of the chapter as a whole:

It was as if she knew somehow that time was short, that autumn was almost upon her, without knowing yet the exact significance of autumn. It seemed to be instinct alone: instinct physical and instinctive denial of the wasted years. Then the tide would ebb. Then they would be stranded as behind a dying mistral, upon a spent and satiate beach, looking at one another like strangers, with hopeless and reproachful (on his part with weary: on hers with despairing) eyes.

Or again:

At first the beginning of the night was always a flood, as if the hours of light and of separation had damned up enough of the wasting stream to simulate torrent for a moment at least. But after a while the stream became too thin for that: he would go to her now with reluctance, a stranger, already backlooking; a stranger he would leave her after having sat with her in the dark bedroom . . .

But it is in Faulkner's gift for rendering selective incident, for the isolation of that critical moment in experience which, once seen, lights up the wastes behind and the darkness ahead, that *Light in August* strikes its full power. Though Faulkner may be wasteful in disposing of incidents, most of them are constructed internally with a firm economy. I have remarked on the frequency of confrontations in *Light in August*, and it is the confrontation which, in this book as in others, is a major resource in the composition of scenes. There is the rending moment Byron Bunch asks Hightower to save Christmas, and the two men stand face to face, aware that an irrevocable choice has to be made. There is the meeting between Christmas and the "leatherhard woman"—is it not between Christmas and the entire alien world?—when he asks, "Can you tell me what day this is?" There is the dialogue, nervous and amusing, between Armstid and his wife after she decides to give her egg money to Lena—a page of incomparable prose. There is the brush between Burch and the old Negro woman who is to send his message to the sheriff for "a dollar cash." And others: moments of climax, two human beings revealed in urgency.

Such incidents occur within a progression of scenes, some dramatic and others pictorial. The dramatic scenes, like Christmas himself, are all turbulence and motion. The pictorial scenes, forming compositions of contrast, are projected in static depth: Lena Grove on the road, a picture light-filled, airy, pastel; Percy Grimm over the body of Christmas, a picture stroked with darkness.

Finally, there is one other source of the novel's power: In *The Sound and the Fury* and *As I Lay Dying* everything is subordinated to the voices of the characters—the voices are the characters. But in *Light in August* a new voice is heard, partly Faulkner's own and partly, as it were, an over-voice speaking for the memories and conscience of a people. Sounding again and again a characteristic note of anguish, lingering over the spectacle of heroism and failure, this voice records the entire Yoknapatawpha story. It will be heard again, in Faulkner's later books.

V

Pylon

Pylon, A STORY OF RECKLESS AND DISTRAUGHT RACING
pilots, leans upon an important idea, evokes a notable
setting, and reflects some of Faulkner's deepest concerns. Though set beyond Yoknapatawpha, the book is
hardly a venture into alien territory. No other American
writer has known so much about the life of the racing
pilots or been so sensitive to their estrangement from
society, both as a problem in itself and a possible occasion for larger themes. New Orleans, the locale of the
novel, was familiar to Faulkner, and he was not likely to
spoil it with second-hand effects, as he later would some
of the Northern scenes in *The Wild Palms*. Yet these
possibilities are seldom realized in the work itself: *Pylon*
is a strained and ineffectual novel, alternately sluggish
and frenetic in quality. What went wrong, and where?

Pylon appeared in 1935, after a prolific half-decade
in which Faulkner had published four remarkable novels and many stories. A decline of energies was neither
surprising nor alarming: *Pylon* is far less ambitious in
scope and technique than its predecessors. This, however, is merely to say that it comes in a smaller frame

than *Light in August,* not yet to inquire why the frame is poorly constructed.

The central themes of *Pylon* are so close to us that any critical statement runs a risk of puffing the book beyond its intrinsic merit. Racing pilots, to be sure, are now a disappearing breed, and they would hardly occur to us as the most likely representatives of that rootless existence which Faulkner wished to present in *Pylon.* Yet, at least while reading the book, it is not too hard to assent to them as modern instances of *anomie,* that extreme state of estrangement which leaves men without attachment, value or place. Nor is it hard to see that Faulkner is trying to capture not merely their local qualities but also their essential condition of lostness. Through the unnamed reporter who serves as a central observer in *Pylon,* Faulkner provides a wry description of the pilots which, if not quite meant to be taken literally, does release a major theme:

> They aint human, you see. No ties; no place where you were born and have to go back to it now and then even if it's only to hate the damn place good and comfortable for a day or two. From coast to coast and Canada in summer and Mexico in winter, with one suitcase and the same canopener because three can live on one canopener as easy as one or twelve.—Wherever they can find enough folks in one place to advance them enough money to get there and pay for the gasoline afterward. Because they dont need money; it aint money they are after anymore than it's glory because the glory can only last until the next race and so maybe it aint even until tomorrow. . . .

This idea, one feels, should have proved fruitful for a novelist like Faulkner; yet in practice it did not. *Pylon* raises expectations, but mostly because of the large possibilities of the subject. It leaves a few strong impressions, but mostly impressions of disarray. It touches us, but mostly on our nerves.

One reason is that Faulkner, if he is to communicate his sense of a distinctly "modern" restlessness, needs the contrasting substance and stability of a known community—and precisely this contrast is what he lacks in *Pylon*. His best books are those set in Yoknapatawpha, not merely because it is the place he knows most intimately but also because it enables him to stand apart from, to gain some coherent relation to, his own awareness of all that we find distressing in our time. The locale, as it were, grants him some perspective on the subject. For while Faulkner is surely a modern writer, he is not really a writer of the modern city, and his capacity for evoking it never equals that of other, less gifted American novelists. His awareness of *anomie* (which we usually think of as an urban condition) comes through not in portrayals of the city, but in his marvellously concrete evocations of how the values and troubles of city life penetrate a town like Jefferson and even a hamlet like Frenchman's Bend. In *Pylon*, however, Faulkner can find no way of gaining sufficient distance from his materials, for he lacks the counter-principle of an established community and style of life. A book intended as a criticism of modern disorder thus comes to seem an example of it.

At the center of *Pylon* stands an anonymous reporter, "a scarecrow in a winter field." Through his eyes we observe the unhappy trio of Roger Shumann, flier, Jack, the jumper, and Laverne, the wife they share; and since the story largely exists in the reporter's sense of it, we must extract its meaning largely from our sense of him. But Faulkner is not quite sure what to do with this reporter, who sometimes speaks as if he had been reading too much early Eliot and sometimes as if he had been subjected to an excess of Hollywood movies about newspapermen. Highly elusive, more a literary indulgence

than a created figure, the reporter is alternately a sentimental version of the modern hero of sensibility and a
caricature of that hero. This uncertainty of intention
carries over into the treatment of the racing pilots,
so that we are never quite certain whether to regard
them as tragic victims or inert clowns. Worse still,
Faulkner uses the reporter as a vehicle for quasi-poetic
outbursts, jokes and rhetorical flourishes, all of which
may have a mild interest of their own but are decidedly
barriers to establishing a firm point of view or narrative
line. Whenever Faulkner turns to the reporter it is with
a flare of hyperbole, as if the very thought of this creature sent his rhetoric soaring: "the reporter loomed from
the hips upward for an incredible distance to where the
cadaverface hung against the dusty gloom of the city
room's upper spaces." A prostitute, suddenly endowed
with Faulkner's vocabulary, claims that taking money
from the reporter "would be like assessing the invoked
spirit at a seance. . . . with a covercharge." In effect,
the character who should order and light up the action
proves to be a grotesque figure eclipsing it—and not
even a very interesting grotesque.

There are other weaknesses. The by-play between the
reporter and his hardboiled editor is a predictable nui-
sance, in its own way as much a sign of how damaging
American "folklore" can be as some of Faulkner's rumi-
nations about the nature of women. The writing often
slips into poor Joyce: linkage ("shieldcaught" and
"propellerblurs") and dizzying runs of concrete nouns,
which presumably are to create effects of vividness but
actually clog and slow the prose. At intervals Faulkner
inserts prose-poems which could be set to verse. However, even when effective, they impede a novel which
tends to circle rather than develop its subject. Much too
long for its meager portion of incident, the book continues for sixty pages beyond the death of Roger Shumann, and the result is inevitably an anti-climax.

All these are signs of hesitation, unconscious devices

for evading a full view of the racing pilots. To form a
continuous action from lives which by necessity are dis-
continuous, is a problem to baffle any novelist. To
dramatize a situation which has already reached dead-
end, is equally troublesome. It is as if the subject were
being withheld, as if Faulkner could name but not enlarge it, so that *Pylon* comes to seem a pale signature of
another, unwritten, far more arresting book. Between
writer and reader there accumulates a cloud of tension
—language quivering far beyond any need of the narrative, language made to do more than it possibly can.

What *Pylon* might have been, Faulkner himself suggested in a review he once wrote of a test pilot's memoirs: "I had hoped to find a kind of embryo, a still
formless forerunner or symptom of a folklore of speed,
the high speed of today. . . ." But for all his passionate
interest in "the high speed of today" Faulkner could
not convert this subject into a coherent drama; the material remains hot, amorphous, unformed in his hands.
There are of course some fine touches: the "family" of
Shumann, Jack and Laverne, so baleful a travesty of
the bourgeois family yet with a last-ditch integrity of its
own; the frightfulness of their submission to the machine and its speed, from which they still manage to
derive something like a human way and a human order.
Faulkner shows no lack of kindliness toward the pilots,
nor does he hasten to judge them; the trouble is that,
having begun with his perception of so "far-out" a version of mankind, he cannot do very much with it in the
novel. Perhaps no one could; perhaps there are some
perceptions a novelist should reach only at the end of
a book, not at the beginning. In any case, *Pylon* is a
prime example of the way a subject intimately known
can master the artist who knows it.

Once before Faulkner had turned to this subject, and
far more successfully, perhaps because he had kept it
tightly reigned in a short story, where development matters far less than initial shock of presentation. "Death

Drag," a small masterpiece, examines the life of stunt pilots with a terseness and fluency *Pylon* lacks. Swooping quickly onto a Southern town, much as might the fliers themselves, the story limits itself to a single incident and single locale. Attention is forced upon one figure and kept there: a Jewish merchant whom bankruptcy has driven to the extreme resort of stunt jumping. He is ready to risk his neck again and again, but with the final stubbornness of Faulkner's characters he insists that each risk is worth a hundred dollars. He will not jump for less.

The idea of a Jewish merchant, turned stunt jumper, might well have been dismissed—it probably could not even have been imagined—by a novelist more familiar with the urban middle class; but as so often in Faulkner's work one is grateful here for his indifference to the plausible. Precisely the savage incongruity of his conception allows him to dissolve the problem of verisimilitude and give the story a certain weird power. Its hero comes to seem a large aching figure of modern loneliness, Jew and stunt jumper, alien by birth and need. Disliking and admiring, warring upon and uniting with his protagonist, Faulkner is able to establish a firm point of view through harsh economy and ironic qualification —exactly what he does not do in *Pylon*.

VI

Absalom, Absalom!

FROM ITS PLACE AT THE CENTER OF THE YOKNAPATAWPHA
chronicle, *Absalom, Absalom!* gains an unsuspected stature; what might in isolation seem a stylized frenzy becomes a tone essentially right, even if all but unbearable. How else, one must concede, could Faulkner manage this lacerating return to the past? how else invest
his one great story—the story of the fall of the homeland—with that foaming intensity which might warrant
still another recapitulation?

Because the material of *Absalom, Absalom!* was so
oppressively close to him, Faulkner had to find a device
by which to hold it, so to speak, in suspension; and that
device, perhaps the only possible one, was Gothic. To
see the purpose and shape of the novel one must understand why Faulkner draped it in Gothic remnants; that
much done, as I have attempted in earlier pages, the
book can be judged as a solitary work of art and its
three main elements examined: the character of Sutpen,
the formal arrangement of its parts, and its uses of language.

In several of Faulkner's books a character is quickly
placed beyond the perimeter of the ordinary; he stands

apart from and towers over the smaller creatures of his world. But no other Faulkner character rules a book so completely as does Sutpen in *Absalom, Absalom!* To be sure, there are several striking figures in the novel: old Mr. Coldfield starving himself in protest against the War; Wash Jones cackling the news of Charles Bon's death and years later cutting off Sutpen's head; Velery Bon marrying a lamp-black Negro woman so as to flaunt his own ambiguous status before anyone, whatever his color. But these figures are not meant to be more than full-scale. Present even when not seen and dominating whether seen or present, Sutpen fills the novel with his smoldering resolution. Ike McCaslin may be great in renunciation but is certainly no hero of action; Lucas Beauchamp shows a touch of greatness, more in what he refuses to do than what he does. Sutpen, by contrast, would force the world to his ends, butting his will against society and sluggish matter. This single-mindedness is less fanaticism than a grandiose solipsism. He is ready to exalt his purposes above the wisdom and convenience of society not because he despises it but because it does not exist for him; and he has the terrifying gift for hurrying to his fate without an interval of self-doubt.

Given his energy, his commitment to a mythic role, his impersonality in behalf of personal vindication—given all this, what could the mirror of his mind reflect but a rigid duplicate of his behavior? Faulkner's neglect of his inner consciousness is, therefore, no failure at all; for this hero need not be analyzed, he need only be stared at from a distance as he lives out his destiny.

Few things in Faulkner astonish more than Sutpen's power to make himself continuously felt, shading each scene, altering the lives of all who touch or cross him. The most frightening evidence of this power is Miss Rosa Coldfield's narrative; as she rises to a hysteria of eloquence in castigating Sutpen, she unwittingly declares herself still subject to him. Were Sutpen to call from the grave, she would run to him, an appalled accessory to his diabolism. Everything in the novel, from Charles Bon's doglike yearning for acceptance by his father to Wash Jones's ultimate rearing-up to manhood, is a function of Sutpen's will. Even Shreve McCannon, the Canadian boy who helps Quentin Compson unravel the story, acknowledges the spell of this "djinn."

Throughout the book Sutpen is finely controlled, his doom an inevitable culmination of his first clash with the world. In a curious sense Sutpen is innocent: he cannot fully reckon the consequences of what he does, the hunger that impels his "design" remains obscure to him. He harms no one out of malice or sadism, and he is not without sense, particularly in the hysterical years after the War. These very qualities serve only to intensify his destructiveness, for Faulkner realizes that a premeditated and impersonal act of evil can be more dangerous than a quick impulse to hurt.

Sutpen's life is a gesture of *hubris*; what prevents him from rising to the greatness of the tragic hero is a failure in self-recognition. For such a climax the stage seems ready: few heroes fall as low as Sutpen, selling candy sticks in a backwoods store, drinking with Wash Jones, trying to perpetuate his line through Wash Jones's granddaughter. But Sutpen is not struck by a weight of knowledge; he neither searches the source of his fall nor assumes responsibility for its consequences. Because he is incapable of that rending of the self and tearing out of pride which forms the tragic element, Sutpen dies as he lived, a satanic hero subject only to his own willfulness and the check of fate. He is one of the few heroes in twentieth-century literature who rejects the passive role, but his creator is sufficiently a writer of the century to withhold from him the cleansing ritual of tragedy.

Sutpen cannot be grasped through a single apprehension; he must be reached through ambush and obstacle, confusion and delay. Only gradually do we accustom ourselves to a man who is large and grand in his evil, and from this complexity in his character follows the technique of the novel. Suspensions of incident, apparent mystifications, calculated affronts to continuity—all are used in behalf of Faulkner's executive purpose. Not that every patch of rhetoric or device of structure springs from ineffable necessity; Faulkner is a craftsman all too ready to indulge his excesses. But the remark of one critic that Faulkner's complex structures derive "from an obscure and profligate confusion, a manifest absence of purpose rather than from an elaborate and coherent aim" is, at least with regard to *Absalom, Absalom!*, wrong.

Of all Faulkner's novels *Absalom, Absalom!* most nearly approaches structural perfection. By presenting the effect of an action on spectator or narrator long before the action itself, the novel creates sudden eddies of confusion but also arouses large and exciting expectations; the emotional response of the characters, instead of stemming from the action, prepares for it. As long as action is adequate to expectation there need be no complaint, and for the most part it is—though one occasionally feels, as in reading Conrad's *Heart of Darkness,* that nothing could possibly satisfy all the hungers the author has stirred.

The scrambling of narrative cause and emotional response, like the circling back and forth in time, is warranted by the material itself. Faulkner is probing the under-tissues of the past, fearful that he will locate some secret evil—and that is hardly to be done with brisk directness. Were he merely trying to render the past in pictorial breadth and immediacy, *Absalom, Absalom!* would surely contain many more dramatic scenes than it does; but since Faulkner and his central narrator Quentin Compson refuse to surrender to the past even as they cannot tear themselves away from it, the story is told rather than shown. And since the past is to be seen as a "dead time," an almost incredible passage of nightmare, it must be presented in a ghostly flatness.

The sense of time established by the novel is thus extraordinarily complex and ingenious. Through a delicate interaction of past times, the novel creates an illusion of timelessness within a strongly felt present. Time stops; the past is not recaptured in flow—that would be too dangerous—but broken, as it were, into a series of stills. And is this not one reason for Faulkner's use of Gothic—to stare at the "old ghost times" from a preserving distance?

For the details of this scheme there can be only praise: for the flares of inventiveness (Charles Bon's love letter, written with stove polish captured from Northern stores); for the moments of scenic vividness (Sutpen taking his bride through the Yoknapatawpha mob while his Negro slaves follow with burning pine knots); for the shrewd placing of cues in the first chapter (by the first fifteen pages the novel has been presented in miniature); for the balanced relation between chapters, each carrying its fraction of the story and together forming a comprehensive pattern; and for the skill with which Faulkner deploys shocks of climax (Judith watching the Negro wrestlers in the stable, Wash Jones announcing Bon's death, Miss Rosa Coldfield revealing her suspicion that Henry Sutpen has returned to the abandoned Sutpen's Hundred).

While several characters are employed as narrators, they are not sharply distinguished, their voices blending in a drone of eloquence. Mr. Warren Beck has claimed that Faulkner "does make some differences among these voices: Miss Rosa rambles and ejaculates with spinsterish emotion, Mr. Compson is elaborately and sometimes parenthetically ironic, Quentin is most sensitively imaginative and melancholy, Shreve most detached and humorous." These differences are indeed present, though not drawn quite so sharply as Mr. Beck formulates them. It does not very much matter, since Faulkner is trying not to identify the narrators as individuals but to arrange them as parts in a chorus. They seem, in the structure of the book, echoes of a master ventriloquist rather than individual voices attuned to Jamesian distinctions.

The style of *Absalom, Absalom!* is a style of oratory. Since *Light in August,* Faulkner's books have been filled with the cadences of a voice distinct from the voices of his characters. In *Intruder in the Dust* the oratory is "official," groaning with echoes of addresses to Southern state legislatures and Fourth of July speeches in town squares. In *Absalom, Absalom!* it is quite different: private in source and accent, and uncongenial to public expectation. The voice we now hear speaks for an afflicted imagination, a grieved mind familiar with the springs of evil. If the oratory of *Intruder in the Dust* echoes the facile rhythms of public persuasion, the oratory of *Absalom, Absalom!* evokes an image of a man rasping from the heart, perhaps to no one but himself. Its effect is similar to that which Morris Croll, in a fine essay on "The Baroque Style," attributes to certain sixteenth-century rhetoricians: "Their purpose was to portray, not a thought, but a mind thinking, or in Pascal's words, *la peinture de la pensée.* They knew that an idea separated from the act of experiencing it is not the idea that was experienced." The convolutions of Faulkner's prose mirror the reactions of his narrators to the events they uncover. And Faulkner's reactions too; the voice of the ventriloquist laments in romantic cadence and lifts to appalled shriek. *Absalom, Absalom!* is packed with the incongruities and complexities of consciousness, each sentence approaching, remembering, analyzing and modifying the material that has preceded it. "To this end," remarks Warren Beck, "the sentence as a rhetorical unit (however strained) is made to hold diverse yet related elements in a sort of saturated solution. . . ." And sometimes, one might add, supersaturated.

The uses to which Faulkner puts this prose are surprisingly varied, though *Absalom, Absalom!* is not a book likely to shine in isolated quotation. But for all its dragging periods, its lifeless Latinisms, its shrillness of pitch, the writing is often capable of fine modulations of tone and a wide range of effects. The prose can specify place and thing, forming a sensuous composition of objects, as in this description of the Sutpen cabin. The boy Sutpen sees it after being humiliated at the planter's house:

> . . . . home, as he came out of the woods and approached it, still hidden yet, and looked at it—the rough partly rotten log walls, the sagging roof whose missing shingles they did not replace but just set pans and buckets under the leaks, the lean-to room which they used for kitchen and which was all right because in good weather it didn't even matter that it had no chimney since they did not attempt to use it at all when it rained, and his sister pumping rhythmic up and down above a washtub in the yard, her back toward him, shapeless in a calico dress and a pair of the old man's shoes unlaced and flapping above her bare ankles and broad in the beam as a cow, the very labor she was doing brutish and stupidly out of all proportion to its reward: the very primary essence of labor, toil, reduced to its crude absolute which only a beast could and would endure. . . .

A tumbling series of images is suddenly pulled short by a colon and then capped by a general statement, Faulkner's language summarizing what the boy has already seen as picture. Another characteristic device is the rendering of human figures in nonhuman terms, the writhing prose suddenly coming to an intense stop, as in this portrait of Sutpen the man:

> A man with a big frame but gaunt now almost to emaciation, with a short reddish beard which resembled a disguise and above which his pale eyes

had a quality at once visionary and alert, ruthless and reposed in a face whose flesh had the appearance of pottery, of having been colored by that oven's fever either of soul or environment, deeper than sun alone beneath a dead impervious surface as of glazed clay.

A full stop emphasized, the passage resumes from a greater removal in space and time, and the writing consequently loses some of its feverishness:

That was what they saw, though it was years before the town learned that that was all which he possessed at the time—the strong spent horse and the clothes on his back and a small saddle bag scarcely large enough to contain the spare linen and the razors, and the two pistols . . . with the butts worn smooth as pickhandles and which he used with the precision of knitting needles. . . .

Voices are recorded with rending clarity. Here is Wash Jones, who has overheard Sutpen's insult to his granddaughter:

" 'But I never expected that, Kernel! You known I never!' until maybe the granddaughter stirred and spoke querulously again and he went and quieted her and returned to talk to himself again but careful now, quiet now since Sutpen was close enough to hear him easy, without shouting: 'You know I never. You know I never expected or asked or wanted nothing from arra living man but what I expected from you. And I never asked that. I didn't think hit would need: I just said to myself *I don't need to. What need has a fellow like Wash Jones to question or doubt the man that General Lee himself said in a hand-wrote ticket that he was brave?* Brave' (and maybe it would be loud again, forgetting again) 'Brave! Better if narra one of them had ever rid back in '65' thinking *Better if his*

*kind and mine too had never drawn the breath of
life on this earth. Better that all who remain of us
be blasted from the face of it than that another
Wash Jones should see his whole life shredded
from him and shrivel away like a dried shuck
thrown onto the fire. . . ."*

At its most intense, the prose of *Absalom, Absalom!*
summons the very quality of pain. The following lines
on the marriage of Velery Bon, which blend effects of
great mass with great speed, should be read as if they
were being cried out by an overwrought voice:

. . . . there followed something like a year composed of a succession of periods of utter immobil-
ity like a broken cinema film, which the white-col-
ored man who had married her spent on his back
recovering from the last mauling he had received,
in frowzy stinking rooms in places—towns and cities
—which likewise had no names to her, broken by
other periods, intervals, of furious and incomprehensible and apparently reasonless moving, progression—a maelstrom of faces and bodies through
which the man thrust, dragging her behind him,
toward or from what, driven by what fury which
would not let him rest, she did not know, each one
to end, finish, as the one before it so that it was almost a ritual. The man apparently hunting out situations in order to flaunt and fling the ape-like
body of his charcoal companion in the faces of all
and any who would retaliate: the negro stevedores
and deckhands who thought he was a white man
and believed it only the more strongly when he
denied it; the white men who, when he said he was
a negro, believed that he lied in order to save his
skin, or worse: from sheer besotment of sexual
perversion; in either case the result the same: the
man with body and limbs almost as light and delicate as a girl's giving the first blow, usually un-

armed and heedless of the numbers opposing him, with that same fury and implacability and physical imperviousness to pain and punishment, neither cursing nor panting, but laughing.

For its major fault in style—the absence of change of pace—only the book itself can serve as illustration. It lacks, and badly needs, those intervals of quiet and warmth provided in other Faulkner novels by such characters as Lena Grove and Dilsey. But a second characteristic weakness, a forcing of imagery, can be shown by quotation. The child Rosa Coldfield is facing Sutpen:

> The face, the smallest face in the company, watching him across the table with still and curious and profound intensity as though she had actually had some intimation gained from that rapport with the fluid cradle of events (time) which she had acquired or cultivated by listening behind closed doors not to what she heard there, but by becoming supine and receptive, incapable of either discrimination or opinion or incredulity, listening to the prefever's temperature of disaster, which makes soothsayers and sometimes makes them right, and of the future catastrophe in which the ogre-face of her childhood would apparently vanish so completely that she would agree to marry the late owner of it.

Faulkner himself seems uncertain about the communicative value of this sentence: how else explain the parenthesis? "Rapport with the fluid cradle," "temperature of a prefever," "the unfortunate soothsayers"—all are signs of language being driven to do the work of imagination. Sometimes the writing breaks down in an excess of abstraction, as in sentences which cannot be read but must be deciphered:

It was probably just peaceful despair and relief at final and complete abnegation, now that Judith was about to immolate the frustration's vicarious recompense into the living fairy tale.

But the distinctive vice in the writing of *Absalom, Absalom!* is that the prose is whipped into a fury so habitual as to become mechanical and dull, a mere surrender to the monstrous. The following passage, a romantic debris, illustrates Gautier's remark that "the decadent style is the last effort of language to express everything to the last extremity":

> *Or perhaps it is no lack of courage either: not cowardice which will not face that sickness somewhere at the prime foundation of this factual scheme from which the prisoner soul, miasmaldistillant, wroils ever upward sunward, tugs its tenuous prisoner arteries and veins and prisoning in its turn that spark, that dream, which, as the globy and complete instant of its freedom mirrors and repeats (repeats? creates, reduces to a fragile evanescent iridescent sphere) all of space and time and messy earth, relicts the seething and anonymous miasmal mass which in all the years of time has taught itself no boon of death but only how to recreate. . . .*

These quotations may suggest somewhat the range of style in *Absalom, Absalom!*; and while their juxtaposition is necessary for a properly modulated judgment, it must be remembered that the book is an integral work of art in which success and failure can be distinguished but not separated. An artist deserves to be accepted, ultimately, in his completeness—his clarity and obscurity. Faulkner's greatest risk, *Absalom, Absalom!* is never likely to be read widely; it is for *aficionados* willing to satisfy the large and sometimes excessive demands it makes upon attention. Wild, twisted and occasionally absurd, the novel has, nonetheless, the fearful impressiveness which comes when a writer has driven his vision to an extreme.

VII

The Wild Palms

MOST OF FAULKNER'S INFLUENTIAL CRITICS HAVE AGREED that *The Wild Palms* is a failure and that its two intersecting stories—"Wild Palms" and "Old Man"—need not be printed together as they were in the original edition. In his *Portable Faulkner* Malcolm Cowley reprints "Old Man" by itself; other editors and publishers have followed his lead. I propose to question this view, both as regards the structure and value of the novel. By looking somewhat closely at their plots, it should be possible to see whether the two parts of the book are genuinely bound together through theme and atmosphere.

A study in middle-class romanticism, "Wild Palms" is probably the most depressing and painful narrative Faulkner has ever written, if only because the self-destruction of its characters proceeds from a desire in itself admirable. The story opens at the point where the disintegration of its leading figures is almost complete. Charlotte Rittenmeyer, a young woman of powerful ego and compulsive sexuality, and Harry Wilbourne, a rather pliant hospital interne, leave New Orleans after a brief, intense love affair. Charlotte abandons a conventional marriage, Harry the promise of a conventional career. Together they seek a life beyond the city, uncertain whether their rebellion is against bourgeois norms or the very fact of society itself. This confusion of purpose is to be a major source of their troubles, for only if controlled by a precise awareness of both goal and limits could their flight possibly succeed. Soon their behavior seems a painful demonstration of how perilous the romantic view of life can be, how violently it can exhaust and then consume those who are most loyal to it—romantic in this instance signifying a refusal to live by any terms except those which cannot be enforced. As Charlotte tells Harry:

> "Listen; it's got to be all honeymoon, always. Forever and ever, until one of us dies. It can't be anything else. Either heaven, or hell; no comfortable safe peaceful purgatory between for you and me to wait in until good behavior or forbearance or shame or repentance overtakes us."

Charlotte is not a fool; if she were, "Wild Palms" could not build up to the tension it does. She can be so fanatically self-destructive as to demand "all honeymoon, always," but she can also express her outlook in terms that are more impressive: " 'They say love dies, between two people. That's wrong. It doesn't die. It just leaves you, goes away, if you are not good enough, worthy enough. It doesn't die; you're the one that dies.' "

The two young people believe they are turning to a blazing sensuous life, an utter purity of instinct and touch. Their relationship is eagerly, programmatically physical; only the clash of bodies, they feel, is an act free of social deceit. Charlotte wants no disabling or melting tenderness. She makes love to Harry by "striking her body against him hard, not in caress but exactly as she would grasp him by the hair to wake him from sleep." The comparison is acute. Vital enough to strain

for a release of suppressed energies, courageous and admirable in her readiness to take chances, Charlotte de-
ceives herself only in supposing that an unencumbered
act of natural living, an embrace of the sun, can be a
sufficient means toward personal fulfillment.

Charlotte and Harry wander off to Chicago; they
have difficulty in finding work but that is not their most
vexing problem. What really troubles them is that in
rejecting the impersonality of the city and the deadness
of middle-class existence they cannot find a way of life
that might transcend the violence of their rejection.
They trap themselves in a frozen gesture of protest, beyond which they cannot move. As soon as they begin
eating regularly they wonder if they are not in danger
of sliding into bourgeois complacence. To avoid this
danger they abandon the city, moving to a desolate
mining camp in Utah. Faulkner is crucially involved in
this flight, for he has nothing in common with the
middle-aged wisdom—perhaps merely middle-aged resignation—which would sneer at it. He is always ready
to extend his sympathy to anyone who lives to the limit
of power or desire. Yet he is also perceptive enough to
see that the flight of Charlotte and Harry is fundamentally incoherent; and in a biting passage he shows the
civilization from which the lovers had fled seeping into
the remote mining camp—Harry is cheated of his wage,
he has to perform an illegal abortion on the supervisor's
wife: again, the moral ugliness of the city.

Destitute, the lovers drift south, back to the Mississippi basin, where Charlotte reveals herself to be pregnant and Harry performs his second abortion, this time
a failure. Now, in the opening scene of the novel, the
couple is living in penniless inertia, Charlotte resentful
and broken, Harry a cartoon of the independent man
he had hoped to become. When Charlotte dies after
the botched abortion, Harry is taken off to prison, there
to nurture memories of love, in safety and emptiness—
yet not total emptiness, for in some desperate way he

remains faithful to the vision he could not live by. In jail he experiences a moment of overwhelming, perhaps fulfilling, reflection:

> . . . . and in the night he could face it, thinking *Not could. Will. I want to. So it is the old meat after all, no matter how old. Because if memory exists outside the flesh it won't be memory because it won't know what it remembers so when she became not then half of memory became not and if I become not then all of remembering will cease to be.* —*Yes,* he thought, *between grief and nothing I will take grief.*

Thrusting its characters into a fierce, somewhat muddled yet ultimately impressive struggle against reality, "Wild Palms" elevates that struggle to a principle of life: "Love and suffering are the same thing . . . the value of love is the sum of what you have to pay for it . . ." But the story also complicates and partly abandons this romantic view. The destination of flight proves as unacceptable as its starting point, perhaps because finally there is not so much difference between the two. Neither society nor isolation can satisfy Charlotte, and Harry's satisfaction is but a dependency of hers. Living too rigidly by a preconceived code, which transforms her passion for freedom into a mode of self-tyranny, she destroys both herself and her lover. The destruction, as I say, is impressive, far more so than the usual run of adjustments; still, it is destruction. So streaked is the life of Charlotte and Harry with the neurotic colors of the world they refuse, so fanatical is their fear of a settled existence, that they render themselves unfit for the natural haven to which they would retire. In the most extreme rural isolation they continue to live by the standards of the city, and at the end it is Harry's ineptness at abortion, a technique of civilization, which causes their catastrophe. Between the city from which they would escape and the natural world they dream of finding, there is no intermediate area of shade and rest. The act of rejection having consumed their energies, nothing remains for the act of living.

A simpler story, "Old Man" concerns an unnamed Mississippi convict. "About twenty-five, flat-stomached, with a sunburned face and Indian-black hair and pale, china-colored, outraged eyes," this tall convict, as he is called, is one of Faulkner's natural men. Limited in mental power, he is superbly in control of his immediate environment and endowed with a fine, even over-acute sense of moral obligation. He has, however, grown so accustomed to the harsh security of the prison-farm that he does not take his freedom when he can.

Brought with other convicts to the Mississippi River to help control a flood, the tall convict is instructed to rescue a woman perched on a cypress snag and a man stranded on a cotton-house roof. Rowing furiously, he finds the woman, who is far gone in pregnancy, and through his instinctive skill in adapting himself to the river they manage to drift crazily down the flood waters. Neither intimacy nor affection sweetens the life of convict and woman; two people thrown together, they must cooperate if they are to survive, but more they will not do. It is a kind of honesty, free of the language of romanticism.

The woman, helped by the convict, has her baby. At the first mouth of the river they end their journey, settling in Cajun country where the convict becomes the partner of an alligator hunter and again, with his marvellous affinity to natural life, proves highly successful. For the first time freedom tempts him: "*Yes. I reckon I had done forgot how good making money was. Being let to make it . . . I had forgot how it is to work.*" But a malicious twist of circumstances forces him to leave the alligator country and return to the prison area. "Yonder's the boat," he tells the prison guard, "and here's the woman. But I never did find that bastard on the cotton house." A final cut of injustice, the climax of "Old Man" is the sentencing of the convict to ten more years for "attempted escape." What impresses him more than this injustice, however, is his memory of how difficult it was to rid himself of the pregnant woman during his time of freedom. As in most Faulkner novels, freedom proves to be elusive, and when found, limited.

Simply sketched, these are the plots of "Wild Palms" and "Old Man." Faulkner has divided each story into five parts, alternating a part from one with a part from the other. To follow the pattern of the novel, envisage an interweaving of the following sections:

"WILD PALMS"	"OLD MAN"
1. Failure of abortion, Charlotte close to death.	2. Convict leaves for flood.
3. Flashback: Charlotte and Harry leave New Orleans.	4. "Lost" in flood.
5. Flashback: drifting from country to Chicago.	6. Drifting with pregnant woman on flood waters.
7. Flashback: haven in a mining camp.	8. Haven with Cajun.
9. Charlotte's death, Harry's imprisonment.	10. Return to prison.

Is this crossing of stories mechanical and arbitrary? That Faulkner may have composed them separately and then spliced them together is not very important; the problem is, why did he connect these two stories in so unusual a way? He has said that "I did send both stories to the publisher separately and they were rejected because they were too short. So I alternated the chapters of them." But he has also referred to *The Wild Palms* as one story of "two types of love," and has recently declared that he wrote "Old Man" to bring the other

story "back to pitch" by contrast with its "antithesis."
The remark is very shrewd, for "Wild Palms" by itself
is almost intolerably painful and needs very much to be
brought "back to pitch." [3]

Even a glance at the above pattern of the novel
should show some rough parallels between the two
stories. There is the possibility that if taken together
they will yield a dissonant irony or "counterpoint"
which neither could yield alone. The possibility that
any two stories by the same writer could be made to
yield interesting contrasts and continuities cannot be
denied; but at stake here is a relation much more detailed and intimate. Each story charts an escape from
confinement to a temporary and qualified freedom and
then to an ultimate, still more confining imprisonment.
Two opposite intentions—one derived from extreme
romanticism, the other a grudging response to circumstances—lead to the exhaustion of both intern and convict, and in that exhaustion there is a kind of common
fate. Coincidence this may be, but the correspondences
and joined oppositions between the two stories are so
numerous and suggestive that we are obliged to take
them seriously, as elements of a literary design.

[3] *Interviewer:* "Are the two unrelated themes in *The Wild
Palms* brought together in one book for any symbolic purpose? Is
it as certain critics intimate a kind of esthetic counterpoint, or is
it merely haphazard?"
Faulkner: "No, no. That was one story—the story of Charlotte
Rittenmeyer and Harry Wilbourne, who sacrificed everything
for love, and then lost that. I did not know it would be two separate stories until after I had started the book. When I reached the
end of what is now the first section of *The Wild Palms*, I realized
suddenly that something was missing, it needed emphasis, something to lift it like counterpoint in music. So I wrote on the *Old
Man* story until *The Wild Palms* story rose back to pitch. Then I
stopped the *Old Man* story at what is now its first section, and
took up *The Wild Palms* story until it began to sag. Then I raised
it to pitch again with another section of its antithesis, which is
the story of a man who got his love and spent the rest of the book
fleeing from it. . . ."

Paris Review, Spring 1956.

Both the intern and the convict are socially homeless men who discover how intractable the world can be and how little one's hopes and ideas can move it. They are radically different men, but in the end the differences do not count for much. The convict is more resourceful and creative than the intern, perhaps because he is able to float upon the wave of circumstance rather than to dash himself against it. Where the convict helps bring new life into the world, though admittedly life for which he has no more than an abstract responsibility, the intern can only abort—and that unsuccessfully. In "Old Man" the life principle does rise to a rueful sort of triumph, yet it brings neither resolution nor satisfaction: it is a triumph that simply keeps the circle of existence turning. In "Wild Palms" a diseased hunger, not merely for life but also for clamping a rigid scheme upon life, becomes the catastrophe.

Still, in noting such contrasts we should not succumb to any pat assumption that Faulkner favors the convict over the intern, primitivism over civilization, nature over the city. The survival of the convict, ambiguous triumph though it may be, has been purchased at the price of a self-denial of personality, a rather awesome suppression of natural desires, and a loss of the vision of freedom—none of which either the characters of "Wild Palms" or Faulkner himself could tolerate. If in some sense the convict proves to be more durable than the intern, there is no reason (except an indulgence in literary primitivism) to ignore the cost of that durability. At the end both men are trapped, and the familiar distinction between will and fate, character and circumstance tends to be dissolved into an ironic perception of their gradual merger.

Faulkner, I think, lends conditional assent to the rebellion of Charlotte and Harry, but with the tacit warning that rebellion becomes suicidal if pressed to a fanatic grasping for total freedom. "Old Man," with a good many sardonic qualifications, proposes a counterterm of acceptance, but this too is carried to an extreme by the convict. Rebellion and acceptance, by the end of the book, shrink in importance beside the over-whelming fact of exhaustion.

In both stories the imprisonment of the leading char-acter is at least partly due to excesses of conscience and ideal, and Faulkner's implicit conclusion—one may de-cide—is that our emotional economies thrive best on restraint. But when reading the novel itself, this is hardly the impression one is left with. The idea of re-straint as a possible resolution seems, for this book, too distant and contained, inadequately rooted in the ac-tual happenings, not a genuine option. At some points it may dimly visit us, but the true and overpowering energy of the book is directed toward another idea: that a suffering man encounters his fate through a total fulfillment of his chosen task. Both intern and convict are caught up in floods, the one a flood of passion, the other a flood of nature, the one a flood wilfully sought after, the other a flood that cannot be escaped. It hardly matters, the novel seems to say, which kind of flood a man lives through; in the end it will break him, and his humanity will be marked by the fullness, the courage of his struggle against it.

The Wild Palms points to the gap between aspiration and realization, the way in which the incommensurable becomes man's fate; and it suggests that this fate can-not be avoided through rebellion or acceptance, aggres-sion or passivity. In the world of this novel, as perhaps in the world of all Faulkner's novels, emotion exceeds possibility, response fails situation, and for the welling of human passion there is never a properly receptive object. It is perceptions such as these which lie behind the strain and fury of Faulkner's prose, and which it is the function of the double plot in *The Wild Palms* both to release and qualify.

By starting "Wild Palms" near its climax, Faulkner magnifies its painfulness, for once he turns to trace the history of Charlotte and Harry it is impossible to feel any hope for them. "Old Man," beginning at its chronological outset and sweeping forward with a humorous and rhythmic equanimity, serves as emotional ballast. The two stories, it should be noted, are of unequal merit and interest, "Old Man" being much superior simply as a piece of writing and "Wild Palms" touching upon problems that are likely to seem more urgent to a modern reader. "Old Man" releases Faulkner's gifts for the fabulous, a mode of narrative in which a human action can be subsumed under, and gain magnitude from, an imposing event in nature. "Wild Palms," because so much of the behavior of its two lovers is caused by a wilfulness bordering on stupidity, cannot reach the tragic limit toward which it strains. Uncertain in its treatment of Northern locale, the story suffers even more seriously from a grating hysteria, an eagerness to hoard and multiply pain, and Faulkner's desperate— yet in some ways admirable—involvement with the two lovers. But whatever one's judgment of the stories, they do sustain each other through a counterpoint of response and should be printed, as they were offered, together.

Probably of little use to anyone but himself, Faulkner's device of alternating sections of the two stories may be judged a *tour de force* that partly succeeds. The novel can hardly be considered one of Faulkner's major works: it will not bear comparison with *The Sound and the Fury* or *Light in August*. But neither is it the negligible effort or outright failure it is too often taken to be. A serious, occasionally distinguished book which contains some admirable parts and is arresting in its general scheme and intent, *The Wild Palms* merits our respect.

VIII

The Hamlet

The Hamlet, LIKE *Go Down Moses,* IS AN EPISODIC novel, its four long sections self-contained yet interrelated in theme and plot. This structure has aroused a certain amount of skeptical inquiry about the "looseness" of the novel—a skepticism that is to be preferred in principle to the wide-eyed exegesis which for some years became a staple of Faulkner criticism.

Like other critical terms, "looseness" is embarrassingly vague, and it frequently involves a confusion between description and judgment. In speaking earlier of the looseness of *Light in August* I suggested that within the scheme Faulkner chose for the novel its parts are arranged with insufficient economy; and this, whether right or wrong, constitutes a critical judgment. But to say that *The Hamlet* has a loose frame is merely to describe, or begin to describe, the organization of the book, not yet to determine its propriety or effectiveness. The episodic form can of course be used to great effect: one need only think of the picaresque tales or read such a masterpiece as Lermontov's *A Hero of Our Time.* Picaresque, by its very nature, inclines toward the episodic, and in *The Hamlet* a strand of it is present—the rise of Flem Snopes being an inverted and sinister picaresque adventure. A strand of the tall tale is also present, and that genre too, with its need to court its subject through indirection, inclines toward the episodic.

To condemn *The Hamlet* because it is loosely strung is, therefore, pointless: for that is the way it was meant to be. What we do have a right to suggest is that at several points Faulkner's use of the episodic form proves unsuccessful, that there is a looseness in the sense of wasteful construction. Several episodes, particularly the flashback to the Varners and the account of the fanatical schoolteacher, Labove, may be necessary to the total scheme of the novel, but they do not carry sufficient weight, either as additions to or complications of the central story, to justify their length. The idiot's affair with the cow and the account of Houston's marriage, while fascinating in their own right and necessary to the development of the book, suffer from verbal overrichness, Faulkner's growing fondness for letting a good passage run wild. Still, these are minor quarrels with the way Faulkner has employed his scheme of organization, not with the scheme itself.

However imperfect, *The Hamlet* is a unified piece of work. It unfolds a major theme—the demoralization of Frenchman's Bend by the Snopes clan—and directs attention to it with reasonable frequency. I say, reasonable frequency because in this kind of novel we cannot expect the close patterning of behavior and reflection which a novel by James or Conrad teaches us to follow, nor the accumulation of dramatic and substantiating material which a naturalistic novel offers. Faulkner spirals his narrative with a leisurely amusement, a relish in seeing it spin and twist through the hands—and mouths—of a variety of characters. Its rhythm is that of Frenchman's Bend, not Memphis and not Jefferson. But if the method is one of calculated wandering, the effect is that of utter inexorability. The spiralling, the circling, the meandering, all have a way of coming back, with a comic exasperation and finality, to the steady growth of Flem's power. Given Flem, there can hardly be any choice.

If the novel does not progress on a strict and austere plot line, there are within each section parallel sets of events, rotating, as several critics have remarked, about the economics of trading and the hazards of love, public and private activities which both occasion and mirror Flem's history. Thus a kind of progression is to be observed, a progression through slow and apparently haphazard increment or—to change the figure—through a series of ambushes, all of which reveal that, no matter what the situation or who opposes him, Flem Snopes cannot be stopped in Frenchman's Bend.

Still more important for creating a unity of effect is the presence of Ratliff, weaving in and out reassuringly in his buck-board and watching, first with a mildly contemptuous amusement and then with growing alarm, the descent of the Snopeses. The best drawn and most intelligent of Faulkner's observers, Ratliff provides a fineness of response which, until the very last section of the book, keeps it from collapsing into mere anecdote. And together with Ratliff there is a strongly felt community—felt all the more as we witness its decay—which serves as the locus for the physical and spiritual action. In *Light in August* the community is also a powerful force, but in a negative way: it is the background against which a drama of isolation is enacted, it represents the unsatisfied desire of the characters for a place that is truly theirs. From the community's indifference, its failure to recognize Christmas and Hightower, follows the tragedy of the book. In *The Hamlet*, however, the community is in the forefront of the action; Will Varner is its economic center at least until Snopes takes over, the bench before the Varner store is its meeting place, and Ratliff, though a back-country traveler occasionally passing through Frenchman's Bend, serves the farmers as spokesman, critic and defender. The shift of power from Varner to Snopes is, in an oblique sort of way, a social revolution; while the Varners may be ambiable parasites, the Snopeses are deadly reptiles; and once Flem and his cousins are done with it, Frenchman's Bend has been shattered. It is a shift of power which Faulkner depicts with his customary shrewdness. Will Varner is not very kind, he cheats his customers regularly, he behaves with an almost feudal imperiousness. Flem Snopes mimics the manners of the Varner family in a way that is at once comic, pathetic and ominous; but soon it becomes clear, as the neighboring farmers sense uneasily, that he is a creature of an entirely different cut, a grotesque who is beyond ordinary comprehension or assuagement. Flem shows neither affection nor anger, he wastes no time in friendly chatter, he acts with impersonal correctness and he conspicuously avoids cheating the customers. On the spectrum of values that the book establishes Flem stands at the opposite pole from Ratliff, and in the intensifying opposition between the two, which finds its way into almost all the stories and anecdotes, there is still another source of structural unity.

But I doubt that the true values of *The Hamlet* can finally be apprehended through discussions of structural unity. For this is a novel that needs most of all to be appreciated as a performance or a series of performances, in somewhat the same way that one appreciates the novels of Dickens. Of all Faulkner's works *The Hamlet* is the most brilliantly colored, the most racily inventive. Only a virtuoso superbly indifferent to the cautions of his craft would bring together such a pell-mell of genres and perspectives, of tones and emotions: the hilarious tall tale of Ab Snopes and Pat Stamper swapping a horse that had been blown up with a "bicycle pump valve under its hide just inside the nigh fore-shoulder"; the dithyramb, at once touching and repellent, of Ike Snopes's romance with a cow; the fierce

Western humor of the spotted horses story (perhaps
Faulkner's greatest feat of virtuosity) followed directly
by the pathos of Mrs. Armstid's begging her husband
not to waste her last five dollars on one of the ponies;
the fury of the Houston episode juxtaposed to the
macabre grubbiness of Mink Snopes's feud with his
more successful cousin; the fantasy in which Flem
Snopes routs the devil out of hell; the outrageous by-
play of Mrs. Varner's complaint that Eula's pregnancy
is disturbing her nap; and the skepticism, humane and
troubled, with which Ratliff watches, intervenes, and
then falls in defeat. A prose extravaganza striking almost every pitch and mood, among all of Faulkner's
books *The Hamlet* is the most astonishing testimony
to his native endowments, his sheer abundance of imaginative gifts. It is, in the very best sense, Faulkner's
last great display.

Yet for all its brilliance, this very mixture of tones occasionally seems gratuitous, a surplus of splendor. That
Ike Snopes's affair with Houston's cow should be cele-
brated in a style both the extreme and parody of romantic prose, that this prose should nevertheless convey the
moral superiority of poor befuddled Ike over the ice-
blooded Flem, is all very fine; we realize that the section is meant as an ironic fantasia, the high romantic
lyricism blended to a subject matter poor and pathetic,
and soon we learn to respond to both elements, keeping
one in a firm relation to the other; yet, as it goes on and
on, page after dazzling page, it defeats its own end, the
parody by its very excess parodying itself. The thun-
derous proliferation of images, the swooning rhythms,
the mere incidental tumults of vividness:

Now he can see again. Again his head interrupts,
then replaces as once more he breaks with drinking
the reversed drinking of his drowned and fading
image. It is the well of days, the still and insatiable
aperture of earth. It holds in tranquil paradox of

suspended precipitation dawn, noon, and sunset; yesterday, today, and tomorrow—star-spawn and hieroglyph, the fierce white dying rose, then gradual and invincible speeding up to and into slack-flood's coronal of nympholept noon. Then ebb's afternoon, until at last the morning, noon and afternoon flow back, drain the sky and creep leaf by voiceless leaf. . . .

Such excesses—for all that we know they are meant to be excesses and to amuse and dismay us as excesses— seem too wilful, too completely mere displays of virtuosity. Occasionally they transform the novel into an exercise in verbalism alternately brilliant and blinding, for Faulkner is all too ready to honor distractions, all too ready to let his language drag him passionately where it will. Even as the novel has a clearly and deeply articulated theme to which he returns with a bravado impossible to dislike, even as the recurrent matching of kinds of love and kinds of trades provides a series of accretive variations on the theme, the book itself is often directionless in its movement from word to word.

The strength of *The Hamlet*, a strength typical of Faulkner, lies in its characterization. The Snopes horde is etched with a bitter precision. What could provide a finer insight into human character than the picture of Flem helping Varner at his yearly settlement with the farmers, "Varner and Snopes resembling the white trader and his native parrot-taught headman in an African outpost"? Or the picture of Mink Snopes thinking, after he has been thrown into a cell with a group of Negroes, "Are they going to feed them niggers before they do a white man?" Seldom has Faulkner noted manners with more ease and humor than in his description of the way two farmers, Bookwright and Tull, share a meal in a Jefferson restaurant; seldom has he more strikingly shown that even in so narrow a world as Frenchman's Bend there can be an immense range of conduct and character.

Finally, however, it is Ratliff who is the triumph of the book, a major even if a marred triumph at the end. For the habitual Faulkner reader it comes as a decided pleasure to find at the center of the novel a truly intelligent and rational man who neither moons nor rants, who is not overwhelmed by neurotic fantasies, who is capable of disinterested observation, who has a highly developed moral sense yet extends his sympathy to those he judges, even to some of the Snopeses. It is a pleasure Faulkner himself seems to share, as in this quick notation of Ratliff during his telling of the Ab Snopes—Pat Stamper tale:

> He laughed, for the first time, quietly, invisible to his hearers though they knew exactly how he would look at the moment as well as if they could see him, easy and relaxed in his chair, with his lean brown pleasant shrewd face, in his faded clean blue shirt, with that same air of perpetual bachelorhood. . . .

Ratliff is an extremely likable man in a way few of Faulkner's people can be said to be; weaving in and out of the book like a cooling stream, he brings the clarity of his mind and the wit of his speech to the turbid struggle of Frenchman's Bend.

Precisely because he is so impressive, it comes as something of a shock when Ratliff finally succumbs to avarice—or perhaps to the "game" of his struggle with the Snopeses—and allows himself to be taken in by Flem. Suddenly, without sufficient warning or preparation, Ratliff proves as gullible as Flem's other victims (they have been fully prepared in their roles as victims) and, like them, is deceived by the hoary trick of "salting" the earth with hidden treasure. But how, one wonders, can this be? In the absence of fuller evidence or explanation, can we credit so extreme and disastrous a conversion of character? One understands why Ratliff's collapse is needed at the end of the book to round off Flem's triumph; but one questions the plausibility, within the terms of behavior set up by Faulkner himself, of Ratliff's sudden loss of intelligence and wit.

Raised by the text, these questions are not answered by it. Nor can they be dismissed as a request for extra-literary information of the kind desired by people who speculate, say, as to whether the marriage between Emma Woodhouse and Mr. Knightley proved successful. What is wanted here is an explanation of an event within the novel, not outside or after it, and Faulkner's failure to provide the necessary grounding is another mark of the carelessness and perhaps worse, the arbitrariness which accompany his prodigious talent. That it is possible, indeed quite easy, for critics to offer *post hoc* rationalizations for Ratliff's sudden collapse—e.g., he too has been caught up in the corruption of Snopesism, a corruption that stains everything in its path— hardly disposes of my objection: for this tells us why Faulkner should have wanted the ending he chose, not whether he has adequately prepared for it. That a Ratliff might "really" succumb is no matter: for in a crucial sense the requirements of probability are more stringent in a novel than in life.[4] No, it will not do:

_____

[4] One Faulkner critic, Viola Hopkins, trying to justify Faulkner's treatment of Ratliff at the end of *The Hamlet*, has remarked that "Varner, in the first part, tells Ratliff that the Frenchman's mansion is the only thing he ever bought that he could not sell to anyone. Ratliff is thereby convinced of its value; his faith in Varner's shrewdness is so deep that he never doubts that 'Uncle Will' has deliberately not sold it because the land has secret assets. This makes it plausible that Ratliff should fall prey to Flem's trick in the last book, for he is prepared to believe that treasure has been buried there . . ." I do not think this will suffice. For if Ratliff is so convinced of Varner's shrewdness, how does he explain to himself Varner's readiness to let the presumably valuable property go to Flem Snopes? And shouldn't this readiness lead Ratliff to reexamine his faith in Varner's shrewdness?

Ratliff, one of Faulkner's finest characters, is marred at
the end of *The Hamlet*, as he will be even more so in
The Town.

In *The Hamlet*, then, Faulkner's strength and weakness are most glaringly contrasted. The strength mani-
fests itself in those sections in which he does not eclipse
his characters with clouds of rhetoric but allows their
speech and gestures to emerge freely. The talk of the
novel is superb—richly idiomatic, virile, brimming with
high humor. When Faulkner confines himself to concrete presentation, be it of the wild chase of the ponies
or the chatter of I. O. Snopes or the conversation of
Ratliff, *The Hamlet* achieves the order of creative
genius. Distinctly American in idiom and observation,
heavily sprinkled with the salt of folk humor, the book
releases its theme with an ease that is a sign of true
seriousness. In its relaxed flow of anecdote and comedy
lies its depths of meaning—in the passage, for example,
in which Flem and Ratliff, cagily trading, face each
other in the store, their very gestures reflecting the social and moral meanings of their struggle.

The weakness—again characteristic of Faulkner—appears in those sections where language overruns matter.
The "voice" that was heard in *Light in August* and
Absalom, Absalom! is now, at times, disastrously magnified—and without reason or necessity; for whatever
justification the subjects of these earlier novels may
have provided for their varying allotments of rhetoric,
the subject of *The Hamlet* provides little indeed. In
the earlier novels Faulkner's uncertain relation to his
protagonists and their inability to live up to their roles
may have been a cause for the rhetoric in and out of
quotation marks; but in *The Hamlet* Ratliff certainly
needs no help, he speaks well enough for himself, and

More important, however, is the trumped-up, rather childish
nature of this denouement for a book which deals with decidedly
serious issues. As is often to be the case in Faulkner's later novels,
the plot is inadequate to the matter it is meant to convey.

Faulkner's distance from him is exactly right, permitting both affection and irony. One now has the impression that the famous Faulkner style has become so involved in a romantic infatuation with words as words, so much an object fascinating in itself, that it undermines the intention behind the work.

Once made, these discriminations may be put a little to the side. For with all its faults, *The Hamlet* is a superb comic novel. As a product of the American folk imagination, with its sharply jostling exaggerations and silences, its broad jokes and sudden tenderness, *The Hamlet* ranks second only to *Huckleberry Finn*. Of all the literary modes, humor is notoriously the most indifferent to critical inspection, and in the end there is little to do but point and appreciate. Confronted with Faulkner's marvels, the critic must feel that his task, though not irrelevant, is all but helpless; and may wish to cry out with the judge in the novel, "I can't stand no more. I won't! This court's adjourned. Adjourned!"

IX

The Bear

FOR THE MODERN CRITIC, *"The Bear"* BRISTLES MIGHTILY with temptations. It is a pivotal work in Faulkner's career, the first sign of emergence from the despair of his major novels; it invites a multiplicity of subtle readings; it shares in certain qualities of myth; it carries a religious aura, mixing Christian sentiment and natural piety; it is constructed in a manner alternately pleasing and puzzling; and it is often a lovely, as sometimes an exalted, piece of writing. The elements of the story are complex and at times even discordant, but they all seem designed to impress upon us one decisive meaning, one striking effect, one final gesture. Any reader who persists through the difficult stretches of "The Bear"— even if meanwhile losing some of the detail—will apprehend this encompassing gesture in Isaac McCaslin's moment of repudiation and renewal, his choice of a private incarnation by which to break past a heritage of guilt and modestly assume a new life.

So resonant is the story and so large the temptation to read it as Faulknerian scripture rather than as a work of the imagination, that there may be some advantage in applying to it a literary version of Occam's Razor.

Some advantage, that is, in wilfully narrowing one's critical scope, dismissing many aspects of the story that merit discussion, and focussing upon a single problem of structure. I do this on particular and pragmatic grounds, not from a belief that "structual analysis" is quite the magical key to literature that some critics suppose. In the case of "The Bear" we can gain a better sense of its value and possible weakness by asking: What is the relation between its two main parts?—between the sections devoted to the hunt and the counterbalancing Section IV in which Isaac McCaslin, parrying the conventional views of his cousin Edmonds, decides to renounce his patrimony?

Something has been said in earlier pages about the significance of "The Bear," both as a solitary work and with regard to its place in Faulkner's development. Several interpretations of the story are possible, though not all are equally cogent. Finding in Faulkner's earlier books "an atmosphere like that of the Old Testament" —a comparison useful only if taken somewhat lightly, —R. W. B. Lewis describes "The Bear" as Faulkner's "first sustained venture toward the more hopeful and liberated world after the Incarnation." It may also be read as a story about the disappearance of the Southern frontier in the 1880's, a portrait of "a boy growing up and growing wiser along the border between the civilized and the still unspoiled," and "another American *bildungsroman* of a boy growing up in America, with all the special obstacles to moral maturity which our culture has erected. . . ."

There are other possibilities: perhaps, as with *Moby Dick*, too many. But it should be remembered that such readings take one (the figure is a matter of choice) very deeply into the work or very far from its surface of narrative. In its more successful half, "The Bear" is primarily a story about a group of Southern men and a young boy who go off on a yearly hunt—a story that can hardly be grasped if taken in narrowly realistic terms, but cannot be grasped at all if those terms are dismissed. Symbolic elements pertaining to myth, anthropology, and psychology are surely present in the story, and it needs no more than the usual second-hand acquaintance with *The Golden Bough* to notice that the bear lends itself to totemic uses. That such elements are present in "The Bear" is clear enough, Faulkner himself referring to it as a "pageant-rite." But the sophisticated reader, he more than others, is in danger of neglecting the literal surface of the story, the story as a performance, in behalf of the meanings that can be dredged up from it. He is in danger of forgetting that the bear, like the white whale, is a "real" animal, not a specter of allegory, and in this case an animal with fur and four legs. An important critical issue is at stake here: that the critic should be loyal to the surface of the text, persist in treating it in its own terms as much as he possibly can, and "convert" to other terms only when and if there is no alternative.

The point is worth remembering as one turns to the story's structure, section by section. The first three present the hunt in full magnificence and awe. Each year the boy, Isaac McCaslin, accompanies several Yoknapatawpha men as they go off to the wilderness to encounter Old Ben, the great and aged bear. The hunt becomes a kind of ritual-game in which the virtues of restraint, honor, and comradeship are embodied. Finally, during a hunt that occurs in Isaac's sixteenth year, Old Ben is killed and an era in the life of the community concluded. Section IV then presents Isaac five years later, at the age of twenty-one, when he is to receive both the money and land of his family. In a long discussion, often a harangue, with his cousin Cass Edmonds—which includes a flashback to a time five years earlier when he discovered, by leafing through family records, the guilts that stain his heritage—Isaac decides to repudiate money, power, status. Section V, which concludes the story, occurs during Isaac's eighteenth year, that is, three years earlier than Section IV. It shows him returning to the wilderness and finding the community of hunters dissolved, the forest invaded by the lumber companies and the one remaining hunter reduced to a petulant incoherence. Nothing has survived of the traditional comeliness and grace of the hunt.

Now it is not difficult to see why Faulkner violated strict chronological order and placed the events of Isaac McCaslin's twenty-first year before those of his eighteenth. The return at eighteen to the violated forest is a cue withheld and thereby all the more eagerly awaited, which helps bring together the implications suggested by the preceding parts of the story. Given what Isaac McCaslin has been trained to be in the first three sections, a youth who will prove worthy of Sam Fathers and Old Ben, it follows that his moral gesture in Section IV should seem right and inevitable—particularly when we learn, in Section V at the end of the story, what happened to him at eighteen. As often in other books, Faulkner presents the consequence of an action before allowing us to apprehend its full cause, thereby involving us in a process of discovery together with one or more central figures of the work.

To say this, however, is not yet to confront the problem which troubles many readers of "The Bear": what to make of the *relation* between Section IV and the rest of the story. If "The Bear" is considered primarily in thematic terms—that is, if we think of its parts primarily as tokens in a conceptualized scheme—it is easy enough to establish the necessity for Isaac McCaslin's long debate with Edmonds and the spray of memory that accompanies it. Isaac's earlier experience with Sam Fathers and Old Ben is a kind of baptism or initiation into the manly, heroic possibilities of life: it educates him, sets a model for him. His gesture at twenty-one then becomes a fulfillment of the vow to virtue which constituted the "ritual-pageant" of the

earlier pages. The decision in the commissary to remove himself from the continuity of social power is
foreshadowed and even made inevitable by the events
of the wilderness.

Now these claims for Section IV have a considerable
appeal, but I would submit that it is in the nature of the
literary experience that they cannot be decisive. What
finally matters is not our ability to tie together the parts
of the story by thematic or conceptual links; what matters is their worked-out, their dramatic relation. And
this relation is always more problematical, both more
and less successfully achieved, than any structural paraphrase can suggest. Indeed, it may be impossible to
give an adequate description of the structure of a novel
or poem without at the same time proposing some
valuation of both the work as a whole and its parts.

If Section IV were omitted, "The Bear" would profit
in several ways: the narrative would flow more evenly
toward its climax; there would be a more pleasing unity
of tone; and the meaning, never reduced to the brittle
terms of Isaac's political and moral speculations, would
be allowed to rest in a fine implication. Since Section
IV is, so to speak, contained in the previous three, it
might be desirable for the story to resolve itself on the
plane of the implicit, with the ritual in the wilderness
suggesting, but no more than suggesting, its relation to
the life of Yoknapatawpha. And in fact, this is pretty
much the way Faulkner first printed "The Bear" in its
magazine version.

The loss, however, would also be considerable. What
Section IV now does is to give the story social and historical density, the ceremony in the forest reverberating
into the life of the town; it provides an abrasive disruption of the idyllic nostalgia previously accumulated;
and it keeps Faulkner's meaning from the confinements
of abstract morality. As we now have it, "The Bear"
comes to seem a dialectically richer, more troubling
work that demands greater energy and attention from

its readers than did the earlier version—perhaps a less perfect work but also a more interesting one.

But whatever the justification for the presence of Section IV, there can hardly be any doubt that as a piece of writing it is much inferior to the other parts. The first three sections, a chanted recital of the "pageant-rite" in the wilderness, comprise one of Faulkner's major achievements in style, a style at once richly chromatic and singularly direct. Of Faulkner's more important literary techniques—the stream-of-consciousness in which the character's voice takes over and the stream-of-eloquence in which an anonymous voice assumes control—"The Bear" is second only to "Red Leaves" as a happy example of the latter. The voice in "The Bear" is that of an observer who knows all the actors, Isaac McCaslin and Sam Fathers and Major DeSpain; more important, it is the voice not so much of an individual as of the community itself, the collective conscience of Yoknapatawpha. First heard in *Light in August* it pervades most of Faulkner's later books, its very pitch and inflection conveying moral judgment.

Section IV, by contrast, represents a sharp drop in both composition and content. Its style is also a style of eloquence, but often inflated to Confederate rhetoric. The dialogue between McCaslin and Edmonds, fanciful, flowery and pretentious, is of a kind seldom heard on heaven or earth. As sheer narrative, the section breaks down several times, forcing the reader to fumble his way through cryptic references and opaque prose. It may be urged that similar demands are made by other works of literature, and this is true; the only question, here as elsewhere, is whether the reward is worth the labor. Whenever Faulkner troubles to dramatize Section IV, as in Isaac's visit to the freed slave Fonsiba, the writing is unforgettably strong; but the bulk of the section is merely an exchange of sentiments, frequently interesting but slowed and stopped by passages of turgidity. The hunt sections present an image and the

commissary section records a discourse. The two are related somewhat like poem and paraphrase; and while
there is no need to suppose that in literature discourse
is always inferior to image, for Faulkner something of
the sort is usually true.

At the end "The Bear" returns to its opening style:
"He went back to the camp once more . . ." Just as the
story began with a glimpse of the bear prowling through
the wilderness, so it ends with an equally powerful
vignette: Boon Hogganbeck, the man who killed the
bear, sitting beneath a tree, his gun dismembered and
his mind shriveled by hysteria. Nothing in Section IV
—neither the entries in the family record-book nor the
eloquence of Isaac McCaslin as he castigates the sins of
the South and praises the virtues of the Negroes—nothing can equal these images: the bear in the forest, the
man beneath the tree. Perhaps it is the point and purpose of the story to show that nothing can.

X

A Note
on the Stories

ONE OF FAULKNER'S CRITICS, MALCOLM COWLEY, HAS
argued that he is "best and most nearly himself either
in long stories like "'The Bear' . . . and 'Spotted
Horses' . . . ; or else in the Yoknapatawpha saga as a
whole. He is most effective in dealing with the total
situation that is always present in his mind as a pattern
of the South; or else in shorter units that can be conceived and written in a single burst of creative effort."
Faulkner, writes Cowley, "is not primarily a novelist;
that is, his best stories do not occur in book-length units
of 70,000 to 150,000 words."

Despite its obvious exaggerations—can one believe
that the author of *The Sound and the Fury* and *Light
in August* "is not primarily a novelist"?—Cowley's
statement does contain a valid insight. The insight, as I
take it, is that Faulkner has shown himself a master of
a certain kind of narrative which lies somewhere between the short story and the novel in length
and approach. Among twentieth-century writers only

D. H. Lawrence displays a comparable assurance in handling fictions of this length, though the uses to which he puts them are of course radically different from those of Faulkner. Lawrence composes miniature novels or novelettes while Faulkner writes long tales: the first suggesting the compactness and impersonality of formal art, the second an expansiveness and inclusiveness which often seems, though it is not, merely artless.

Certain sections of *Go Down, Moses* and *The Hamlet*, the rhapsodic intervals of *Requiem for a Nun*, perhaps even some parts of Faulkner's more conventionally put-together novels—these may be seen as long tales, which by their nature can forgo the strict requirements of the short story or the somewhat less strict requirements of the novel. In the tale there is no inescapable need for either that economy of effect which is essential to the short story or for those complications of social behavior that are often depicted in the novel. Sharing some of the qualities of fable and myth, the tale inclines toward simplicity of action, spaciousness and freedom of invention, and the elaboration of familiar or folk anecdote. It can spin or wander off on its own, in a flexible style that allows for a wide variety of effects, ranging from bardic eloquence to native humor.

If there is some justification for distinguishing between the tale and the novelette, there is at least as much for distinguishing between the short story and the tale. Faulkner, to be sure, has narratives which overlap both of these latter types and cannot easily be lodged in either. Yet it is more than pedantry to claim some usefulness for the distinction: if only to suggest, for the moment, that Faulkner is a master of the tale but no more than occasionally distinguished in the short story.

During the years in which he published his novels Faulkner also wrote several dozen stories, most of which were collected in one large volume in 1950. As a testi-

monial to Faulkner's zeal for experiment and devotion
to craft, the book has a certain impressiveness. It displays several facets of his work that are somewhat hidden in the novels; it helps a great deal in filling out the
fictional world of Yoknapatawpha; it shows his ability
to handle a genre for which he is not naturally suited;
it ranges in feeling, like the novels themselves, from
blazing intensity to mild affability; it contains a half-
dozen brilliant pieces of writing and another dozen
reasonably good ones; but it does not persuade one that
Faulkner, the story writer, is nearly as important or
original as Faulkner, the novelist. Let me put the matter
somewhat drastically: had Hemingway not written his
short stories, the history of the genre in America and
Europe would be radically different from what it is,
while if Faulkner had not written his stories that history
would not have been seriously affected.

The rhythms of Faulkner's imagination are too spacious—they can seldom be contained within a whole
book—for him to achieve the symbolic or dramatic concentration required by the story. Where a "natural"
story writer like Hemingway secretes his meaning in a
few phrases, a few spare notations of gesture and speech,
Faulkner allows his impressions and thoughts to spool
their way through multitudes of incident and labyrinths
of language. Hemingway tends to see his material as an
event self-contained and compact, Faulkner as a history
sprawling into the past and future. Hemingway labors
to exclude all but the barest essentials, Faulkner to pack
in whatever may qualify, complicate and enrich. Hemingway turns to the moment of revelation, Faulkner to
whatever made it possible and whatever may come beyond it. Hemingway tries to light up the living moment
with a sudden ironic or poignant flare, Faulkner prefers
to peel away layers of the past. The kind of imagination that dips into history and brings up legend or myth
is naturally at home in the long tale but not likely to be
at ease with the short story.

For the Faulkner student, a number of stories quite trivial in themselves take on a special interest through their relation to the Yoknapatawpha novels, as sidelights on those we already have and possible scenarios for those yet to come. "There Was a Queen," though its intrinsic value is slight, helps one to understand Faulkner in his aspect of traditional Southerner: it is a good corrective for those critics, like the author of this book, who tend to be impatient with that side of Faulkner. "Centaur in Brass," a story in which a Snopes is defeated by two Negro laborers, provides insight into the Faulkner who is something more than a traditional Southerner: it is recommended to other critics. Though valuable in illuminating the novels, such stories are rarely notable in their own right. Lacking in Faulkner's customary plasticity, and often intended as fictional memoranda or footnotes that had better be hurried onto paper, they seem hardly to possess a life of their own.

Two other groups of stories should be noted briefly. One consists of several experiments in writing about the supernatural, and as a rule these are both uncertain in purpose and embarrassingly "soft" in quality. The other is concerned, more importantly, with the life of soldiers in the First World War. Though skillful enough, these stories read like specimens of a class rather than uniquely achieved works of art: specimens of the war story in which a writer, facing an experience impossible to order, invokes its terror and pity through tense announcements and pregnant understatement. They are essentially derivative stories, crowded with echoes of the literary generation of Cummings, Dos Passos and inevitably, Hemingway. What, asks a character in "Ad Astra" of his soldier friend, "what is your destiny except to be dead?"

Finally, there remains a small group of stories that merit inclusion in any choice of Faulkner's best work. Without pretending an exhaustive analysis, which in any case they do not need, I should like to single them out, roughly in a rising curve of merit.

"Death Drag" is one of the few Faulkner stories that creates a dramatic fable with a distinct beginning and a firm end, and creates it in terms of the emotional urgency that the story form requires. Faulkner's inclination to circle about his material, to rehearse his ideas again and again, to brood over his dilemmas and his people—a great strength in his novels but not finally appropriate to the short story—is here suspended, simply because the central idea or *donnée* of the story is so conclusive there is no need for him to do anything but allow it to move, uncluttered, toward its end. "Mountain Victory," probably Faulkner's best piece of writing about the Civil War, also develops a self-sufficient and economical action. As it describes a meeting between a Southern officer making his way home from defeat and a Tennessee family sympathetic to the North, "Mountain Victory" becomes an instance of Faulkner's gift for dramatizing conflicts between styles of life, in this case between plantation aristocrat and poor-white mountaineer. The story is controlled by one of Faulkner's most personal and authentic insights: the way an encounter between strangers can overwhelm their lives, or perhaps more accurately, the way such an encounter seems to become a force apart from and superior to their individual wills, shaping their existence with a kind of sublime ruthlessness. Not only does "Mountain Victory" dramatize this encounter between aristocrat and mountaineers as they clash in fear and strangeness; it also brings together two sides of Faulkner's imagination, that which cherishes a conventional image and that which digs to the bed-rock of realism. The Southern officer blends chivalry and wisdom in the accredited Faulkner prescription; his Negro servant of the "ole massuh" school is vivid enough to be faintly annoying; but the Tennessee family is superbly rendered, harsh, violent, gaunt in its loveless poverty.

"A Rose for Emily," Faulkner's most famous though hardly his best story, invites treatment as a parable and arouses strong responses, sometimes acute revulsion, because of its dependence on the power of shock. The effort to read the story in terms of the relations between South and North, with Miss Emily representing the decadent South and Homer Barron the rapacious North, seems to me ill-conceived in general and indefensible in particular. Still, a story so pointed and glaring in its effects does solicit a stringent line of interpretation. Perhaps the one least likely to do violence is that it presents a generalized parable about the decay of human sensibility from false gentility to genteel perversion, which has its obvious historical references but not those alone. Simply as a story, "A Rose for Emily" may seem too dependent on its climax of shock, particularly in its hair-raising final sentence. The shock, however, is largely justified by the theme of the story—given this theme, there can be no way of realizing it except through shock. Notable for its control of atmospheric detail, the story is a *tour de force*, and for all its undeniable power, too cunningly a *tour de force*. While reading it one is reminded of those chill fables in which Hemingway and Ring Lardner score moral points but do not let quite enough "life" break through the taut surface of their prose. Perhaps one's sense of the story's limitations can be summed up by saying that finally it calls our attention not to its represented material but to the canny skill with which Faulkner manipulates it.

Two of Faulkner's best stories are related to his novels, "Wash," which he later wove into *Absalom, Absalom!*, and "Barn Burning," which concerns the Snopes clan. "Wash" is a taut narrative, violent and self-contained, which depicts the death of Colonel Sutpen at the hands of Wash Jones, a poor white hanger-on who had served Sutpen for decades, had allowed him to seduce his granddaughter not merely with easy consent but even with a sort of pride, but now finally rebels against the arrogance Sutpen displays upon discovering the child is a girl. Only to a slight extent is the story dependent on *Absalom, Absalom!*, where we can learn more fully the reasons for Sutpen's disappointment at not having a male heir. But the significance of Sutpen's contempt for Milly Jones and of the ultimate rebellion, the final trace of dignity in Wash Jones—these are fully and bitterly evoked in the story itself.

Equally dramatic is "Barn Burning," a story about the boy, Sarty Snopes, who is one of the very few Snopeses treated sympathetically by Faulkner. As it uncovers Sarty's dismay over learning his father is an arsonist, "Barn Burning" is a story painful to read in the way any story must be which records a boy's discovery that he is trapped in the soiled and dishonest world of his elders. Between the violent father, overwhelmed by his sense of humiliation, and the boy who wishes to be loyal even while recognizing him as a wrongdoer, there is a forceful and often poignant counterposition of feeling; and the story is saved from trickiness by Faulkner's control, his mute understanding of the father and sympathy for the boy.

Faulkner's two best stories—the two that may, I think, be called "great"—are "That Evening Sun" and "Red Leaves." The first of these, told by Quentin Compson, portrays the fear of a Negro servant that her estranged husband will murder her during the night. Written in dialogue which flits about the action but never quite touches it, the story evokes an aura of primitive terror—the image of a human being waiting to be killed by another. Basically, however, "That Evening Sun" is not about the Negro characters at all. In the end it becomes clear that the incident of the Negroes has been used merely as a test for the moral stamina of the Compsons. Throughout the story the Compsons "do" virtually nothing, but in their reactions to the closeness of death—their pity or indifference, their generosity or selfishness—they are brought to distinct being. "That Evening Sun" is a triumph of indirect presentment, art by ricochet.

"Red Leaves" deals with the death of the Indian chief, Issetibbeha, in early Yoknapatawpha, and the flight and eventual capture of his Negro body servant, who must be buried, according to the custom of the tribe, with his master. This story—unquestionably a masterpiece—has the air of a folk tale or miniature epic. Composed with delicate gravity, it encompasses Faulkner's most genuine themes: the cycle of flight from and reconciliation to one's fate, the use of submissiveness as a means of self-preservation, the value of dignity in defeat and tact in victory. Neither rhetorical nor underwritten, "Red Leaves" employs a swaying bardic prose and a few symbols—the snake, the mud, the gourd—with precise economy. In twentieth-century American fiction only one or two short pieces— "The Snows of Kilimanjaro," "The Triumph of the Egg"—form so compact and inevitable a fable of life. More than any other of his stories, "Red Leaves" embodies Faulkner's feeling for the outrageous mixture which is human experience, its ultimate worthiness and desperate finality.

XI

A Fable

Only a writer of very great talent, and a writer with a sublime deafness to the cautions of his craft, could have brought together so striking an ensemble of mistakes as Faulkner has in *A Fable*. An ordinary novelist, even if he were to think of doing a book about a Second Coming in the trenches of France during the First World War, would quickly brush the idea from his mind. He would notice the temptations to the solemn and the pretentious inherent in the subject; he would sense how the overarching presence of the gospels, forcing upon him an intolerable comparison, might make his own work seem petty and insipid; he would reflect upon the grave difficulties, perhaps even the undesirability, of using the Christ as a central figure in a serious novel. True, it was precisely by ignoring cautions of a comparable, though admittedly lesser, kind that Faulkner wrote some of his best novels. *A Fable* suggests, however, that even a genius can push his audacity too hard.

Neither quite a fable nor a novel, an allegory nor a representation, *A Fable* is an example of the yearning so common to American writers for a "big book," a

summa of vision and experience, a final spilling-out of
the wisdom of the heart. Structured as a modern shad-
owing of the passion of Christ, it lacks the charm and
humane suppleness of the Gospel according to Mat-
thew, the text on which it partly depends. Meant as an
affirmation of man's powers and capacities, it never
resolves the contradiction between its high-minded pos-
itives and the bleak implications of a "reenactment" of
the passion. Inviting consideration as a fable, it lum-
bers through a maze of Faulknerian plot complications
and rhetorical entanglements, so that the one quality it
most conspicuously lacks is the unilinear directness of
the fable. A *Fable*, one regretfully concludes, is still another of those "distinguished" bad books that flourish
in America.

Its action takes place in France, a few months before
the end of the First World War, during a facsimile of
Holy Week. The troops are exhausted from years of
slaughter; the war drags on as a self-perpetuating mechanism tended by the general staffs on both sides. Now,
in May 1918, a French regiment has been ordered to
make an attack which the general staff and the local
commander know is doomed to futility and can lead
only to further bloodshed. But neither humane nor, as
it seems, strategic considerations matter any more; apparently beyond human check or control, the war has
acquired an insane rationale of its own.

On the Monday morning in May that the attack is
to begin, the assigned regiment simply refuses to move
from the trenches. A shadowy foreign-born corporal,
flanked by twelve disciples, has persuaded the regiment
to lay down its arms. For some time now this mutinous
platoon has been spreading the secret word of peace
and fraternity not merely among the Allied armies,
where it moves with inexplicable ease, but still more
mysteriously, among the Germans. Every enlisted man
at the front knows of this platoon and has begun to
absorb something of its message, yet the officers remain

in total ignorance, so fierce is the mute solidarity which binds the men against those above them.

Once the regiment refuses to attack, the Germans in the facing trenches also drop their guns. In a few hours the front is strangely quiet, as if life were returning to the rhythms of sanity; the troops have made their own, their separate peace. Now—it is at this point that the book opens, to dart back and forth in time—the entire regiment is hurried to the rear and the mutinous thirteen are thrust into prison. A secret conference is arranged between the Allied and German generals, which decides that ordinary soldiers must never be allowed, in violation of all the rules, to end a war at their will. But word has already spread through the ranks, and no mere imprisonment of the mutineers can so easily stop the men from trying to take their destinies into their own hands. One British soldier, formerly an officer and now through his own choice degraded to the rank of a runner, serves as Paul for the Christ-like corporal. On one level, though not the deepest level, it is he who speaks the "message" of the book:

> "Don't you see? If all of us, the whole battalion, at least one battalion, one unit out of the whole line to start it, to lead the way—leave the rifles and grenades and all behind us in the trench: simply climb barehanded out over the parapet and through the wire and then just walk on barehanded, not with our hands up for surrender but just open to show that we had nothing to hurt, harm anyone; not running, stumbling: just walking forward like free men—just one of us, one man; suppose a whole battalion of us, who want nothing except just to go home and get themselves into clean clothes and work and drink a little beer in the evening and talk and then lie down and sleep and not be afraid. And maybe, just maybe that many

Germans who don't want anything more too, to
put his or their rifles and grenades down and
climb out too with their hands empty too not for
surrender but just so every man could see there
is nothing in them to hurt or harm either. . . ."

Meanwhile the French marshal who commands the
Allied armies begins his investigation of the mutiny
by confronting the corporal in private. There occurs
between them an astonishing dialogue, heavy with the
echoes of past literature and rigid with Faulkner's straining toward ultimates, in which the marshal reveals that
the corporal is really his illegitimate son. As he delivers
orations to this new-found son on the nature and destiny of man, the marshal comes to seem a curious
mixture of historical, legendary and Biblical figures—
it is hard to say whether through deliberate intent or
mere incoherence. Acknowledging his paternity of the
Christ-figure who stands captive before him, the marshal can be seen as God the father, the stern yet just
patriarch of the Old Testament facing the prince of
peace from the New Testament. Wielding his temporal
power over millions of men with complete assurance,
he has his obvious resemblances to Marshal Foch.
Speaking of the malleability and weakness of the human
mass, he becomes a latter-day version of the Grand
Inquisitor. And as he offers the corporal his freedom on
condition he renounce his martyrdom, the marshal takes
on some of the qualities of the great Tempter. Perhaps
it is enough to say that in his power, his weariness and
his wisdom—but ultimately a limited wisdom—he is
meant to be an inclusive embodiment of the principle
of authority.

No sooner does the marshal make his offer than the
corporal rejects it, and indeed the marshal has not
really desired that it be accepted. Each of the two men
—I should say two figures or shades, since in A *Fable*

they appear as more or less than but not merely human —is driven by a sense of impersonal destiny; both feel they are reenacting a great drama and must, therefore, abide by its fated patterns. The corporal believes that the very principle of his existence requires a refusal of freedom at the price it is offered him, while the marshal knows that only if the corporal refuses can the principle for which he will be martyred receive its vindication. It is this overwhelming consciousness of repetition—both in Faulkner and as it seems, some of his major characters—which makes A *Fable* less a dramatic narrative than a sort of literary pageant entirely predictable in its dependence on the idea of fatality.

In one of the better and least overwritten scenes, a last supper is held in a jail cell, with the dirty, ignorant and unexalted mutineers fumbling for the words of grace. A Judas is revealed; a disciple named Piotr denies the corporal and later, weeping, falls before his feet; two women named Marthe and Marya wait patiently for the moment of agony; the corporal is thrust into a cell with two thieves and then shot between them. Finally, the possibility of a resurrection is suggested, though Faulkner is careful here, as throughout the book, not to insist upon a miraculous or supernatural interpretation. The aura of piety is heavy, but the demand upon belief slight.

This, in skeleton, is the main plot line of A *Fable*, and perhaps the best that can be said for the book is that Faulkner creates some moving effects whenever he remembers to stay close to this plot line. The Christian story is a forever affecting one, both to believers and skeptics, and it is possible to imagine a fiction which would depend for its power on a quiet repetition of that story unencumbered by moral or psychological novelties. That, conceivably, would be a genuine fable: simple, swift, without strain or pretension, and allowed to move on its own momentum of memory and association. To the small extent that Faulkner has written such a story—it is really a book lost within the book we have—A *Fable* has its moments.

But Faulkner, unfortunately, has not been content with anything so modest or restrained: he does not stay with the simple story at the center of his book. Whether from rhetorical self-indulgence (though one feels that in his late style Faulkner, like the sorcerer's apprentice, is no longer able to contain the torrent), or a misconceived desire to render things profound, or a failure to grasp the requirements of the fable as a form, he has chosen to work a number of subplots, set-pieces and miscellaneous passages of reflection into the book. The subplots vary from humorous byplay to rather cheap theatrical effects, from the lively tale about the racehorse which set records in the South running on three legs[5] to an immoderate quantity of tedium about French generals bowing, scraping and saluting as if they were extras in a Chaplin satire about military life. In any case, whatever the particular value or interest of these subplots may be, in their sum they seriously mar the book. Faulkner was unable to decide whether he was writing a novel or a fable, whether he was trying for a complex representational richness or a bare line of event and significance; and the result is an inharmonious mixture of the two genres. The point is not, of course, that genres must remain pure, but that the particular mixture Faulkner attempted here is almost impossible to bring off.

This problem—it is the main one, I think, in the structuring of the book—can be noticed in several ways. The Christ-figure, for example, is conceived as a strong natural leader exerting his authority with placid self-command, a man entirely without dogma or theol-

---

[5] Unquestionably this episode must have a variety of recondite implications, probably of a trinitarian nature, but since it happens to be one of the few good Faulknerian stories in the book, which can be read with pleasure and ease, I shall refrain from explicating, interpreting or symbolizing. In fact, I shall leave it alone.

ogy or even visible religion, and unlike Faulkner, free from the vice of preaching. Brought back in chains to face an inflamed mob, the corporal reveals "a face merely interested, attentive, and calm, with something else in it which none of the others had: a comprehension, understanding, utterly free of compassion, as if he had already anticipated without censure or pity the uproar. . . ." For a book that was merely concerned with depicting a mutiny among a group of soldiers and was not pressing for a whole range of multi-level meanings, such a characterization might well do. But for a book which insistently thrusts before us parallels with the story of Christ, it simply will not suffice to make the corporal into a contained but inarticulate leader. A *Fable* rouses, but does not satisfy, a desire for some detailed evidence that the corporal possesses at least some of the ethical power and *charisma* which all of Faulkner's analogical buttressing leads us to expect; that in some modest degree he shares the intellectual resources and emotional depths of the Jesus we know from the Bible. If not, the corporal is merely a naïf inspiring stricken naïfs, and the whole machinery of Biblical correspondences proves irrelevant. As it is, one suspects that Faulkner has succumbed to the sentimental heresy of regarding Christ as a divine but rather dumb ox.

Somewhat parallel strictures need to be made about the marshal. If the corporal says too little, the marshal says too much. If the corporal seems too shadowy and distant, the marshal soon comes to seem disastrously familiar, an old Faulknerian speech-maker rising to a still higher pitch, Gavin Stevens raised to the "nth" power. And if the corporal is too monolithic, a mere flat block of conception, the marshall is too protean, a mere pastiche of literary possibilities. In his visible character, as distinct from those attributes Faulkner would have us accept on faith, the corporal remains disconcertingly far from his prototype; the marshal, by contrast, runs too close to an excessive number of prototypes. For a fable the marshal is inappropriate, and for a novel he is inadequate.

Throughout the book Faulkner labors to establish a good many Biblical likenesses: the corporal's birth in a stable, his death at thirty-three, the Judas with his thirty pieces, the crown of thorns (barbed wire), the three crosses, the last supper, a series of trinities, and much more. These likenesses function in the book somewhat like rhyme in a poem: they set up a series of formal expectations which we are quite justified in wishing to have fulfilled. But too often Faulkner turns needlessly inventive or "fancy" and thwarts the very expectations he had himself aroused (as with the marshal, who does not readily fit the pattern of Biblical likenesses which in other respects is so close and detailed.) If, however, the book is seen as a novel rather than a fable, the whole structure of likenesses becomes so much dead matter interfering with the dramatization of a unique experience. H. H. Waggoner, a critic much more sympathetic than I am to Faulkner's religious impulses, has some remarks on this point which seem beyond disputing: "The effect of the realistic texture in which the Biblical allegory is embedded is to destroy the allegory. Reading the book, we have constantly to readjust our understanding as passages of vivid, but not meaningful, realism give way to Biblical echoes. A character is about to come alive for us, is almost created; but suddenly we are reminded that he is Peter or Judas or the Devil tempting Christ, and the likeness fades, the allegory seems questionable, and we find ourselves objecting that Peter or whoever was almost certainly not like this. . . . Insofar as the events and people become lifelike, fictionally real, they cease to be credible allegorical types. What moves these people is never in the last analysis anything but the author's opinions."

But what those opinions are is not so easy to say. A *Fable* is surely the book which speaks most devotedly for the later Faulkner, enlarging upon the themes of his recent pronouncements, orations and letters to newspapers. Yet, despite its many statements and mottoes about man's capacity to endure, the book suffers, I would maintain, from intellectual uncertainty and incoherence.

Critics seeking the implications of A *Fable* usually devote themselves to its elaborate network of Christian reference: that, certainly, is the place to end but perhaps there is some value in beginning elsewhere, with the neglected affinities the book has to a political-literary tradition. The idea of fraternization across the trenches was advanced during the First World War by extreme radicals like Karl Liebknecht and later became a rallying cry for such anti-war novelists as Henri Barbusse. Faulkner himself is about as removed from this tradition as any writer could be, yet in some indirect and essentially literary way it seems to have reached him in Mississippi, perhaps through some of the anti-war novels of the 'twenties. However that may be, a good part of the central action and even outlook of A *Fable* bears a remarkable closeness to the tradition of the radical or pacifist anti-war novel. That A *Fable* also contains a heavy weight of Christian material complicates but does not invalidate this point, since the main happenings of the book can be seen as quite compatible with a strict naturalism.

Presumably, then, some order and coherence might be gained for the book from its dependence on this tradition. But Faulkner, in at least two major respects, denies himself whatever advantages he could have received from it. I leave aside, as another question, whether by the mid-twentieth century it was a tradition that still had very much to offer him.

The idea of a Second Coming that is doomed to fail-

ure sets up an atmosphere of fatality and a behavior of
ritualized limitation which are in the sharpest opposition to the very rhythm of the anti-war novel that Faulkner is, in part, composing. A doomed Second Coming
means a novel that is fundamentally static, its fatalism
of conception making it into a series of set-pieces for
an action already determined, indeed, an action already
known and completed. The rhythm of the anti-war
novel however, requires an opposite assumption, for no
matter how despairing its tone or ending may seem,
it must finally be committed to the possibility of human
innovation and the value of the human will. The idea
of A *Fable* signifies limitation; the pattern of its narrative, potentiality. In terms of novelistic structure and
intellectual coherence, neither of these is necessarily
superior to the other, and Faulkner, like anyone else, is
quite free to choose between them. What he could not,
or should not have tried to do, was to choose both.

At least as damaging is the incongruity between the
asserted pacifism of A *Fable* and Faulkner's recurrent
fondness for apostrophes to military derring-do. His
work has always been troubled by a conflict between a
romantic celebration of honor and a mature reliance
upon integrity, but never in quite so severe a way. Had
he deliberately tried, Faulkner could have found no
better strategy for exposing all the triviality of his talk
about Bravery and Honor, all his boyscout admiration
for those ramrod French generals, than by a juxtaposition to the rhythm of the Passion. That this disharmony
of value mars A *Fable* is a pity; that Faulkner seems
unaware of it, a disaster.

What holds for Faulkner in regard to the tradition of
the anti-war novel is also and more importantly true in
regard to the tradition of Christian symbolism and belief.

Faulkner's attachment to Christianity in A *Fable* is of
a large and solacing kind. He is moved by symbols as-

sociated with his childhood, upbringing and region; he is moved by stories that seem to embody those human potentialities he has wished to celebrate in recent years; and above all, he is moved by the image of man as victim, man on the cross. Perhaps this last is Faulkner's deepest "conviction" about the human lot—that finally each man reaches his cross. But in itself it does not yet come to, for all that it greatly depends upon, Christian belief.

Faulkner's use of Christian materials in A *Fable* is clearly more than a literary convenience or strategy; it stems from intimate and cherished personal feelings. But the way in which he uses these materials—transforming them from the imperious claims of religion into the loose affirmations of a stoical humanism—does come to seem exceedingly "literary." He succumbs to the fault one finds in so much recent writing which tries to lean on Christian symbolism: that of regarding religion not as an absolute view of the universe, but as a "usable myth" to be appropriated in convenient portions for literary purposes. Lavish as Faulkner is in duplicating the details of Holy Week, solemn as he is in soliciting an atmosphere of pious grandeur, he is maddeningly vague—and perhaps worse, maddeningly indifferent—when it comes to Christian belief itself. In a phrase from André Gide, he wallows in the approximate. He can neither accept the Christian view of existence as literally true nor dispense with those symbols and stories which, to take on their full and proper meaning, require such an acceptance. It is a problem that strikes one on almost every page of A *Fable*, the very momentum of the narrative forcing a constant inquiry as to its terms of credence.

Faulkner repeatedly falls back upon a version of Hawthorne's "multiple-choice" technique: the technique through which the reader is allowed to interpret events as either naturalistic or miraculous. But there is an enormous difference in the way the two writers use

it. Hawthorne used it in representing human fantasies
and delusions, Faulkner in creating a replica of the
story of Christ. Intense as his affection may be for the
Christian epos, Faulkner finds himself embarrassed by
the problem of miracles, which is to say, the problem
of the supernatural, the problem of religion. The non-
chalance with which he dismisses it is, in the context of
an elaborate Christian allegory, nothing less than
breathtaking. Thus, in the dialogue between the marshal and the corporal, which is close to Faulkner's Nobel
Prize speech, we must assume that they speak for him:

> "I don't fear man. I do better: respect and admire
> him. And pride: I am ten times prouder of that
> immortality which he does possess than ever he of
> that heavenly one of his delusion. Because man
> and his folly—"
>
> "Will endure," the corporal said.
>
> "They will do more," the old general said proudly.
> "They will prevail."

And the runner, echoing the words of Nancy in *Requiem for a Nun*, declares that "Maybe what I need is
to have to meet somebody. To believe. Not in anything:
just to believe."

There are a good many remarks of this kind in A
Fable, most of them spoken by the positive characters
and, therefore, one presumes, meant to be taken seriously. In their sum they seem little more than an
example of that assuaging religiosity which has been so
characteristic of our era and is finally no more than a
symptom of the will to faith or, often enough, the
absence of faith.[6] That Faulkner cares to endorse

---

[6] That Faulkner personally accepts this religious sentimentalism
comes through quite clearly in his interview with the *Paris Review*. Christianity, he says,

> is every individual's code of behavior by means of which he
> makes himself a better human being than his nature wants

"belief" regardless of its nature and object or whether it even has a nature and object; that he puts himself on record affirming his confidence in man's capacity to endure and even prevail—such declarations may and obviously do move some of his readers. Others, like myself, remain unmoved and unimpressed as long as Faulkner fails to tell us what, how and why man should "believe," and as long as he fails to tell us anything about the terms of man's "prevailing"—it all seems much too much of a vagueness. But insofar as A *Fable* itself is concerned, it must now be evident that its essential "message" is a statement of worldly, humane and stoical optimism, and that, consequently, there is no organic relationship in the book between this ideological content and the elaborate system of Christian reference. The relationship is a factitious one: the Christian correspondences, the evocation of the Christ-figure, even if he be largely dumb, the reenacted crucifixion, all lend an aura of emotional sustenance and solemnity to a point of view which logically can be developed without reference to Christianity at all. As a result, I would contend, the whole pattern of religious allegory proves irrelevant to, a needless weight of imposition upon, the central matter of the book.

Nor is that all. Between the affirmation of faith in man and the rhythm of the action in A *Fable* there is a serious discrepancy. The idea of a "reenactment" of the Second Coming is not merely, as I have already noticed, a static and fatalistic one; it is also an utterly desperate one. How it can be reconciled with a proud faith in man's prevailing—except as it becomes a literary equivalent of pie-in-the-sky—is hard to see. For to imagine a Second Coming which is essentially a repetition of the original agony; to see the Christ figure again scorned by the crowd, again betrayed and deserted by

---

to be, if he followed his nature only. Whatever its symbol—cross or crescent or whatever—that symbol is man's reminder of his duty inside the human race.

his followers, again crushed by the state; to conceive of
a Christ who knows he is doomed, who offers neither
hope nor a belief in hope; to present this as a necessary
condition of man, so that, in effect, the repetition of
the agony could as well be the Third or the Tenth,
history itself coming to seem no more than a cycle of
hope betrayed and faith misused—all this implies a
vision of despair that largely undercuts not only the
assumptions of Christianity but also those statements of
affirmation which Faulkner would like us to take away
from the book. The result is incoherence.

XII

The Town
and The Mansion

SEVENTEEN YEARS INTERVENED BETWEEN THE PUBLICA-
tion dates of *The Hamlet* and *The Town*, years not
merely of honors, prizes, public declamations and com-
muniqués, but also of a slowly mounting crisis in Faulkner's career. Formally the two books comprise parts of a
trilogy for which *The Mansion* is the concluding volume, and there is profit in so regarding them if one's
main interest is to gain a commanding view of the
history of Faulkner's themes and the development of
his feelings toward Yoknapatawpha County. But when
examined strictly as individual novels, *The Hamlet* and
The Town have rather little in common: they are written in different modes, the first being exuberant humor
and the second a sober narrative; they take different attitudes toward what seems to be a common body of
material; indeed, they can almost be regarded as the
work of two different writers, the Faulkner who is a superb novelist and the Faulkner whose imagination is

too often distracted by the mottoes of his Nobel Prize speech.

After *The Hamlet* and *Go Down, Moses* Faulkner did not succeed—at least until 1960—in writing a fully-sustained, first-rate novel. The books he published in the years after the war contain many fine and even brilliant parts, but on the whole they are forced, anxious and high-pitched, the work of a man, no longer driven, who must now drive himself. *Intruder in the Dust* is marred by patches of dead Southern oratory, *Requiem for a Nun* by a play meant to be dramatic but frequently declining into inert statement. A *Fable*, which may come to hold a place in Faulkner's work somewhat analogous to *Pierre* in Melville's, is a book admirable in conception but hollow in execution.

What went wrong? It is risky to say and at most we can only speculate, but let me note a few symptoms of the trouble. In all these works there is a reliance upon a high-powered rhetoric which bears many of the outer marks of the earlier Faulkner styles, but is really a kind of self-imitation, a whipped-up fury pouring out in wanton excess. The very abandon with which Faulkner now uses language seems itself calculated and predictable, a device in the repertoire of a writer who senses the dangers of relaxation even as he approaches the dangers of exhaustion.

There is also in these novels a tendency to fall back upon hi-jinks of plot, a flaunting arbitrariness and whimsicality of invention—as if Faulkner, having examined and brooded upon human life for so long and with such pain, now felt that "anything" is possible to men, verisimilitude being a mere mask for our trepidation; or as if Faulkner, wearied of telling stories and establishing characters, were now determined to break his own spell and betray an impatience with his own skill at the very moment of their appearance. At least one part of Faulkner, the man you see in the photographs dressed in a natty grey topcoat, looking dapper and reserved, has entered or reentered the familiar workaday world in which you and I live; and no longer is it possible to imagine him, like Balzac, calling on his deathbed for a doctor—"get old Doc Peabody!"—from his own novels. His creative journey, begun with the nihilism of the twenties in *Soldiers' Pay*, has led him, not as his conservative critics have maintained, to the security and strength of a traditional morality, but to the perilous edge of the nihilism of the fifties. Faulkner, in the ripeness of his honor, is in many ways as baffled and perplexed as when he published his first melancholy poems.

Faulkner has become our contemporary. He can no longer work within his established means; one senses bewilderment spreading through his pages, by which the subjects of his earlier novels now become a force constraining his later ones. How else can one explain the frantic verbal outpourings of Gavin Stevens, the District Attorney with a degree from Heidelberg and a passion for rant, who unhappily can seem like Faulkner's "alter ego"? Anyone with a touch of feeling, to say nothing of respect, must respond warmly to this new Faulkner who so evidently shares our hesitations and doubts. But in truth this is no longer the man who wrote *The Sound and the Fury* or *The Hamlet*. For by the time Faulkner turned back to the Snopeses, completing the trilogy in the late 1950's, he could sustain neither his old fury nor his old humor. Both, to be sure, break out repeatedly in *The Town* and *The Mansion*; there are sections which, if torn out of context, read nearly as well as anything he has done in the past. But they need to be torn out of context.

Nor is the difficulty to be found in the over-all design of the trilogy. Faulkner has a fine grasp of the social probabilities of Snopesism. He sees how Flem Snopes must strive for the appearance of respectability in order to gain public sanction for his wealth, and how, in turn, the appearance of respectability, as soon as it seems within grasp, will rob him of a portion of his demonic powers and narrow him into an ordinary sort of creature. Faulkner also sees how Flem, though quite able to handle any attacks from the "traditionalist" moral leaders of the county, must meet his destruction at the hands of a Nemesis from within his own tribe. All this is clearly projected through the scheme of the trilogy: there can be no serious quarrel with Faulkner's conception of the rise and destiny of the Snopeses.

One can anticipate scores of essays which will trace the ways in which each incident or episode in the trilogy contributes to the total scheme and which will thereby create the false impression that a satisfying congruence exists between the conceptual design and the novels as they actually are. Yet, as regards both *The Town* and *The Mansion*, such a congruence is not to be found, for only fitfully do these novels realize the needs and possibilities of Faulkner's over-all design.

A minor example may prove revealing. In *The Mansion* one of the Snopeses, cousin Cla'ence, running for Congress in 1945, suddenly declares himself an opponent of the Ku Klux Klan. This maneuver, apparently made in response to the changing atmosphere of the South, greatly upsets Ratliff and Gavin Stevens, who fear that the tiny and unseasoned group of Yoknapatawpha "liberals" will now be taken in. Ratliff then arranges that, at a picnic in Frenchman's Bend, a gang of dogs should mistake Cla'ence for a familiar thicket which they visit regularly each day—and this dampening of the candidate makes him appear so ridiculous, he must withdraw from the race. For as Uncle Billy Varner, the Croesus of Frenchman's Bend, says: "I aint going to have Beat Two and Frenchman's Bend represented nowhere by nobody that ere a son-a-bitching dog that happens by cant tell from a fence post."

Simply as an anecdote, this comes off beautifully. It has a plausibility of its own, and a self-sufficiency too. Faulkner can tease this sort of joke along better than anyone else writing in America, just as he knows the mind of a grasping petty demagogue like Cla'ence Snopes better than anyone else. But in the context of the trilogy the incident seems inadequate and perhaps damaging, for there is a serious discrepancy between the problem raised by Cla'ence's masquerade of enlightenment and the means Ratliff employs to cope with it: a discrepancy between two modes and eras of social existence. The incident suggests that the threat of Snopesism can easily be deflected by the country shrewdness of a Ratliff—an assumption which all the preceding matter has led us gravely to doubt and which, if now we do credit it, must persuade us that the danger embodied by the Snopeses need not be taken as seriously as the whole weight of the trilogy has seemed to argue. The incident is fine, so is the scheme of the trilogy; but the relationship between the two is troubling.

There are more important examples. Through both *The Town* and *The Mansion* Flem Snopes drives steadily toward economic domination in Jefferson. The meaning of this is fully indicated, but Flem himself, as a character in a novel, is not nearly so vivid in these books as he was in *The Hamlet*. Partly this seems due to a flagging of creative energies, partly to a propensity for avoiding the direct and dramatic. The action of *The Town* and, to a large extent, *The Mansion* is usually strained through the blurred and blurring consciousness of Gavin Stevens, surely the greatest wind-bag in American literature, and Charles Mallison, who shows promise of becoming the runner-up. It is as if Faulkner, once so fertile and free in his technical innovations, were now their prisoner, driven to go through the motions of virtuosity and to complicate the point of view from which his story is told, regardless of inner need or plausibility. *The Town* and *The Mansion* both enjoy a textbook sophistication in technical matters which is quite superior to that of *The Hamlet*; and it does them little good.

Especially in *The Town* is this difficulty irksome. *The Town* is a novel that dutifully satisfies its obligations to the trilogy, following up the proper thematic cues and moving the action to the point where *The Mansion* can take it over, but seldom winning our affection, seldom bursting into vividness or fire in its own right. In *The Town* Ratliff, by far the most attractive and successful of Faulkner's commentators, is made to withdraw into the background and is not allowed to speak with the authority he commanded in *The Hamlet*. Now there is perhaps a thematic reason for this: Ratliff in modern Jefferson cannot act with the ease and knowledge he enjoyed in Frenchman's Bend. He is a figure from an earlier time and another kind of life who is not really at home in the present moment. But if the withdrawal of Ratliff is abstractly plausible, the concrete literary results are unfortunate. Most of the time, in *The Town* and *The Mansion*, we see the action through the coarsening vision of Stevens and the callow vision of Charles Mallison, and we find ourselves yearning for the cool humor, the kindly humaneness and the simply maturity which Ratliff brought to *The Hamlet*. Even when Faulkner does allow Ratliff to move into sight, it is too often as a secondary reflector for Stevens and Mallison, rather than as the prime narrator and observer. There are times, decidedly irritating ones, when we see Ratliff only third-hand, through Mallison's sense of Stevens's sense of him. Compounding the problem is the fact that Faulkner so seldom establishes any critical perspective upon—that so much more often than the reader he is deceived by—Stevens and Mallison, whom he usually regards as a quixotic moralist and a fine young man inheriting the stories and the wisdom of the Yoknapatawpha experience. In *The Mansion* Faulkner does begin to show some signs of awareness that Stevens is very far from what he has tried to persuade us he is; but then Mallison becomes more annoying. The likable boy of *Intruder in the Dust* is now a Harvard graduate mimicking his elders in cracker-barrel portentousness, as in his remarks about the probable sex life of Stevens and Linda Snopes: "Are they bedded formally yet or not? I mean is it rosa yet or still just sub, assuming you assume the same assumption they teach us up here at Harvard that once you get the clothes off those tall up-and-down women you find out they aint all that up-and-down at all." Nothing in the text, so far as I can see, provides any ground for supposing that Faulkner takes a caustic view of this sophomoric widsom, or that he wishes us to see Mallison in any but a sympathetic light.

Such a complicating and rarefying of perspective tends to be inherently undramatic, unless the observers themselves contribute tension and energy to the story. In *The Town* it sets up a technique that is a good deal more involuted than the matter requires, and thereby a technique that harasses and frets the matter. One comes to feel in *The Town*—and to a lesser extent in *The Mansion*—the uneasy presence of an ingenuity searching for but not quite finding a subject on which to exercise itself. And meanwhile Flem Snopes, whom we yearn to see in diabolic motion, free and on his own, without the explanatory or intervening remarks of anyone, let alone Gavin Stevens, fades further and further into the background: Flem who should be the great commanding figure, as he was in *The Hamlet*, of the whole trilogy!

In fairness, one should admit that the very perfection of malevolence with which Faulkner established Flem in *The Hamlet* posed an extremely difficult problem for him. How could Flem be made further to develop, how could he appear to enlarge his field for aggrandizement without becoming merely melodramatic or a fiction of sociology? Apparently aware of this problem, Faulkner tried to outflank it in both *The Town* and *The Mansion* by keeping Flem in the background, a figure we barely see though one we are meant always to sense through his impact on the other characters. It does not always work, however, because there is a conflict between what the trilogy requires of Flem—that he withdraw into respectability—and what Faulkner's local strategy of depiction requires of Flem—that he continue to exert a malevolent hold upon all those about him. That Flem Snopes, of all the marvellous monsters in American literature, should end up seeming shadowy and vague—who could have anticipated this?

Faulkner has made the mistake of softening Flem; he verges at times on a sociological and psychological explanation for his behavior, which Flem would be the first to scorn—and which is as unfortunate as if Ben Jonson broke into tears over Volpone. When the Flem we see or, alas, more often hear about is "the old fish-blooded son of a bitch who had a vocabulary of two words, one being No and the other Foreclose," all is nearly for the best in the best of all Faulknerian worlds; but when it is a Flem who becomes still another item in the omniverous musings of Gavin Stevens, then he suffers a fate worse than even he deserves.

In composing *The Mansion* Faulkner seems to have been unwilling to face the possibility that Flem, having reached the top of his world, might snugly remain there, or more simply, that it would make for a better novel to let him remain there. The insistent but somewhat willed optimism which came over Faulkner in the years after the Second World War could not sustain— it could barely countenance—that marvellously wry disenchantment which in *The Hamlet* led him to write about the rise of Flem Snopes as if it were somehow beyond help or judgment and nothing could be done but to witness and even relish the catastrophe. By the time Faulkner came to completing *The Mansion*, he seems to have felt a strong need to destroy Flem, not, to be sure, from any fatuous assumption that Gavin Stevens or the likes of him could ever prove a match for the Snopeses, but out of a desire to affirm those

positive values—charity and kindness and endurance—
which he had been expounding in his public statements.
There was, as I have noted, the quite legitimate and
controlling scheme of the trilogy itself: that Flem's passion for respectability would prove his undoing. But
when one examines closely the plot of *The Mansion*, it
becomes clear that there is no necessary causal relation
between the over-all scheme of the trilogy and the
manner in which Flem is finally disposed of, between,
that is, the general theme of respectability and the immediate revenge of Mink upon his cousin. In terms of
moral satisfaction, as also perhaps of social verisimilitude, the ending of *The Mansion* may be quite acceptable. But in terms of the comic impetus released by the
earlier Snopes stories and *The Hamlet*, the development
and perhaps even the denouement of the trilogy suffer,
since what first pleased one in reading about the
Snopeses was not any absurd assumption that they con-
formed to social reality, but that through fantasy, extravagance and a kind of surrealism they illuminated a
whole area of modern life, as indeed a whole kind of
human behavior.

Only occasionally does this comic impetus break out
in *The Town* and *The Mansion*. On the whole *The
Mansion* is a better novel, more dramatic and "rendered" than *The Town*, if only because it contains the
description of Mink Snopes's journey from prison back
to Jefferson. But in *The Town* there are a few sections
and episodes which recall the old humor and the old
zest better than anything in *The Mansion*. Some of
these sections and episodes are reworkings of such earlier Faulkner stories as "Mule in the Yard" and "Centaur in Brass." The first of these, as it is spun out in *The
Town*, is an especially happy piece of nonsense. It concerns I. O. Snopes, the word-mangler, who had worked
himself out a scheme for planting mules on a blind
curve of the local railroad and collecting $60 for each of
them when they were run down by the trains, but who

is now in a high state of outrage because he has not got-
ten his fair share of the $8500 insurance money which
the wife of his partner, Hait, had collected after Hait,
poor soul, had happened to join the mules on the track.

Better still is the concluding section of *The Town*,
in which Byron Snopes, the loose-fingered bank-teller
who had run off to Texas with several thousand dollars,
sends four of his children by an Apache squaw to Flem.
In these monstrous children, who almost burn cousin
Cla'ence alive, break into a Coca-Cola factory without
tripping the burglar alarm and show a mature familiarity with switch knives, the pure Snopes destructiveness, what might be called *ur*-Snopesism, comes through
with an unmodulated zealousness. They are, as Ratliff
remarks, "the last and final end of Snopes out-and-out
unvarnished behavior in Jefferson," and even Flem,
now trapped and implicated by civilization, has to ship
them back to Texas in self-defense. High-spirited and
brilliant, the episode strikes the note one had learned to
look for in stories about the Snopeses—a note which,
perhaps because of Faulkner's new sobriety and responsibility, is not struck often enough in either *The
Town* or *The Mansion*.

The greatest trouble, finally, with both of these books
is that Faulkner is obliged to give a large portion of his
space to material that does not directly involve the
Snopeses. Again, there is a conflict between the needs
and designs of the trilogy and what Faulkner can bring
off at the moment of composition. And a good part
of this necessary material—necessary for setting in motion the machinery of plot—tends to be rather flatly
stated or summarized, rather than dramatically presented.

Perhaps the best example of this flatness occurs in
the middle section of *The Mansion*, which deals with
Stevens's relation to Linda Snopes, stepdaughter of
Flem and daughter of Eula Varner Snopes. The New
York locale, Linda's venture into Communism, the

snooping of an FBI man—these are not matters that
Faulkner handles with authority. The relationship between Gavin and Linda—they love, but in vain, and
they neither marry, for reasons not clear, nor do anything else a man and woman in love might be expected
to do, for reasons still less clear—this relationship is
never allowed to settle into quiet clarity. At most it
elicits a mild pity, since Faulkner never seems able to
face up to whatever remnants of Southern chivalry,
romantic ideology or plain ordinary repression drive
him to think of love as invariably a grandiloquent
"doom." The truth, I suspect, is that Faulkner cannot
treat adult sexual experience with a forthright steadiness, despite the frequency with which sex appears in
his earlier books as a symptom of disorder and violence.
Only at the end of the novel, as Stevens and Linda
kiss goodbye and he slides his hand down her back,
"simply touching her . . . supporting her buttocks as
you cup the innocent hipless bottom of a child," does
Faulkner break into the candor for which this whole
section cries out.

If the Snopes trilogy is both imposing and seriously
marred, *The Mansion* taken more modestly, as a novel
in its own right, has some splendid parts. Perhaps the
reader who is not steeped in Faulkner's work and cares
nothing about its relation to his previous books is in the
best position to accept it with pleasure. For whenever
Mink Snopes appears, the prose becomes hard, grave,
vibrant, and Faulkner's capacity, as Malcolm Cowley
has put it, for "telling stories about men or beasts who
fulfilled their destiny," comes into full play. Like the
convict in *The Wild Palms*, Mink drives steadily toward
his end, without fear or hope, unblinking and serene.

The portrait of Mink is beyond praise: a simple
ignorant soul who sees existence as an unending struggle between Old Moster (God) and Them (the
world), with Them forever and even rightly and naturally triumphant, always in control of events as they

move along, yet with Old Moster standing in reserve,
not to intervene or help but to draw a line, like Mink
himself, and say that beyond this line no creature, not
even a wretched little Mink, dare be tortured or tried.
Mink's is the heroism of the will, a man living out his
need, the last and in some ways the most moving embodiment of what I have earlier called the Faulkner
gesture.

In the opening part of the novel, as well as in its brilliant final pages—where Mink goes to Memphis to buy
a gun, gets caught up in a superbly rendered revivalist
sect led by Marine Sergeant Goodyhay, mooches a quarter from a cop, supposes this is one of those new dis-
pensations he had dimly heard described as "the WP
and A" and finally, as if in a pageant of fatality, returns
to Jefferson to kill his cousin—in these pages Faulkner
is writing at very close to the top of his bent. It would
be straining things to suggest that every fine and author-
itative touch is required by the design of the trilogy,
and there is a way in which one can regard the final
section of *The Mansion* as a brilliant set-piece, a flare
of virtuosity which establishes its own meanings and
its own rhythms, a heroic recall of Faulkner's earlier and
most indigenous gifts, such as we had come to know in
"Old Man" or parts of *Light in August*. Now the pages
quiver with evocation, the language becomes taut, and
Faulkner's sense of the power of human life as it floods
a man beyond his reason or knowledge, becomes overwhelming. Here is Mink in a moment of reflection:

> In 1948 he and Flem both would be old men and
> he even said aloud: "What a shame we cant both of
> us jest come out two old men setting peaceful in
> the sun or the shade, waiting to die together, not
> even thinking no more of hurt or harm or getting
> even, not even remembering no more about hurt
> or harm or anguish or revenge,"—two old men not
> only incapable of further harm to anybody but

even incapable of remembering hurt or harm. . . .
But I reckon not he thought. *Cant neither of us
help nothing now. Cant neither one of us take
nothing back.*

And Mink approaching Jefferson after 38 years, as he
rests on a truck:

He was quite comfortable. But mainly he was off
the ground. That was the danger, what a man had
to watch against; once you laid flat on the ground,
right away the earth started in to draw you back
down into it. The very moment you were born out
of your mother's body, the power and drag of the
earth was already at work on you. . . . And you
knew it too.

Reading such passages in the fullness of their context, is like returning to a marvellous world that had
gone a little dim but now is once more full of clarity,
brilliance, power; and then all seems well.

XIII

The Reivers

DURING THE LAST TEN OR FIFTEEN YEARS OF HIS CAREER, Faulkner came to be surrounded by an aura of solemn adulation that did neither his work nor himself much good. A false impression grew up that his books are neatly planned segments in a mosaic of symbolism and morality, rather than acts of creative passion and, sometimes, disorder. Faulkner himself, in some of his later novels, became quite ponderous, as if overwhelmed by the thought of his own wisdom. And so intent were many of his critics upon milking every drop of meaning from his work, they tended to forget that before all else he was a literary *performer*, a self-made virtuoso aiming to dazzle, incite, and give pleasure. They forgot, above all, that he could be a brilliant comic writer, blessed with a repertoire of gifts for folk extravaganza, deadpan humor and surrealist hijinks.

Faulkner's last novel, *The Reivers*, ought to put some of these facts in a clearer light. ("Reive" is an archaic word meaning to plunder.) It is a deliberately minor work, the playful last note of a writer who knows he has struck all his major ones. Here Faulkner does not strain to compound a total vision of life; but perhaps for that very reason, it is almost entirely successful. Relaxed in narrative tone and strategy, clear in diction, full of amusement at the power of human beings to entangle themselves in endless webs of mischief, *The Reivers* is a comic novel at once easy-spirited and pleasurable. In part it follows the traditional pattern of "the novel of education"—how an inexperienced youth makes his way into the world and through a shock of exposure comes to know its multiple dangers—and in part it provides a parody of that traditional pattern.

The novel forms a quite simple fable, transparent in its significance but adorned with dark, violent, and, at times, obscure complications of plot. The fable this time consists of an adventure set in 1905, when three Mississippi innocents—Lucius Priest, an eleven-year-old white boy; Boon Hogganbeck, a hulking and bumbling half-Indian; and Ned McCaslin, an old Negro curmudgeon—"borrow" from Lucius' grandfather one of those charming new toys called automobiles and head straight for Memphis. Not that grandfather Priest accepts the utility or even plausibility of the automobile; it is just that the other leading banker of Jefferson had already bought one of the fool things, so that he, grandfather, had no choice but to buy one too, conspicuously tucking it away in the stable, where Boon would tend it lavishly and on ceremonial occasions be allowed to drive it gingerly.

The adventures of Lucius, Boon, and Ned bring into play one of Faulkner's most cherished themes: the relaxation of the sense of social duty, the need every once in a while to play hookey, so that men can bear going back to the tedium and trouble of life. It is a theme that received its gravest and most profound expression in "The Bear" (in which Boon Hogganbeck also figures prominently); and now, in *The Reivers*, it comes through as a sly appreciation of the sheer waywardness, the saving cussedness, of human nature.

As Faulkner pleasantly fills in his picture of the old Mississippi countryside, his trio of travelers finishes the first day's journey and stops at Miss Ballenbaugh's place, "a small store with a loft above it containing a row of shuck mattresses each with its neat perfectly clean sheets and pillow cases and blankets for the accommodation of fox- and coon-hunters and fishermen." The next morning, refreshed, they set out for Hell Creek bottom, and here Faulkner springs one of those marvelous country tales that will remind at least some readers of the humor of "the old Southwest" in nineteenth-century America.

At Hell Creek bottom a shrewd redneck has set up his private version of the feudal tollbooth. He cultivates what Uncle Ned McCaslin calls a "well-traveled mud-hole" in which the infrequent autos of the day are certain to mire ("Mud's one of our best crops up this-away"), and he stands by patiently, waiting with a team of mules to rescue drivers for a superbly unreasonable fee. There follows a bout of bargaining in which Boon tries to argue that the charge for his "passengers" is excessive, since one of these "ain't even white." Unmoved by this turn of Southern logic, the keeper of the mudhole replies, "Son, both of these mules is color-blind."

Once in Memphis, the travelers get down to some fancy reiving. They lodge—it is Boon's bright idea—in the brothel run by the trimly elegant Miss Reba, a lady one remembers from *Sanctuary*. Uncle Ned, a bit cautious until now, suddenly comes into his own, bursting with pungent talk and vivid schemes, and full of a shrewdness about Memphis life that reveals his sense of being at home in its half-visible Negro sub-world. He trades grandfather's car for a somewhat battered race-horse, since he feels that any sensible person can detect the superiority of live horse flesh over dead metal; and when Lucius and Boon erupt in panic at the thought of having to explain this transaction to grandfather Priest, Ned calmly shows himself a master of the long-shot gamble. Through a bewildering series of deals and maneuvers, he arranges a race in which the horse—an experienced loser named Lightning—will run against a horse owned by the man who now has the car. Thereby, he calculates, he will win back the car, keep the horse, and make some cash on side bets.

What follows reminds one, happily, of Einstein's remark about a Kafka novel: nothing could be that complicated. Uncle Ned wins a race through some thaumaturgical passes with a sardine; he himself, loquacious and cool, spends several hours in jail; Boon gets into a brawl with a sheriff who has been molesting one of Miss Reba's nicest girls; Lucius, in an idyllic interlude, visits with a Negro family in the country (one of those retreats to moral ease which occur periodically in Faulkner's novels); and then Lucius' folks turn up, with consequent further betting, drinking, and sharp talk, a marriage for Boon, an educational hiding for Lucius and glory of sorts for Ned.

Throughout these carryings-on Faulkner, obviously enjoying himself, acts as a kind of ringmaster who brings on a fresh act whenever there is a sign the audience may be tiring. A lively group of background figures—some characters, some caricatures—keep weaving into the action: Mr. Binford, lover and landlord of Miss Reba, a paragon of respectability whose "sole and only vice was horses running in competition on which bets could be placed"; Miss Corrie, the darling of Boon despite the inconveniences she causes by turning straight at the last moment; Minnie, Miss Reba's Negro maid, a "nature-minded" girl with a wicked gold tooth in the middle of her mouth; and Otis, a fifteen-year-old dwarf with a heart of poison who manages to steal Minnie's precious tooth. Hovering over all these figures stands Ned, a fine grump who combines an innocence of feeling that makes him the apt partner of an eleven-year-old—together with a sharpness of observation testifying to those powers of humanity he has preserved beneath the mask of the pliant Negro.

Perhaps the best things in *The Reivers* are the snatches of talk: crisp, racy, idiomatic. Miss Reba complains about the children who perversely clutter up her establishment: "You know as well as I do that Mr. Binford disapproves like hell of kids using houses for holiday vacations; you heard him last summer when Corrie brought that little s. o. b. [the insufferable Otis] in here the first time because she claims he dont get enough refinement on that Arkansas tenant farm. Like Mr. Binford says, they'll be in here soon enough anyway, so why rush them until at least they have some jack and are capable of spending it."

And here is Ned answering Boon's complaint at the beginning of the journey that Ned, having stowed away under the tarpaulin at the back of the car, doesn't offer to help Boon lift it out of the mud: "And hot under there too, mon. . . . I dont see how I stood it. Not to mention having to hold off this here sheet-iron churn from knocking my brains out every time you bounced, let alone waiting for that gasoline or whatever you calls it to get all joogled up to where it would decide to blow up too."

Or Otis moaning over his delayed discovery of city advantages: "When I think of all them years I spent over there on a durn farm in Arkansas with Memphis right here . . . and I never even knowed it. How if I had just knowed when I was four or five years old, what I had to wait until just last year to find out about, sometimes I just want to give up and quit. But I reckon I wont. I reckon maybe I can make it up."

With the warning that it is a light novel, a dash of country froth, I think it worth suggesting that the most interesting idea in the book concerns the role of Uncle Ned. At its heart, *The Reivers* is an excursion into the pleasure of fantasy, an act of comic praise to the refreshments of mischief. For Faulkner the official world of business, money, and women has always been the world of the white man: an arena of frustration, vanity, and pain. But when the time for joy comes, when the freedom of play begins, then it is Uncle Ned, the Negro, who takes over, as an impresario of vitality. To press this point would be silly; to ignore it as a key to Faulkner's sense of American life would be neglectful.

The last of Faulkner's major novels, *The Hamlet* and *Go Down, Moses,* came out in the early forties, and since then he seemed increasingly caught up in a severe crisis of belief and perception, partly a result of his slow emergence from the trials and comforts of Yoknapatawpha County. His sense of the radical disorder, the ultimate unbearableness, of human existence became increasingly acute, but he could not always find ways of embodying that sense in his later novels. Sometimes, as in *The Fable,* he drove himself to an almost hysterical portentousness; other times, he lapsed into country-store jocosity. *The Reivers* represents not a solution, but an evasion, of the moral and literary problems besetting Faulkner's late work. To say "an evasion" is not to pass any sort of adverse judgment, for by the time he came to write *The Reivers* Faulkner had fulfilled himself as a writer. He had confronted the terrors of the world and the demons of self as much as any other writer of our century, and he was clearly entitled to the charming grace note with which he ended his career.

A Concluding Note

WILLIAM FAULKNER'S REPUTATION HAS GONE THROUGH some astonishing shifts, both during and after his lifetime. By 1940, after a brilliant decade of work, several of Faulkner's best books were out of print; during the last part of his life, though his work largely declined, he won an enormous amount of critical admiration; and since his death, there has been a steady accumulation of critical studies, though apparently a decline in popular interest. Nevertheless, Faulkner's place in American and indeed world literature seems assured.

In point of inventiveness Faulkner is at least the equal of the twentieth-century European masters. He is—to use a troublesome word—a genius. His work abounds and overflows with native power; even in his later, somewhat uncertain books there remains evidence of his fertility in creating lively situations and characters. He has the primary gifts of the novelist: to imagine a situation and tell a story. Faulkner is the most impressive living American novelist, certainly the best since Dreiser and perhaps since James. Yet, except in a few novels and stories, there are certain elements of greatness missing from his work—the kind of ultimate mastery that can be found in the novels of Joyce, Proust, Kafka, and Lawrence.

Where Faulkner disappoints, whether in whole books or in parts of them, it is usually through a failure of intellect. It may well be objected that a writer able to construct so marvellously complex and serious a work as *The Sound and the Fury* cannot be deficient in intellect or that the man who conceived and nurtured the whole Yoknapatawpha chronicle surely commands an impressive measure of mind. This, so far as it goes, is true; but when we speak of the quality of a writer's mind we mean something more. We mean his capacity for a high order of comment and observation *within* the structure of his work, his ability to handle general ideas with a dramatic cogency equal to his ability to render images of conduct.

These are capacities as choice as they are rare, and only a very few novelists—Stendhal, Dostoevsky, Tolstoy, George Eliot, to name the greatest—fully possess them. It is in this department of fiction, as important in its way as the delineation of character and the heightening of drama, that so many gifted American novelists conspicuously fail, particularly those "natural talents" of Faulkner's generation who are unstained by the imprint of literary tradition or training. Their failure is a failure in the explicit, in precise statement and intellectual coherence. It is related to their romantic fear of the literary vocation and literary stance; and it breaks out in their language, which they often force to assume the labors rightfully belonging to the mind. In *Doctor Faustus* Thomas Mann remarks that in art "the highest and profoundest claim to feeling is to a stage of intellectuality and formal strictness." The greatest art, he suggests, represents a fusion of feeling and thought, Dionysian passion and Apollonian lucidity. There are of course a number of works—*The Sound and the Fury, As I Lay Dying, Light in August*—in which Faulkner realizes this fusion; but at other times, because of his weakness in those areas of composition that call for the orderly and the abstract, he is forced to fall back, far too much, on his brimming imagination.

Why this should be so is a complex and difficult problem that remains to be discussed by historians of American culture; but an interesting hint has been provided by John Crowe Ransom, the Southern poet and critic. Faulkner, he writes, "has not had the advantages of the society of his literary peers discussing the realistic novel and performing it, nor that of intellectuals with their formidable dialectic, permitting him to give to his creation so vast and controlled a spread as Dostoevsky did."

Within these limits the rewards are remarkably high. Alone among American writers of the present century Faulkner has filled out a complex world of the imagination in which we recognize the moral qualities and lineaments of our time; a world that reappears, enlarged and replenished, from book to book. Though confined to a provincial area and, therefore, devoid of many significant types of American character and many significant issues of American conduct, the world of Yoknapatawpha is unequaled in recent American writing for imaginative density and spaciousness, for the fierce intensity of its realization. No American novelist —and none of those who are, in some ways, superior to Faulkner—has been so absorbed, with a passion reminiscent of Dickens or Balzac, in asserting and validating the reality of an imagined scene. In an almost literal sense, Faulkner has widened the boundaries of our world and our existence.

Faulkner has given us an astonishing variety of characters, unforgettably striking in their attitudes and traits, their speech and posture. One thinks of Benjy, Jason Compson and Dilsey; Darl, Cash and Addie Bundren; Popeye and Temple; Joe Christmas, Lena Grove and Hightower; Sutpen; the tall convict; Ratliff and Flem Snopes; the whole brood of Snopeses; Ike McCaslin and Lucas Beauchamp; and in his short stories, Miss Emily, the Negro fugitive, the Jewish stunt jumper, the Tennessee mountaineers. Becoming part of our experience, enriching and complicating it, they thrive in memory.

In his best work Faulkner has striven with themes of a depth and consequence seldom approached by his American contemporaries. He has grappled with the inherited biases of his tradition, breaking through to a tragic realization that, at least in part, they are inadequate and wrong. He has dramatized, as have few other American novelists, the problem of living in a historical moment suspended between a dead past and an unavailable future; dramatized it in his own terms, as a clash between traditional mores no longer valued or relevant and a time of moral uncertainty and opportunism. He has told us again, as every honest creative writer of our day tells us and with the dramatic force available only to the creative writer, of the devastation of our world, the estrangement of man in an inhuman milieu, the barrenness of a commercial culture and a loveless ethos. An authentic moralist when not moralizing, he has tried to reach, in images of character, the meaning of human virtue: of pride and forbearance, humility and truth. And he has seen the human enterprise as a risk forever undertaken and forever renewed, a risk in which the true measure is not success but exposure.

As an artist he has not remained content with the familiar and well-worn. No other writer of our time except Joyce has so brilliantly exploited the stream-of-consciousness technique, and none has so successfully resisted the tendency of this technique to dissolve into its flow the structures of plot and character. No other writer in America has rebelled so vigorously against the "common style," the cult of understatement and tepid irony; and if the price of his rebellion has come high in rhetoric, so has the gain in poetry. One thinks again of the rolling power of the convict's Mississippi journey, one remembers Joe Christmas's plunging flight through the marshes, one summons the rhythms of "The Bear" as they register the very tone and tension of the hunt.

All significant virtues, all enough to lend enduring value to Faulkner's work. Yet none of them matters nearly so much as Faulkner's special contribution to twentieth-century American literature. At a time when our characteristic writing had been clipped and constricted, and a fear of showing emotion had become a sign of good manners or even good morals, Faulkner unashamedly expressed and represented the strongest passions. He restored to our writing a full range of feeling, a readiness to accept the extremes of response, that had largely been lost. He has not been afraid to howl, to scream, to bawl, to make himself appear ridiculous. In novel after novel he shows how fearful is the cost and heavy the weight of human existence, yet he illustrates how fulfillment and perhaps even salvation may come to those who stand ready to bear the cost and suffer the weight.

APPENDIX

A Note on *Flags in the Dust*

IN ITS ORIGINAL, MANUSCRIPT VERSION, *Sartoris* WAS A good deal longer than the novel as it appeared in 1929. The complete text, Faulkner's first major venture into Yoknapatawpha County, remained unavailable until 1973, when Random House published it under the title, *Flags in the Dust*. Preferred by Faulkner himself, the original title of the novel is surely more evocative than *Sartoris*.

Faulkner had started working on the book in 1926. Completed a year later, it was rejected by a dozen publishers, and when accepted by Harcourt Brace, a condition for publication was that it be sharply cut. This task was given to Faulkner's agent, Ben Wasson, who trimmed away about a quarter of the text. In 1929, the reduced version came out as *Sartoris*.

Flags in the Dust is slower in pace, more discursive in character, and richer in texture than *Sartoris*. The original version focuses not only on the Sartoris clan but more fully than the cut version on a range of subsidiary families and figures, thereby revealing both the scope of Faulkner's early ambition and his inability, as yet, to realize it. For the Faulkner student *Flags in the Dust* is valuable since it indicates that even at the beginning of his career Faulkner had clearly in mind a good portion of the materials, attitudes, and even developments of the Yoknapatawpha chronicle. The sense that he is working with—and possessed by—a received body of anecdote, legend, and myth is stronger in *Flags in the Dust* than in *Sartoris*.

Still, it would be an exaggeration to say that simply as a novel to be read in its own right, *Flags in the Dust* is decisively better than *Sartoris*. Cutting brought both gains and losses. If *Sartoris* is more disciplined than *Flags in the Dust*, some of the sentences worked into the cut version as bridges over deleted material are decidedly inferior.

Wasson had the good sense not to trim more than an occasional phrase or sentence from the more vivid sections of the book, such as the anecdote about "the other Bayard" in the Civil War and the pastoral interlude with the MacCallums. Sometimes, the editing hand is heavy. *Flags in the Dust*: After Sartoris rides back wildly to the Northern lines, the "captive Northern major" says: "Forward, Sir, I beg . . . What is one man, to a paladin out of romance?" *Sartoris*: "the captive Northern major" says: "Forward, Sir, I beg . . . What is one man to a renewed belief in mankind?" Clearly the original phrasing is more appropriate to the general tone of the novel.

In neither complete nor cut version, however, does the book strike one as a successful or first-rate novel; its importance remains as a somewhat ill-constructed prelude to the great novels that were soon to come.

Index